MANAGING SPORT FINANCE

All good managers working in sport need to have a clear understanding of the principles of finance and accounting. Whether working in the private, public or voluntary sectors, a firm grasp of the basic concepts and techniques of financial management is essential if a manager is to make effective decisions and to implement those decisions successfully. *Managing Sport Finance* is the first book to offer a comprehensive introduction to financial management and accounting specifically designed for managers working in sport.

The book assumes no prior knowledge of finance or accounting on the part of the reader. It clearly and succinctly guides the reader through each key concept and practical technique, including:

- balance sheets;
- financial statements;
- costing systems and decision-making;
- capital investment appraisal;
- budgeting and budgetary control;
- double-entry bookkeeping;
- funding for sport;
- annual reports.

Using a rich variety of case studies, examples and data from the real world of sport management, the book places each concept into a managerial context, ensuring that the reader understands why that concept is important and how best to employ each technique. Each chapter also contains a range of useful features, including chapter introductions, learning objectives, activities, summaries, review questions and further reading. This is the most useful, comprehensive and accessible introduction to financial management for sport currently available and is essential reading for any student of sport management or sport development.

Robert Wilson is a Principal Lecturer in Sport Business Management at Sheffield Hallam University. His subject specialisms are financial reporting, management accounting and economic decision-making in the sport industry, and his research interests are in the financing of professional team sport and the economics of major events. He is the co-author of *Finance for Sport and Leisure Managers: An Introduction*, and a recognised expert in learning, teaching and assessment in higher education.

MANAGING SPORT FINANCE

ROBERT WILSON

LONDON AND NEW YORK

First published 2011
by Routledge
2 Park Square, Milton Park, Abingdon, Oxon OX14 4RN

Simultaneously published in the USA and Canada
by Routledge
711 Third Avenue, New York, NY 10017

Routledge is an imprint of the Taylor & Francis Group, an informa business

© 2011 Robert Wilson

The right of Robert Wilson to be identified as author of this work has been asserted by him in accordance with sections 77 and 78 of the Copyright, Designs and Patents Act 1988.

All rights reserved. No part of this book may be reprinted or reproduced or utilised in any form or by any electronic, mechanical, or other means, now known or hereafter invented, including photocopying and recording, or in any information storage or retrieval system, without permission in writing from the publishers.

Trademark notice: Product or corporate names may be trademarks or registered trademarks, and are used only for identification and explanation without intent to infringe.

British Library Cataloguing in Publication Data
A catalogue record for this book is available from the British Library

Library of Congress Cataloging in Publication Data
Wilson, Robert, 1980–
  Managing sport finance / by Robert Wilson.
     p. cm.
  1. Sports—Finance. 2. Sports administration. I. Title.
  GV716.W554 2011
  796.0691—dc22   2010034996

ISBN: 978–0–415–58179–0 (hbk)
ISBN: 978–0–415–58180–6 (pbk)
ISBN: 978–0–203–85000–8 (ebk)

Typeset in Zapf Humanist and Eras
by Keystroke, Station Road, Codsall, Wolverhampton

Printed and bound in Great Britain by TJ International Ltd, Padstow, Cornwall

CONTENTS

List of illustrations   xi
Preface   xiii

PART 1   FINANCIAL REPORTING   1

1   FINANCIAL ACCOUNTING IN CONTEXT   3

Introduction   3
Accounting in sport   5
The importance of financial management in sport   9
The users of financial information   13
Legal identity   15
Financial versus management accounts   17
Statutory requirements in sport and leisure   18
Summary   19
Questions for review   19
References and further reading   20

2   REGULATORY FRAMEWORKS IN SPORT   21

Introduction   21
The regulatory framework   23
Accounting rules   29
More accounting terminology   33
The impact of the regulatory framework on sport   34
Corporate governance   36
Summary   37
Questions for review   39
References and further reading   40

3 THE MECHANICS OF FINANCIAL ACCOUNTING 41

Introduction 41
Recording business transactions 44
The accounting equation 45
The double-entry rule 48
Choice of accounts 52
Applying the double-entry rule 53
Summary 57
Questions for review 58
References and further reading 60

4 ACCOUNTING RECORDS IN SPORT 61

Introduction 61
Loan interest 61
Depreciation 64
Discounts 68
Bad debts 70
Returns 73
Disposals of fixed assets 74
Summary 76
Questions for review 77
References and further reading 77

5 FROM 'T' ACCOUNTS TO FINANCIAL STATEMENTS: CONSTRUCTING A TRIAL BALANCE 78

Introduction 78
The trial balance 79
Limitations to the trial balance 82
The trial balance balances! Now what? 82
Summary 85
Questions for review 86
References and further reading 86

6 FINAL ADJUSTMENTS IN SPORT 87

Introduction 87
Cost of sales 88
Mispostings 90
Accruals 91
Prepayments 92
Summary 92

Questions for review	93
References and further reading	93

7 THE FINANCIAL STATEMENTS — 94

Introduction	94
The income statement: measuring financial performance	95
Interpreting the income statement	98
The balance sheet: a snapshot of the financial position	99
Interpreting the balance sheet	101
Relationship between the income statement and balance sheet	103
Cash flow statement	103
Cash versus profit	107
Non-trading (or not-for-profit) organisations	107
Summary	110
Questions for review	111
References and further reading	111

8 ANNUAL REPORTS — 112

Introduction	112
Contents of an annual report	113
Notes to the accounts	115
Summary	120
Questions for review	121
References and further reading	121

9 INTERPRETING ANNUAL REPORTS — 122

Introduction	122
Why analyse annual reports?	123
Dissecting annual reports	125
Introducing ratio analysis	129
The steps of financial ratio analysis	130
Growth	131
Profitability ratios	134
Liquidity ratios	140
Defensive position ratios (long-term solvency)	143
Investment ratios	147
Ratio analysis and its limits	149
Summary	150
Questions for review	150
References and further reading	150

PART 2 FINANCIAL MANAGEMENT   151

10 UNDERSTANDING THE NATURE OF COST IN SPORT   153

Introduction   153
Cost   154
What is cost accounting?   155
Cost control   156
Monitoring routine performance   160
Summary   162
Questions for review   163
References and further reading   163

11 SHORT-TERM DECISION-MAKING   164

Introduction   164
Classifying costs by behaviour   165
What is marginal costing?   165
Marginal costing theory   167
Revenue statements in marginal costing format   167
The role of contribution   168
Contribution/sales ratio   169
Breakeven analysis   171
Establishing the breakeven point in units   172
Establishing breakeven points in revenue   174
Illustrating breakeven analysis   176
Cost structures   177
Margin of safety   178
Application of marginal costing   180
Comparing alternative marketing strategies   180
Extra order profitability calculations   183
Make or buy decisions   184
Summary   187
Questions for review   188
References and further reading   188

12 BUDGETING AND BUDGETARY CONTROL   189

Introduction   189
The meaning of budgeting   192
Applying budgeting to worked examples   201
Comparing actual and budgeted performance   206
Summary   210
Questions for review   211
References and further reading   211

13 INVESTMENT APPRAISAL AND LONG-TERM DECISION-MAKING 212

Introduction	212
The purpose of investment appraisal	213
Project data	214
Payback period	216
The accounting rate of return	218
Net present value: a discounting method	220
Compound interest	221
Discounting	222
Discount factors	224
Discounting tables and formula	224
Net present value	224
Using NPV to evaluate two or more projects	226
Internal rate of return	228
Summary	232
Questions for review	233
References and further reading	233

14 SPORT FUNDING AND FINANCE 234

Introduction	234
Funding options	235
Non-commercial finance options	235
Commercial finance options	239
Alternative finance options	241
The funding process	244
Monitoring and evaluation: key performance indicators	245
Summary	246
Questions for review	246
References and further reading	247

Appendix A: Additional case study	248
Appendix B: Answers to review questions	249
Glossary of terms	259
Index	264

ILLUSTRATIONS

FIGURES

1.1	Tottenham Hotspur Statement of Ambition	6
1.2	Tottenham Hotspur income statement	6
1.3	Tottenham Hotspur balance sheet	7
1.4	Tottenham Hotspur financial highlights	8
1.5	Tottenham Hotspur summary and outlook	9
1.6	Tottenham Hotspur shareholders' funds	15
2.1	Rugby Football Union profit and loss account (or income statement)	23
2.2	Rugby Football Union balance sheet	24
2.3	RFU statement of accounting policies	25
2.4	RFU statement of responsibility	32
2.5	An example of an asset statement	35
2.6	A breakdown of asset figures applying FRS 10	36
2.7	Rugby Football Union corporate governance	38
3.1	Kitlocker.com and their start-up balance sheet	45
3.2	Kitlocker.com balance sheet Mk II	47
3.3	Kitlocker.com balance sheet Mk III	48
5.1	Mike: trading income statement	84
5.2	Mike: balance sheet at end of first trading period	85
7.1	Tottenham Hotspur income statement	97
7.2	Tottenham Hotspur notes to the accounts	98
7.3	Tottenham Hotspur balance sheet	101
7.4	Tottenham Hotspur notes to the accounts	102
7.5	Tottenham Hotspur cash flow statement	106
7.6	British Triathlon Federation income and expenditure account	109
7.7	British Triathlon Federation balance sheet	110
8.1	JJB Annual Report contents	113
8.2	The opening to the Chairman's report	114
8.3	Statement of gains and losses	116
8.4	Statement of accounting policies	117
8.5	Notes to the accounts: revenue	118
8.6	Lack of detail in the financial statements	118

8.7	Notes to the accounts: revenue	119
8.8	Lack of detail in the financial statements (2)	120
9.1	Process diagram for considering financial health analysis requirements	124
9.2	JJB Sports operating results	126
9.3	JJB Sports explanation of exceptional operating expenses	126
9.4	JJB Sports income statement	127
9.5	JJB Sports plc balance sheet	128
9.6	JJB Sports income statement growth analysis	132
9.7	JJB Sports balance sheet growth analysis	133
9.8	Gross profit ratio figure selection	135
9.9	Operating profit ratio figure selection	136
9.10	ROCE ratio figure selection	137
9.11	Turnover: capital employed ratio figure selection	138–9
9.12	Current ratio figure selection	141
9.13	Quick ratio figure selection	142
9.14	Debt ratio figure selection	144
9.15	Gearing ratio figure selection	146
10.1	The private sector health and business club	162
11.1	Graphical representation of breakeven	177
12.1	The budgeting process	193
12.2	Rugby club continuation budget	199
12.3	An income statement	202
12.4	Rugby club annual budget sub-analysed by month	203
12.5	Opening balance sheet, change, and closing balance sheet	205
12.6	Abbreviated cash budget	207
12.7	Actual versus budget comparison	208
13.1	Discounting and compounding	223
14.1	The funding process	245

TABLES

1.1	Users of financial information and their information needs	14
2.1	Manchester United Football Club takeover timeline	28
10.1	The relationship between financial and management accounting	156

PREFACE

Today's sport industry is huge and far more important than people tend to believe. It has also changed at a startling pace over the past twenty years. The Sport Industry Research Centre, based at Sheffield Hallam University, suggests that sport accounts for 2.5 per cent of consumer expenditure and as an industry is worth something in the region of £24 billion per year (Sport Industry Research Centre). Consequently students studying sports-related degree programmes and industry managers need to be acutely aware of how they can manage money, provide value for money and maximise profit in what is becoming an increasingly competitive marketplace.

This book has been written because I believe students and managers need a quick reference guide to finance, as well as a book that doesn't disappear into a world of technical language, obstructive theory and complicated equations. When I wrote *Finance for Sport and Leisure Managers: An Introduction* with John Joyce, it was the first real accounting for sport book in the marketplace. We wrote it because we like students and we like helping them, and we believed that, given the obvious gap on a sport library shelf, one way to help students understand finance was to write a book about it – that way, even the students whom we never saw (and there can be a few these days, given all of the extracurricular opportunities on offer at university) might just see what a great subject this is. It is not that we thought other books were bad or that our book is better. It is that we thought our book would be different – and it was (see Bill Gerrard's review in *Managing Leisure*, 2009).

As a result, this book is written in a similar style to *Finance for Sport and Leisure Managers*. That is to say, it isn't a book that gets bogged down with terminology or formulas to remember; nor is it a book that uses convoluted explanations when simple ones will do. I have tried to make it as student-friendly as possible, and consequently have written it in a less formal style. I hope that you enjoy reading it as much as I have enjoyed writing it, and that you will see the value in using 'real world' examples (some of which have come from my students) instead of fictitious case studies and can recognise that it offers something different to the mountains of academic texts that, in many cases, seem only to make accounting and finance appear difficult.

Managing Sport Finance provides a practical, applied and critical look at the important but often confusing area of public, private and voluntary sector sport finance. The book is specifically aimed at students who have no prior knowledge of financial reporting, management accounting or economic decision-making and seeks to offer a 'one-stop shop' to understanding the bewildering language of finance in a sport context. By adopting a step-by-step approach it will guide you through the maze of financial rules, regulations, concepts and terminology before moving on to take a practical and applied look at finance in progress so that you will understand the meaning and application of finance in the context of sport.

As I have already mentioned, the sport industry is huge and generates in excess of £24 billion in consumer expenditure per annum. The case for the importance of this book and understanding it can rest here! As future or current managers in sport or employees in the wider industry, you need to establish how you can get a slice of this huge cake, whether you are trying to generate profit or help facilitate a community, school or club initiative. Once you get some of the cash you need to treat it with care and confidence, and control and use it so that you can be effective in your job. You should therefore find this book a useful reference text throughout your career and you will certainly be able to use it while studying financial reporting or management accounting on a degree programme, or simply leave it on the shelf as a useful dip-into text. One of the book's genuine strengths is the use of examples throughout the chapters and the activities embedded within them that I ask you to complete. Very often you may need to look at some figures and will have no idea what they mean; I will give you the knowledge and show you how to use that knowledge.

While *Finance for Sport and Leisure Managers: An Introduction* was reviewed well and received glowing reports from students due to the accessibility of the language used and the realism of the case material, the title narrowed the market and the content did not develop enough 'financial management' skills due to the focus on 'accounting'. This second book starts where the first left off, with a coverage of accounting, but it then broadens into financial management, taking into consideration the tools of finance: budgeting, pricing, funding and capital investment appraisal. Consequently, the book is structured in two main parts: financial reporting and financial management. Conceptually this will help you engage with the subject gradually and at a pace that suits you. Once the mechanics of financial reporting are out of the way you will see how finance works in action.

You will find an introduction at the beginning of each chapter that summarises what it is about and how you will be taken through it. As this is a progressive book we will build on the skills you have mastered in each chapter, so don't rush too far ahead (or, as my students tend to do, miss out the odd session or chapter), since this will limit your grasp of the material. Once you have completed Part 1 you should be able to confidently construct a basic set of financial statements and interpret them to help you make decisions based on historical data. Having completed Part 2 you will be able to construct detailed management accounts and plans, make decisions and exercise business control which would be a real asset to any organisation. The emphasis throughout is on the application of key principles, and consequently you can work through things at your own pace, examine some of the issues in depth and see how everything works in practice through the use of industry examples and case studies. You will also find a series of review questions at the end of each chapter so that you can continue to apply your knowledge (you will find the answers in Appendix B at the end of the book).

As I have already mentioned, this book recognises that most of you may not have studied finance before. Therefore you will find that the book is written in an accessible, clear, concise and user-friendly style. I will not take you down blind alleys to explain the meaning of obscure transactions or events but will instead stick to the rules and principles that will be of benefit to you on a day-to-day basis. Where the use of specialist terminology is unavoidable I provide clear explanations and supporting examples where necessary. In addition, all of the key terms are listed in alphabetical order in the Glossary of terms at the back of the book.

Interspersed through most of the chapters are a number of activities. I would strongly advise you to complete these as they are designed to act as the sort of quick-fire questions that I, as a lecturer, would fire at you in the classroom. They also give you an opportunity to check that you understand what has been covered so far.

Finally, and before you start reading this masterpiece, I would like to acknowledge the guidance and support of a number of people who have made this book possible. First, Professor John Joyce who held my hand during my first book and who has agreed to let me use the material on financial reporting here. Second, my long-term mentor Professor Simon Shibli who baptised me into the world of finance as an undergraduate and helped me secure my first teaching post as a 22-year-old (and for contributing to Chapter 12 on budgeting). Third, the students of mine who have given me the motivation to write this book (all of your failings are in here so that others don't make the same mistakes) and those who have helped with the development of some of the material so that it really is user-friendly. Finally, to Sarah, Alfie and our new arrival, Sophie, who have endured the long days and nights while I put the book together.

Welcome to the book.

Rob

REFERENCES

Gerrard, B. (2009) Book Review. *Managing Leisure: An International Journal*, Vol .14, Issue 2. Routledge, London.
Sport Industry Research Centre (2009) *Sport Market Forecasts*. Sheffield Hallam University, Sheffield.

PART 1
FINANCIAL REPORTING

CHAPTER 1

FINANCIAL REPORTING IN CONTEXT

On completion of this chapter you will be able to:

- communicate the purpose of accounting in a sporting context;
- identify and describe the users of accounting information;
- distinguish between financial and management accounts;
- understand the information needs of user groups;
- understand the statutory requirements of sport organisations.

INTRODUCTION

It is important before we start that we establish some ground rules; put simply, finance *is not* just about numbers and you *do not* have to be a skilled mathematician to understand a set of financial statements. Instead you need to understand the guiding rules and principles that help compile and structure a set of accounts. Put simply, accounting is a way of showing to external stakeholders and internal management how well a business has performed over a period of time and its prospects for continuing to operate.

The aim of Part 1 of this book is to focus on how to use accounts and accounting information so that you can understand them, if not necessarily produce them. As managers or future managers you need to be able to interpret and then communicate the meaning of accounts to a variety of people and for a variety of reasons. The identification of the users and their needs provides us with the reasons for the accounts. Without an understanding of why the accounts are being prepared, the numbers and the situation they portray will be meaningless. This chapter therefore aims to put financial reporting into a context that is meaningful and to identify the different user groups and their needs to illustrate why financial reporting is integral to the sport industry.

It stands to reason that you will have come across the terms 'financial statements' or 'set of accounts' but you won't necessarily understand what they actually mean. Indeed, anyone who follows Premier League football in England will have been confronted by such statements regularly over the past few seasons. At the time of writing this book the terms have been used in conjunction with Portsmouth Football Club and Manchester United Football Club on what seems like a daily basis, but many will not appreciate their importance. You may also have wondered who uses accounting information and what the purpose of accounting actually is. Some of you may even have thought that they were meaningless terms, given how professional football clubs seem to run themselves. So before we get stuck into some of the nuts and bolts let us start with a quick overview to help you understand what accounting is all about.

> **KEY TERMS**
>
> ## ACCOUNTING
>
> Is about identifying, collecting, measuring, recording, summarising and communicating financial information.
>
> ## ACCOUNT
>
> A record that is kept as part of an accounting system. It will be a record of the transactions and will be recorded in monetary values.
>
> ## FINANCIAL STATEMENTS
>
> The complete set of accounts. This will include the balance sheet (which shows the organisation's assets and liabilities), income statement (the profit and loss account) and the cash flow statement. Also included will be notes on the accounting policies used and significant activities.

> **ACTIVITY**
>
> Why do you think financial statements and accounts are important?

Hopefully the answer here is straightforward. Financial statements enable us to see what is really going on with money in a particular organisation. Using the examples mentioned above, in Portsmouth FC's case, at the time of writing it is possible to examine the club's financial statements and see that it owes a great deal of money and cannot really afford to pay it, while Manchester United seems to have a significant level of debt (i.e. money owed to other people), although the club has sufficient income to look after itself.

As students or managers who work within the sport industry it is vital that you appreciate the importance of financial management and responsibility, and that you can communicate key financial information to both the internal and external stakeholders. Sport and leisure is now big business. Indeed, the Sport Industry Research Centre (2009) indicates that the sport and leisure sector is worth around £20 billion, which roughly equates to 2.5 per cent of consumer expenditure. By 2011 this is expected to rise to an estimated £24 billion

(SIRC, 2009). This proves that sport and leisure is far more serious and less frivolous than people believe.

ACCOUNTING IN SPORT

Sport finance deals with financial management in all types of sport organisations and, while it is inevitable that much of the literature surrounding the subject is focused on professional team sports as the most high-profile and commercialised part of the industry, sport finance is relevant to all forms of sport organisations as they will all have objectives and will all need to manage their money. Indeed, the commodification and professionalisation of sport has led to vast sums of money being invested at all levels: for example, Tom Walkinshaw's investment in Gloucester Rugby Football Club in 1997 shortly after the sport turned professional; and Malcolm Glazer's £700 million purchase of Manchester United in 2005. Stewart (2007) also identifies that sport and leisure has established itself as a mechanism for creating personal meaning, cultural identity (e.g. the purchase of a replica football shirt) and a lucrative career path for many people all over the world. Deloitte's *Annual Review of Football Finance* (2008) identifies that ten clubs earned in excess of 200 million euros a year, while in the USA many professional sportsmen earn more than US$1 million a year.

Unfortunately, sport has lagged behind other business sectors from a financial management point of view. For the most part sport marketing, planning and strategy have dominated sport business management education and led to a growing maturity in such areas. Financial management has often been overlooked, anecdotally because individuals claim to have some sort of fear of numbers. There are still many sport managers and graduates with sport management degrees who struggle even to understand the basics of an income statement or balance sheet, let alone have the confidence to make informed judgements on the financial health of an organisation. However, every organisation ranging from multi-million-pound operations such as Manchester United Football Club through to small, local, voluntary sport clubs such as the City of Sheffield Swimming Club need to produce a set of financial statements at least once a year. Therefore, if organisations have to do it, the chances are that should managers wish to be successful in employment, they will also have to understand, communicate and use financial information.

The information that is provided in the accounts is concerned with the resources held by the organisation and how they are used. The accounts therefore show the organisation's financial position (something we shall come back to in Chapter 9) at the end of a financial period, an analysis of changes during the period, and point to the future prospects of the organisation. Such information will be of great importance to anyone who has an interest in an organisation because it shows whether or not the organisation is achieving its goals.

It is probably worth having a quick look at some financial statements here. If nothing else, this will show you the financial results of an organisation and how an accountant presents them. In Figures 1.1, 1.2 and 1.3 you will find a paragraph or two about the organisation's goals, the income statement (or profit and loss account) and balance sheet for Tottenham Hotspur Football Club. These are the actual excerpts from the company's annual report and something that I will ask you to think about later. It is important that you don't worry about what everything means here but it is useful if you can see what the two statements are basically illustrating while referring to the club's ambitions (or corporate statement).

> "WE HAVE MADE SIGNIFICANT PROGRESS IN DELIVERING ON OUR LONG-TERM VISION FOR THE CLUB. WE HAVE ALWAYS HAD THREE KEY PRIORITIES AND YOU WILL HAVE HEARD THEM OFT REPEATED – INVESTMENT IN THE FIRST TEAM, A NEW TRAINING CENTRE AND AN INCREASED CAPACITY STATE-OF-THE-ART NEW STADIUM."
>
> Daniel Levy
> Chairman, Tottenham Hotspur plc

Figure 1.1 Tottenham Hotspur Statement of Ambition
Source: From Tottenham Hotspur plc Annual Report and Financial Statements 2009.

ACTIVITY

Using the information that you have on Tottenham Hotspur Football Club (see the next few pages), can you answer the following questions?
- Is the organisation meeting its objectives?
- How has the business performed over the past year?
- What are its future prospects?

CONSOLIDATED INCOME STATEMENT
for the year ended 30 June 2009

Continuing operations

	Note	Operations, excluding football trading* £'000	Football trading* £'000	Total £'000	Year ended 30 June 2008 Total (note 3) £'000
Revenue	4	113,012	–	113,012	114,788
Operating expenses	5	(94,622)	(38,099)	(132,721)	(124,298)
Operating profit/(loss)		18,390	(38,099)	(19,709)	(9,510)
Profit on disposal of intangible fixed assets	8	–	56,500	56,500	16,362
Profit from operations	6	18,390	18,401	36,791	6,852
Finance income	9			4,563	1,797
Finance costs	9			(7,956)	(5,662)
Profit on ordinary activities before taxation				33,398	2,987
Tax	10			(10,234)	(2,018)
Profit for the period from continuing operations	23			23,164	969
Earnings per share from continuing operations – basic	11			25.0p	1.0p
Earnings per share from continuing operations – diluted	11			12.9p	1.0p

* Football trading represents the amortisation, impairment, and the profit/(loss) on disposal of intangible fixed assets and other football trading related income and expenditure.

There were no other gains or losses in either the current or prior year, accordingly no consolidated statement of recognised income and expense is presented.

Figure 1.2 Tottenham Hotspur income statement
Source: From Tottenham Hotspur plc Annual Report and Financial Statements 2009.

CONSOLIDATED BALANCE SHEET
as at 30 June 2009

	Note	30 June 2009 £'000	30 June 2008 £'000
Non-current assets			
Property, plant and equipment	12	**103,338**	74,130
Intangible assets	13	**128,432**	62,423
		231,770	136,553
Current assets			
Inventories	14	**1,172**	1,884
Trade and other receivables	15	**37,738**	41,292
Current tax receivable		**1,104**	2,182
Cash and cash equivalents	16	**19,622**	35,283
		59,636	80,641
Total assets		**291,406**	217,194
Current liabilities			
Trade and other payables	17	**(89,579)**	(77,496)
Interest bearing loans and borrowings	17	**(13,810)**	(7,798)
Provisions	17	**(1,211)**	(5,602)
		(104,600)	(90,896)
Non-current liabilities			
Interest bearing overdrafts and loans	18	**(66,504)**	(57,187)
Trade and other payables	18	**(37,871)**	(14,607)
Deferred grant income	18	**(2,211)**	(2,143)
Deferred tax liabilities	18/19	**(18,157)**	(9,751)
		(124,743)	(83,688)
Total liabilities		**(229,343)**	(174,584)
Net assets		**62,063**	42,610
Equity			
Share capital	21	**4,640**	4,639
Share premium		**11,638**	11,637
Equity component of convertible redeemable preference shares ("CRPS")	22	**3,805**	3,806
Revaluation reserve		**2,240**	2,288
Capital redemption reserve		**595**	595
Retained earnings		**39,145**	19,645
Total equity	23	**62,063**	42,610

These financial statements were approved by the Board of Directors on 9 November 2009.

Figure 1.3 Tottenham Hotspur balance sheet

Source: From Tottenham Hotspur plc Annual Report and Financial Statements 2009.

At this point in the book it is difficult to say what is really going on here as we have no knowledge of what all the terms mean on both the income statement and balance sheet. In fact, unless you have cheated and looked ahead, you probably don't even know what the income statement and balance sheet are! Don't worry; if we apply a bit of logic here we can actually paint a rough picture of what is going on and see through the maze of financial terminology to work up some answers.

The answers to the activity are all interlinked. The income statement tells us that the football club has made a profit of £33.4 million before tax. Moreover, if we compare the figures from 2008 to those of 2009 we will see that the club has increased its pre-tax profit considerably (from around £3 million to around £33 million). Thus, in terms of financial performance the football club is doing well. We should now ask: Why?

In a nutshell Spurs have made a considerable profit due to the increase in profit on player trading (£56.5 million in 2009, up from £16.4 million in 2008). You can probably see the figures if you look at the income statement but as usual the accountants want to make things a little difficult to understand, so they have termed the 'profit on player trading' as 'profit on disposal of intangible fixed assets' – we will come back to this later. The general conclusions that we may draw from this is that Spurs are well set financially for the new season and have the money they need to meet their objectives (i.e. invest in the playing squad, a new first team training centre and increased capacity in a new stadium).

While the income statement tells us about the organisation's financial performance the balance sheet illustrates what the organisation has to use to conduct business (its assets). It also details the money that the organisation owes to others (its liabilities). A quick look at Spurs' balance sheet shows that they have enough assets to cover their liabilities (c. £291 million in assets versus c. £229 million in liabilities in 2009). Again a quick comparison with 2008 shows that the club has increased its assets, principally its property and intangible fixed assets (players), and has also increased its liabilities. If we put these figures into the context of the football industry, and what the media tell us about football finance, I would say that Spurs aren't doing too badly at all. That said, this is only a brief look at their financial statements and we should really examine them in more detail – the tools to do this are covered in Chapter 9.

As future managers, you will need to look at financial information with some confidence and this exercise should have helped demonstrate that annual reports and financial statements aren't actually that scary. Indeed, if you look at the full annual report much of the basic analysis will be done for you; just take a look at Figures 1.4 and 1.5. These excerpts 'highlight'

FINANCIAL HIGHLIGHTS

Revenue
£113.0m
2008 : £114.8m

Profit on ordinary activities before taxation
£33.4m
2008 : £3.0m

Group net assets increased to
£62.1m
2008 : £42.6m

Profit for the year from continuing operations
£23.2m
2008 : £1.0m

Profit on disposal of registrations
£56.5m
2008 : £16.4m

Earnings per share
25.0p
2008 : 1.0p

Figure 1.4 Tottenham Hotspur financial highlights

Source: From Tottenham Hotspur plc Annual Report and Financial Statements 2009.

SUMMARY AND OUTLOOK

- **Record profit before tax of £33.4m**
  - Revenue remains high at £113.0m
  - Player trading profit of £56.5m
  - £119.3m spent on player acquisitions in financial year
  - Group net assets increased to £62.1m from £42.6m at prior year end

- **Planning application submitted** for the Northumberland Development Project, our new stadium and related scheme

- **£61.0m committed** on property transactions in and around current stadium over the past six years

- **Works started** on our new Training Centre for the First Team and Academy at Bulls Cross in Enfield

Figure 1.5 Tottenham Hotspur summary and outlook
Source: From Tottenham Hotspur plc Annual Report and Financial Statements 2009.

the positive points that come from the annual report and financial statements and also detail what the organisation intends to do in the future.

Hopefully what this exercise will show you is that with a little bit of thought and guidance you can understand financial statements. Once you master these skills you will be able to see through the maze. However, it is crucial that you realise that no single statement can give a whole picture: profit and cash, for example, are both important indicators but they are very different. For any business, the ability to pay its debts as they fall due is vital to organisational success or failure: cash may be used to pay the bills but profit cannot.

THE IMPORTANCE OF FINANCIAL MANAGEMENT IN SPORT

The concept behind financial management is not the simplistic idea that you need to manage profit, but more importantly how to monitor, evaluate and control the income and expenditure of an organisation. It is vital for you as sport managers to understand the changing values of the three sectors (public, private and voluntary) and to recognise that a large number of sport services are provided to achieve social objectives, which operate at a loss and which will normally require a government subsidy. This does not mean, however, that proper financial controls are not important. Not surprisingly, it is vital for you to have an understanding of the costs of the products and services that you offer in order to operate as effective business entities to generate profits, or ensure that taxpayers' money is not being wasted on frivolous plans or ideas.

Many organisations will borrow to fund their expansion plans; in fact borrowing is part and parcel of everyday life if organisations wish to remain competitive. Just think about how an average person buys a house if you need proof of this; very few of us are in a position to pay for a house purchase outright; instead we talk to a bank or building society and borrow the money. Borrowing is based on the assumption that future returns will be high enough to cover the loan (and the interest!). However, problems will occur if the organisation fails to meet its obligations to the people it owes money to by not generating earnings high enough to cover its responsibilities. It may seem obvious, but it is a fact that accurate statements and forecasts about the current state of the organisation and its future cash flows are needed. Organisations need financial information to make decisions, although sometimes even with this information the wrong decisions can be made. This is a lesson that a number of professional football clubs have learned the hard way: for example, Leeds United, Leicester City, Southampton, Portsmouth (twice in ten years) and countless others. The problem in football is that no one seems to learn and the problems continue, as we shall see below.

By way of an example – and excuse the number of football references here (but that's where most of the data are) – football is business and big business at that. Over the past ten years general interest in the game has increased, as have amounts of investment, income from television broadcast rights and corporate sponsorship. For example, BSkyB paid over £600 million to Premier League football clubs between 1997 and 2001, before increasing that amount to £1.024 billion for the period 2003 to 2007, just for the rights to televise matches.

In addition to television income, success in European competitions, in particular the UEFA Champions League (UCL), has offered significant rewards to many of the top teams. The winners of the UCL are estimated to earn up to £20 million and with such large sources of cash available to the top teams, a winning team is essential. Only the top four clubs from the Premier League qualify to play in the UCL the following season. Consequently the UCL is not a guaranteed source of income: teams need to perform well to earn their place and the associated cash rewards. On the downside, if a team performs badly there are also cash implications: sources of income will dry up.

Despite the growth in potential financial gains the sport of football has been blighted by a series of high-profile problems. It is believed that only one in four football clubs expects to make a profit. This is mainly due to high transfer fees and the high wages that are paid to attract players in trying to build successful teams. In recent years clubs such as Sheffield United Football Club have published significant losses when pushing for promotion to the English Premier League (EPL) (they reported a loss of £9.6 million that season), and although they hope to recoup this through the new funding streams available in the EPL, it is clear that a game that has been perceived as cash rich is not so. While at the time of writing Portsmouth Football Club had entered administration for the second time in twelve years it is their local rivals Southampton Football Club that can be used to demonstrate what happens when you don't manage your money properly.

CASE STUDY

FINANCE, FOOTBALL AND SOUTHAMPTON LEISURE HOLDINGS

In 2003 Southampton Football Club narrowly lost to Arsenal in the FA Cup Final. By May 2005, after twenty-seven years in the top flight of English football, Southampton FC was relegated to the football Championship. Following this relegation Southampton had a series of new managers, new playing staff and new chairmen. By the time Rupert Lowe resigned in 2006 there was £3.4 million on deposit at Barclays Bank. In addition, there were payments outstanding for players such as Theo Walcott. However, by the time Lowe returned in 2008 the cash deposit had been replaced by an overdraft of £6.3 million, and an overall operating loss of £4.9 million. This was despite receiving £12.7 million profit on the sale of playing staff! Furthermore, and more importantly when we consider financial management, the club was running a player/coach wage bill of 81 per cent of turnover. Basically, this meant that for every £1 of revenue that the club generated, 81 pence was being spent on players and coaches alone, leaving 19 pence to pay for everything else including the upkeep of a 32,000-seater stadium.

What is central to effective financial management is the ability of the organisation to pay its debts as they fall due. Southampton was clearly not in a position to do so. Some further analysis of the organisation's income statement and balance sheet reveals more issues. Broadcasting revenue (often the Achilles heel of a football club) fell from £8.1 million to £3 million, match day revenue from £10.5 million to £7.9 million, commercial revenue from £4.6 million to £3.3 million, while operating expenses saw increases in the cost of players and coaches from £10.5 million to £12.2 million).

Football clubs often gamble finance with on-pitch performance, much in the same way as Leeds United did before they ran into financial difficulties due to the failure to qualify for the UEFA Champions League (see Wilson and Joyce, 2008). For Southampton, promotion back to the Premier League was not realistic in the 2007/8 season; their revenues fell while their costs rose. Disaster was on the horizon both financially and strategically.

Although the loss for the year 2007/8 amounted to £5 million, the value of the company also fell (from £7.3 million to £2.3 million). This compounded an already precarious financial position (a net debt of £19.2 million for the football club) to an overall group net debt of £27.5 million. Most small organisations will go under when they reach a net debt of about £1 million.

On 25 April 2009, Southampton Football Club was officially relegated to League One. Having entered administration, it ensured that Southampton started the next season, but in League One with a 10-point deduction. This is within six years of being FA Cup runners-up, UEFA Cup competitors and finishing eighth in the English Premier League. By the end of May 2009 the club was unable to meet its financial commitments to its staff; i.e. they could not afford to pay people's wages and had to ask employees to work unpaid. The club administrator warned that the club faced imminent bankruptcy unless a buyer was found and, while club legend Matt LeTissier fronted a

> consortium, they were unable to reach agreement to purchase the club. However, by 8 July 2009 a new buyer had been found in the form of Swiss businessman Mark Liebherr. Since then the club's fortunes have improved and by October 2009 Southampton had managed to erase the ten-point deduction and accrue eleven additional points, thanks in part to new signing Richard Lambert. While their future appears stable financially, it remains to be seen if the club can climb out of the relegation zone and reach safety.
>
> (Figures extracted from Southampton Leisure Holdings PLC, Annual Report and Accounts 2008.)
>
> ### Questions
>
> - Do you think the Southampton case suggests that football clubs, or any sport organisation, should avoid borrowing?
> - Do you think there is a right level of borrowing and, if so, how do you think it should be calculated?
> - What were the most significant issues that caused the financial decline of Southampton FC?
> - What strategies could Southampton have employed to ease their financial problems?

Borrowing is not necessarily a bad thing – nor for that matter is debt. The main issue is being able to service the debt. Can you afford to pay your credit card bill? If so, you can service your borrowing and reduce your debt. If not, your debt will grow in much the same way as it did for Southampton FC – they did not manage their finances (or borrowings) very well. So, the answer to the first question in the case study could therefore be, 'No, providing that the clubs and organisations do not borrow more than they can afford to service'.

We can answer the second question in much the same way. The right level of borrowing for any club will be determined by the amounts they can afford to pay back. Think about how a personal mortgage is worked out. If you wanted a mortgage of £100,000 costing £500 per month you would expect to have earning power of at least £1,000 per month. This would allow you to pay for the mortgage without getting into difficulties. On the other hand, if you only had an earning potential of £600 per month you would struggle to have a life and pay your mortgage. It is the same in sport except on a much larger scale. Southampton did not have enough money coming in to pay its bills.

There are two principal issues here to do with financial management. The first is that managers need to make an assessment of the market in which they are operating, as this will offer some direction as to how to deal with cost. In Southampton's case spending 81 per cent of turnover on players' and coaches' wages was not a financially acceptable thing to do. The second issue is to do with debt. Clearly Southampton has operated with a fairly high level of debt compared to the value of the company. However, it was not the concept of debt, nor the concept of borrowing, that led to the company's downfall. The issue was that they could not service the debt and that wealthy owners do not lie around every corner.

The final question is a little trickier. Short of buying better players (which would have cost more), how could they improve on-the-field success to increase the number of fans watching their games? Perhaps by getting a better manager? They tried this two or three times but without any joy. Performance-related pay? This may have worked to motivate players more but they were already tied to contracts. I think the simple answer is 'who knows?' In hindsight it is easy to say that Southampton got it wrong. If they had sorted out the financial packages more effectively they may not have gone so wildly out of control. Hopefully this book will help you to spot similar problems in your working life before it is too late and prevent you from getting into the position that Southampton were in!

THE USERS OF FINANCIAL INFORMATION

Financial information will be useful to a wide variety of stakeholders, who will often span several sectors and each will have slightly different needs for the information. For example, Malcolm Glazer (the owner of Manchester United FC) will want to know how much profit his company has made, to ensure that he can afford the necessary interest payments on the loans he took out to finance his takeover in 2005. Sheffield City Council will want to know how much subsidy they have to provide in order to keep all of their leisure services running across the city, so that their council taxpayers get value for money. The Chairperson of the Cheltenham Swimming and Water Polo Club will want to ensure that enough money is being received through subscriptions and funding to cover their running costs. However, before we move on to examine who the main users of financial information are and why they need such information, have a go at the following activity.

ACTIVITY

Select a business, organisation or club and make a list of who you think will be interested in its financial information. In addition, think about why they might need such information and write it down (allow about five minutes to complete this activity).

Your ideas will generally depend on the type of business you were thinking about. If you were thinking about Gloucester Rugby Football Club you could have identified Tom Walkinshaw as a user of financial information because he will want to see how his company (Gloucester Rugby Football Club Limited) is performing; for example, did he make a profit last year? Alternatively, if you were thinking about your local athletics club you could have identified one of the club's members as a user of financial information because they would want to see how the club was using the income from its subscriptions. As clubs and associations exist to provide a service to their members they must ensure that the money received through subscriptions and fundraising is sufficient to cover the running costs of the club. However, other businesses may exist to make a profit for their owners.

Generally, information relating to the finance of an organisation is of interest to its owners, managers, trade contacts (e.g. suppliers), providers of finance (e.g. banks), employees and customers. All of these groups of people need to be sure that the organisation is strong, can pay its bills, make a profit if it is commercial, and remain in business. An indicative list of users and their areas of interest is illustrated in Table 1.1.

It is widely accepted that the financial statements of any organisation cannot meet all the information needs of its user groups. However, most users will have common requirements: they need to know the organisation's ability to make a profit or loss, how much cash it has (this is called liquidity) and its ability to fulfil obligations to clients.

Accessibility by the general public to financial information will depend on the 'status' of the specific organisation in which they are interested. For example, the sportswear company Kitlocker.com (a case study that we will use throughout this book) are currently operating as a partnership. As a result, they are not required to make any sort of public disclosure of financial information. The main users of their information will be the owners themselves and

Table 1.1 Users of financial information and their information needs

User groups	Areas of interest
Owners of a company	Owners will want to know how well the management of the organisation are doing on a day-to-day basis and how much profit they can take from the organisation for their own use.
Managers	Managers require financial information so that they can make future plans for the organisation and see how effective their decisions have been.
Trade contacts (i.e. suppliers)	Suppliers and other trade contacts need to know if they are going to be paid on time by the organisation.
Providers of finance (i.e. banks etc)	Banks and other lenders of finance need to ensure that any loans and interest payments are going to be made on time before they lend money and during the repayment period.
Her Majesty's Revenue and Customs (UK), Internal Revenue Service (USA) or the Australian Taxation Office, etc.	The tax office needs information about the profits of the organisation so that they can work out how much tax the organisation owes. They also need details for VAT and employees' income tax.
Employees	Organisations' employees often wish to know that their jobs are safe and that they are going to be paid on time.
Customers	It is normal for customers to know if goods/services purchased are going to be delivered/provided. They may also be interested in investing in the company and therefore will want to know whether it is a good prospect.

any managers they appoint. However, a company that is listed on the London Stock Exchange, such as Powerleague (five-a-side football league operators), has a statutory obligation to publish an annual report (which will include financial statements) and send copies to Companies House.

LEGAL IDENTITY

It is important to realise that in accounting, the business and the owners are seen as two separate bodies. You can see this in the notes to the accounts which explain the figures on the balance sheet for Tottenham Hotspur Football Club (see Figure 1.6). This shows the bottom section of the balance sheet and an explanation of note 23 which details the shareholders funds: 'equity (or capital)' is the owner's stake in the business.

This concept is always applied in accounting. In law the business and the owners can be separate. The law recognises that a business may acquire assets and debts in its own right. In such a situation, if the business goes bankrupt the shareholders are not required to pay the deficit: the debts are the responsibility of the business. The owners (shareholders) have limited liability.

Before we look at the different types of businesses you will need to understand that they can take two forms: unincorporated and incorporated. Unincorporated businesses are sole traders or partnerships. Incorporated businesses are public or private companies.

Equity			
Share capital	21	**4,640**	4,639
Share premium		**11,638**	11,637
Equity component of convertible redeemable preference shares ("CRPS")	22	**3,805**	3,806
Revaluation reserve		**2,240**	2,288
Capital redemption reserve		**595**	595
Retained earnings		**39,145**	19,645
Total equity	23	**62,063**	42,610

23. Reconciliation of movements in Group shareholders' funds

	2009 £'000	2008 £'000
Opening shareholders' funds	**42,610**	46,128
Profit for the year	23,164	969
Ordinary 5p shares redeemed during the year	–	(841)
Dividend payment	(3,712)	(3,733)
Conversion of CRPS to ordinary shares	**1**	87
Net addition/(reduction) to shareholders' funds	**19,453**	(3,518)
Closing shareholders' funds	**62,063**	42,610

Figure 1.6 Tottenham Hotspur shareholders' funds

Source: From Tottenham Hotspur plc Annual Report and Financial Statements 2009.

KEY TERMS

LIMITED LIABILITY

Legal protection given to the owners of a company. When a company cannot pay its debts the shareholders will not be liable to contribute more than their initial investment towards the overall debt.

UNLIMITED LIABILITY

In short, the opposite of limited liability. At least one of the shareholders (be it a sole trader or partnership) will be liable for the total debt the company incurs.

LIQUIDATION

This is quite simply the process by which a company ceases to exist. It is a legal status rather than a financial position.

- *Sole traders*: one person owns the business. In this case there is no legal separation of identity between the business and the owner (although there will be for accounting purposes). The debts of the business are also the debts of the owner and there is no obligation for the public disclosure of financial information about the business.
- *Partnerships*: this is when two or more people enter into business together. The liability will be shared between the owners and at least one of them will have unlimited liability for the debts they may incur.
- *Private company (limited company)*: this is a company where the obligation of its owners is limited to the amount that they invested. If the business goes bankrupt the owners will lose their shares but the creditors cannot chase them for the company's debts. To form a limited company it must be registered at Companies House and the firm must have various legal documents including a Memorandum and Articles of Association. There need only be one director. The company must prepare annual accounts and submit them to Companies House. Private limited companies may be a small family-based business or they could be a major international organisation (such as the Virgin group).
- *Public company*: a public limited company (plc) has shares, but the key difference between private and public companies is that the shares in a public company can be purchased by anyone (they are traded on the stock exchange). Ownership is therefore open to anyone who wants to buy shares. Plcs have legal requirements in that they have to produce annual reports and accounts and file them with Companies House. They must have two directors.
- *Not-for-profit*: an organisation that exists for reasons other than to maximise profit. While many professional sport teams, private health clubs and high street stores operate to generate huge revenues intended to make a profit, the majority of sport organisations

are actually interested in servicing the needs of their members – just consider how many local sport clubs there are or sport development agencies! These types of organisations are interested in having a structure that gives not-for-profit status while at the same time protecting their members from creditors. Governments now have in place legislation which allows community sport organisations to register as what are termed 'incorporated associations'. This enables their members to be legally separated from the organisation while allowing tax-free status by virtue of their not-for-profit status. Any surplus will be reinvested in the development of their facilities and services and in the general development of the sport concerned.

FINANCIAL VERSUS MANAGEMENT ACCOUNTS

Essentially there are two types of accounts: financial and management. Depending on the nature of a user's information needs (something that was explored a little earlier) the style of the accounts may be quite different. In addition, we can already see that accounting information can look both forwards (i.e. to the future) and backwards (i.e. to the past) and that there are people both inside and outside the business who use it. In a nutshell financial accounting (what we are predominantly interested in for this book) concerns the preparation of information for external use, and is mainly concerned with reporting past events. When looking backwards (i.e. into the past), it is normal to examine financial accounts as they are prepared for external use and are based on historical information; they are also required by law. A set of financial accounts will, for example, illustrate the past financial position and financial performance of an organisation.

KEY TERM

FINANCIAL ACCOUNTING

The term used to describe the system for recording historical financial transactions and presenting this information in summary form.

However, should managers wish to be more proactive and examine future trends and issues, they will need to examine more forward-looking (future) accounting information. Such information will not be found in financial accounts, hence there are management accounts (i.e. accounts that look forward and are based on providing information for managers to help with the planning, decision-making and control of organisations). Unlike financial accounts, management accounts are not a statutory requirement. It is important that managers understand the distinction between the two types of accounts, as these dictate where they should look for information.

In reality, as managers, you should appreciate that financial and management accounts work together hand in hand. Even though the law stipulates that financial accounts should be constructed within the parameters set out by the International Accounting Standards (IAS), no managers in their right mind would record financial transactions and hope for the best.

> **KEY TERM**
>
> ## MANAGEMENT ACCOUNTING
>
> The term used to describe more forward-looking financial data for planning, decision-making and control purposes.

Instead they will plan their operations, consider the implications of their decisions and control their organisation in such a way that they reach (in most cases) their organisation's objectives. In order to plan and make effective decisions, a manager will have to adopt the principles of good management accounting, for example budgeting, breakeven analysis and costing – all of which will be explored in Part 2 of this book. Consequently, a rounded understanding of how the two types of accounting practice are applied is essential for a successful manager.

The purpose of putting this book together was so that we could examine both areas and see how they impact upon each other. As you will be aware, Part 1 will focus on financial accounting and how to use the information to form a view on how well a business has performed.

STATUTORY REQUIREMENTS IN SPORT AND LEISURE

Each and every sport organisation has a responsibility to produce financial statements: the legal requirements will be determined by the nature of the company (i.e. whether they are a sole trader or a public company, as discussed earlier). Later in the book you will find out how these statements are developed and how to interpret them. However, to end this chapter we will briefly examine the meaning of the two main financial statements that will be drawn up by financial accountants: the balance sheet and income statement (or profit and loss account if you are looking at information from a few years ago before the terminology changed; these were illustrated earlier in this chapter when we looked at Tottenham Hotspur Football Club).

> **KEY TERM**
>
> ## BALANCE SHEET
>
> A list of all of the assets owned by a business and all of the liabilities owed by a business at a specific point in time. It is often referred to as a 'snapshot' of the financial position of the business at a specific moment in time (normally the end of the financial year).

It is worth mentioning here that 'assets' are resources that the business owns, for example buildings, machinery and vehicles. Such resources will be used by the business in its operations. There may also be bank balances and cash. These will hold the funds that the business needs to operate. However, the business may also owe money to its owners, other people or organisations – we call these liabilities. Why not skip back a few pages and have a look at the assets and liabilities for Southampton Football Club and familiarise yourself with what they own and owe?

> **KEY TERM**
>
> **INCOME STATEMENT (profit and loss account)**
>
> A statement showing the profits (or losses) recognised during a certain period. The profit is calculated by deducting expenditure (including charges for capital maintenance) from income.

A limited company will produce a profit and loss account for the period of one year. However, it is not uncommon for internal users to produce income statements on a quarterly or even monthly basis. Income statements that you come across are likely to be in annual reports and will therefore be for a twelve-month period. Organisations that are 'not-for-profit' such as charities produce a similar statement called an income and expenditure account, which will show any surplus of income over expenditure (or a deficit if expenditure exceeds income). Again, look back to the statements for Tottenham Hotspur Football Club and see what is going on there.

SUMMARY

This first chapter has been designed to introduce you to financial accounting. During the chapter I have shown you why financial accounting is important to sport organisations and I have also highlighted the main users of financial information. Furthermore, you have been introduced to the main financial statements – you will learn how to understand and construct these during the remainder of this book.

The main financial statements have been illustrated and explained in brief. Although we will come back to visit these in much more detail later on, it was worth letting you see what the end result of this book will be. You should have by now grasped a few of the basic skills required to read the financial statements and should be able to see why the information is so valuable to businesses, and why it should be so important to you as you embark on a journey to understand finance in sport and leisure.

QUESTIONS FOR REVIEW

1. Why do managers use financial information?
2. List three users of financial information (ignoring managers).
3. What are the four main company types?

4   What type of information does financial accounting examine?
5   The balance sheet helps us determine the profit of an organisation. True or false?

Answers will be found in Appendix B.

REFERENCES AND FURTHER READING

Beech, J. and Chadwick, S. (eds) (2004) *The Business of Sport Management*. Pearson Education, Harlow.
Chadwick, S. and Arthur, D. (2008) *International Cases in the Business of Sport*. Butterworth-Heinemann, Oxford.
Deloitte (2009) *Safety in Numbers: Annual Review of Football Finance*. Sport Business Group at Deloitte, Manchester.
Dyson, J.R. (2003) *Accounting for Non-accounting Students*, 6th edn. Financial Times Press, Harlow.
McLaney, E. and Atrill, P. (2005) *Accounting; An Introduction*, 3rd edn. Financial Times Press, Harlow.
Sport Industry Research Centre (2009) *Sport Market Forecasts*. Sheffield Hallam University, Sheffield.
Stewart, B. (2007) *Sport Funding and Finance*. Elsevier, London.
Wilson, R. and Joyce, J. (2008) *Finance for Sport and Leisure Managers: An Introduction*. Routledge, London.

CHAPTER 2

REGULATORY FRAMEWORKS IN SPORT

On completion of this chapter you will be able to:

- understand and communicate the main accounting concepts, bases and policies;
- use the main financial accounting terminology;
- identify the key regulations for financial accountants.

INTRODUCTION

You will need many facets to be a good financial manager. The first is to be systematic and considered when running an organisation and to provide sufficient resources to ensure that the 'books' are kept up to date. The second is to appreciate the difference between financial reporting (the material we are going through at the moment) and financial management (the material we go through in Part 2). This will ensure that you have correctly 'reported' data on which you can make management decisions. The third is that you become financially literate. In essence this means that you will be able to understand and speak the language of accounting and financial reporting, and, perhaps more importantly in my opinion, be able to accurately interpret financial documentation (such as the income statement and balance sheet that we briefly examined in the previous chapter) and prepare financial material such as budgets, project evaluation reports, costing and pricing strategies, and the main financial statements. The need for all of these skills is now more important than ever when you consider the current issues and blame that can be associated with the legal position of an organisation (just look at what happened with Portsmouth Football Club in the early part of 2010 as an example). As a twenty-first-century manager you need to know where you stand.

Although the aim of this book is not to teach you how to become an accountant, the purpose of it is to show you how to read and understand accounts and financial data so that you can manage an organisation effectively. Consequently, you need an understanding of how accounts are prepared (otherwise the numbers will be relatively meaningless!). The next four chapters will explain the guiding rules and principles and illustrate how accountants use them to construct the accounts. This will give you the necessary skills to prepare basic accounts, should your course or employer require you to do so. This chapter will explain the concepts, statements and guidelines that form the 'rules' of financial accounting.

Chapter 1 outlined that accounting is about identifying, collecting, measuring, summarising and communicating financial information. The information has a purpose – it is to satisfy the needs of users, i.e. the information will be used by someone. As a result it must be fit for purpose, and that is where you can come into your own.

When you looked at the financial statements of Tottenham Hotspur Football Club and those of Arena Leisure (see Appendix A, p. 249), you will have noticed that they contain a great deal of information and highlighted lots of terminology that you didn't understand. However, what you should also have noticed was that while the volume of information was significant the terminology and the layouts that were used were very similar. This is because both companies have to conform to the regulatory framework of accounting. To reinforce the point, look at the excerpts from the Rugby Football Union (RFU) in Figure 2.1. For those of you who don't already know, the RFU is the governing body for all rugby, including the England national team, played in England.

Can you see how the statements use similar terminology and layout? Granted some of the finer details are slightly different, but in general they are the same. This similarity is also highlighted in the balance sheet (see Figure 2.2).

Again, many of the terms and structures are identical. If you think about why this is, and approach the question logically, you will be able to understand both the need for a regulatory framework and the purpose of this chapter. Imagine that you are preparing a list of the top performances by 100-metre sprinters. When you look at the times that the individual sprinters have recorded you will take it for granted that they all comply with certain rules and regulations (e.g. run on a flat track, and not wind assisted). Similarly, when looking at the performance of businesses, you need to be able to form assumptions with a view to making comparisons either from year to year for the same company or to benchmark against other companies. Just like any other type of information, accounts need to be objective, reliable, comparable and understandable.

While medium to large organisations have to follow strict procedures when preparing their accounts, small businesses and local swimming clubs, for example, can prepare their accounts in any style they like. However, it is generally accepted that their accounts will follow certain principles that form an accepted code of practice for accountants so that they match the requirements of 'good information'. However, companies must comply with the requirements of the Companies Act 1985 (CA 1985), as amended by the Companies Act 1989. A major requirement of this act was that each year companies must prepare financial statements that give 'a true and fair view'. This is so that shareholders can see how the company is performing. A copy of these statements will be submitted to Companies House so that if a member of the public wishes to see what is going on they can get access to the information. Generally these statements will be in the form of an Annual Report, which we will look at in more detail later. Company law is just one source of the rules and guidelines that seek to regulate how company accounts are prepared. The other sources will now be introduced.

Group profit and loss account
for the year to 30 June 2009

	Notes	2009 £m	2008 £m
Revenue			
Ticket income		29.2	13.2
Broadcasting		23.4	21.4
Sponsorship		16.1	12.8
Hospitality and catering		29.6	23.8
Merchandising and licensing		5.4	7.9
Travel and leisure		7.2	7.7
Hotel		0.7	–
Other income		7.6	12.3
	2	119.2	99.1
Costs			
Direct		34.1	26.0
Elite rugby		11.8	14.5
Community rugby		17.2	16.2
Business and administration		12.3	13.0
Stadium		12.5	10.5
		87.9	80.2
Operating profit	2,3	31.3	18.9
Allocations to clubs and Constituent Bodies		(22.0)	(19.9)
Share of loss from associated undertakings		(0.1)	–
Net finance (loss)/income	5	(0.2)	0.5
Profit/(loss) on ordinary activities before taxation		9.0	(0.5)
Taxation credit on ordinary activities	6	0.1	2.0
Profit on ordinary activities after taxation		9.1	1.5
Attributable to minority interests		(2.9)	(2.3)
Profit /(loss) for the year	21	6.2	(0.8)

There is no material difference between the profit on ordinary activities before taxation and the retained profit reported in the profit and loss account and the equivalent figures calculated on a historical cost basis.

Figure 2.1 Rugby Football Union profit and loss account (or income statement)

Source: From the Rugby Football Union Annual Report 2009.

THE REGULATORY FRAMEWORK

The regulations for UK company accounts are framed by several sources.

Company law

The major requirements of the CA 1985 were outlined above. The act also recognised 'statements of standard accounting practice' (SSAPs). These were the predecessors of the

Balance sheets
at 30 June 2009

	Notes	Group 2009 £m	Group 2008 £m	Parent 2009 £m	Parent 2008 £m
Fixed assets					
Negative goodwill	8	–	–	–	–
Tangible fixed assets	9	195.5	166.4	190.2	164.6
Loans	10	6.7	5.8	0.2	0.2
Investments	11	0.1	(0.2)	31.1	30.7
		202.3	172.0	221.5	195.5
Current assets					
Stocks	12	1.2	1.4	1.1	1.2
Debtors and prepayments – within 1 year	13	15.8	14.7	22.0	27.4
Debtors and prepayments – after 1 year	13	1.2	0.9	1.2	0.9
Cash at bank and in hand		8.2	10.1	(0.2)	(9.1)
Deferred tax asset	17	0.2	–	0.3	–
		26.6	27.1	24.4	20.4
Creditors:					
Amounts falling due within one year	14	(21.6)	(24.1)	(16.5)	(17.1)
Net current assets		5.0	3.0	7.9	3.3
Total assets less current liabilities		207.3	175.0	229.4	198.8
Creditors:					
Amounts falling due after one year	15	(54.8)	(34.3)	(54.8)	(34.1)
Provisions for liabilities and charges	17	–	(0.3)	–	(0.2)
Net assets excluding pension (liability)/asset		152.5	140.4	174.6	164.5
Pension (liability)/asset	24	(1.8)	1.4	(1.8)	1.4
Net assets including pension asset		150.7	141.8	172.8	165.9
Financed by:					
Debentures 2075-2085	18	94.7	89.3	94.7	89.3
Capital and reserves					
Called up share capital	19	–	–	–	–
Other reserves	20	38.1	38.1	38.1	38.1
Profit and loss account	21	14.7	12.1	40.0	38.5
Total equity funds		52.8	50.2	78.1	76.6
Minority interests		3.2	2.3	–	–
Capital employed		150.7	141.8	172.8	165.9

Figure 2.2 Rugby Football Union balance sheet

Source: From the Rugby Football Union Annual Report 2009.

Financial Reporting Standards (FRSs). Perhaps the most important SSAP was SSAP 2, which covered the 'Disclosure of accounting policies', and dealt with the fundamental concepts of accounting. This has now been 'updated' by FRS 18 which we will look at a little later. The reason for stating this is not to bore you with detail but so that if you happen to hear such phrases as 'In order to comply with SSAP X or FRS Y' you will have an idea of what is meant. Figure 2.3 illustrates the types of claims that the RFU makes in its financial statements so that whoever reads them knows what is going on.

Notes to the financial statements

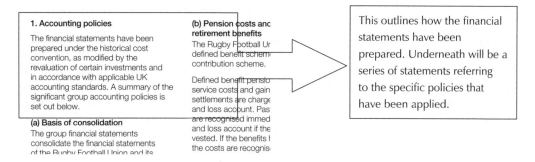

Figure 2.3 RFU statement of accounting policies
Source: From the Rugby Football Union Annual Report 2009.

Financial reporting standards

The increasing complexities of the business world (including sport) meant that there was a requirement to develop accounting standards to prevent the misrepresentation of profits and to narrow the areas of difference and variety of accounting practice. Therefore a body entitled the Accounting Standards Committee (ASC) was set up with the objective of reducing the 'flexibility' that allowed companies to be somewhat 'creative' with financial information. The ASC issued accounting standards, known as SSAPs. Unfortunately the ASC did not have the power to improve the quality of financial reporting, so, in 1990, the Financial Reporting Council (FRC) was established to deal with corporate reporting and governance. However, the ASC was soon replaced by the Accounting Standards Board (ASB), which began to issue accounting standards known as Financial Reporting Standards (FRSs). The aims of the ASB are 'to establish and improve standards of financial accounting and reporting for the benefit of users, preparers and auditors of financial information'.

International accounting standards

The International Accounting Standards Committee (IASC) was established in June 1973 with an overriding aim to coordinate the development of international accounting standards. If you think for a minute you will realise that the international dimension to accounting is of vital importance to sport given that many areas of the industry are not confined to business in the UK. Globalisation, sponsorship and broadcasting have given sport in the UK a platform to establish a worldwide audience. The IASC includes representatives from many different countries from across the globe as well as from the UK. Since its establishment it has, however, been superseded by the International Accounting Standards Board (IASB) which itself issues International Financial Reporting Standards (IFRSs). Since January 2005, companies are required to publish their financial statements using IFRSs rather than domestic standards.

The stock exchange

The stock exchange is a place or 'market' where stocks and shares (i.e. a share of the ownership of companies) are bought and sold. When companies trade their shares this way, they are known as 'listed' or 'quoted' companies. Some UK-based sport organisations are listed themselves, for example Arena Leisure (which we look at in Appendix A), the Blacks Leisure Group (which sells outdoor clothing and equipment) and Ladbrokes. Being listed will allow companies to grow by raising more capital by issuing more shares. It also allows people to buy shares in the company, and obviously allows existing shareholders to sell their holdings. Consequently the ownership, and control, of companies can be bought here. If you are a football fan you may remember what happened to Manchester United plc in the summer of 2004 when the American tycoon Malcolm Glazer first bought a number of shares in the business and then eventually de-listed the company after having purchased all the shares.

ACTIVITY

Go to the *Financial Times* website (www.ft.com/) and have a look at the 'Annual Reports Service' link and select 'Leisure and Entertainment'. Here you will find a selection of different sport and leisure companies that are listed. Once you have done so try to answer the following questions:

- How many sport organisations are listed?
- How many leisure organisations are listed?
- Which sector, sport or leisure, is represented the most on the UK stock exchange?
- Is your favourite sport team listed?

In total there are about thirty listed organisations on the 'free' site. However, don't be fooled, as this is just a small proportion of the actual number. Of these thirty there is only one notable sport organisation: Powerleague Group plc. What this exercise should have shown is that 'leisure' organisations are more likely to list themselves on the stock exchange due to the size of the market in which they operate. Furthermore, when sport organisations float on the stock exchange it can bring about significant problems.

In order for a company to be 'listed' it must conform to the rules and regulations stated by the stock exchange. The company will commit itself to certain procedures and standards, including how information is disclosed. This includes publishing an Annual Report within six months of the year-end and publishing interim results giving profit and loss information. We will have a look at this in a moment but before we move on it is worth illustrating the benefits and drawbacks of a stock market floatation.

CASE STUDY

FOOTBALL, THE STOCK EXCHANGE AND MANCHESTER UNITED FOOTBALL CLUB

Malcolm Glazer, the US sports tycoon and owner of the Tampa Bay Buccaneers (an American Football Team), won full control of Manchester United plc in a £790 million takeover in June 2005. The takeover was not without controversy as many of the club's fans tried desperately to prevent it from happening. However, the opportunity for Glazer came because Manchester United plc was a listed company. Let us have a quick look at why this came about and what the implications have been since the takeover.

After Manchester United was floated on the UK stock exchange in 1990 and following a surge of investment in shares (i.e. small bits of the business that you or I could buy), the club went from strength to strength. Its biggest achievement pre-2000 was the 1999 treble-winning season when it was victorious in the English Premier League (EPL), the FA Cup and the UEFA Champions League (UCL). Such success had turned Manchester United into one of the biggest global brands in sport and made it an unlikely takeover target – after all, the company was estimated to be worth somewhere in the region of £670 million. Rupert Murdoch and BSkyB had attempted a takeover in the past only to be stopped by the Office of Fair Trading.

The main problem for anyone attempting a takeover is to get into a position whereby they can acquire 75 per cent of the shares. At this point an organisation can be de-listed – thereby preventing you and me from buying any shares – and at 90 per cent a compulsory purchase for the remaining 10 per cent of shares can be made. Nevertheless, Glazer managed not only to gain control of the club through his takeover vehicle Red Football, but to convert it into a completely private company.

Although it took some time to achieve, the mechanics of the takeover were quite simple. While keeping his holding ticking over, Glazer knew he would have to persuade the major shareholders to part with their investments. Shares are generally purchased for financial gain, i.e. you buy them to make money. At the beginning of May 2005 a Manchester United share was worth around £2.60, so to get all of the major shareholders to sell he would have to offer more. Glazer effectively mounted his takeover bid by securing the 28.7 per cent stake owned by Irish horse-racing tycoons J.P. McManus and John Magnier. The racing duo agreed to sell their shares for £3.00 each and in doing so made a sizeable profit on their investment. This purchase was in addition to the shares Glazer had already purchased by offering shareholders around 20 per cent more than the company was worth. Hence the stock market value was about £670 million, a clear £120 million less than he eventually paid. The timeline of how this came about is shown in Table 2.1.

Although Glazer was eventually successful with his takeover of the club, in doing so he has had to borrow heavily against the club's assets and take out a number of high-risk loans alongside his personal investment. Manchester United Football Club was a financially stable business that regularly made a profit and had plenty of readily available cash to fund the acquisition of new players and ground expansions. Some will argue that the new position is precarious at best! Glazer has effectively gambled that future

Table 2.1 Manchester United Football Club takeover timeline

March 2003	Malcolm Glazer makes his first move and purchases a 2.9 per cent stake in the club.
June 2004	After twelve months of activity Glazer's stake in MUFC approaches 20 per cent.
October 2004	The MUFC Board receives a bid from Glazer as his holding approaches 30 per cent.
February 2005	A new approach is made by Glazer valuing the club at £800 million.
12 May 2005	Glazer raises his stake to 57 per cent and launches a formal takeover bid.
23 May 2005	Having purchased the stakes of major shareholders McManus and Magnier (28.7%), Glazer now owns more than 76 per cent of the club.
28 June 2005	Glazer secures 98 per cent and therefore total control of the club.

on-the-field success will bring about increased revenues which will enable him to repay the debts quickly. It could be viewed as a good move, however, when you consider that the club is already a successful global brand, attracting huge audiences and generating substantial profits all over the world. If Manchester United is to continue its growth as one of the biggest clubs in the world it will need to maintain its position as a global force.

It has been well documented that Glazer will achieve increased revenue by exploiting TV coverage to a greater extent, increasing ticket prices and arranging lucrative tours to the Far East and the USA. Indeed, by early 2010 all of these strategies had been implemented and consolidated by the club's continued on-the-field success which includes three EPL titles, one UCL title and second final in 2009 alongside several other domestic honours, things are likely to continue despite increasing pressure from fan groups, organised protests using the old green and gold colours of Newton Heath FC (the original name for Manchester United), a well-documented £700 million loan which was used to part-finance the takeover in the first place and the rumours in the media about a £1.5 billion takeover bid by the 'Red Knights'.

Shares in Manchester United were de-listed after fourteen years of trading, and examining how this came about provides a useful insight into how sound financial ideas can have a varied effect. By floating on the stock exchange the Manchester United plc Board was able to raise the necessary funds to mount a serious challenge to the top teams in England and Europe. To some extent the decision was vindicated when you consider the honours that the club has won over the time since floatation. Briefly, these are: eight EPL titles, four FA Cups, one League Cup, one European Cup Winners Cup, one UCL title and one Intercontinental Cup. As mentioned above, the club was an unlikely takeover target due to the value of the business. However, when you list a business on the stock exchange, anyone with a big enough pocket (or in Glazer's case a deep pocket and a secured level of borrowing) can launch a takeover bid.

ACCOUNTING RULES

I mentioned in Chapter 1 that the accountancy profession is engaged in the supply of financial information to a variety of different user groups. In fact, the amount of information required is so diverse and detailed that it is necessary to place some limit on the type of data to be dealt with. Modern-day accounting systems have been derived over a long period of time and have grown out of necessity rather than a theoretical model. As a result, a number of procedures have developed that are best described as first principles or basic rules. Many authors refer to them as assumptions, concepts or conventions but I prefer rules or principles. These principles guide us in the preparation of financial statements and the recording of financial data, so you need to understand what the main ones are and how they are applied to sport.

FRS 18 accounting policies

FRS 18 gives an insight into the rules, concepts and conventions used by accountants, in particular those who operate in the sport industry. FRS 18 deals with the selection, application and disclosure of accounting policies. Its objective is to ensure that for all material items:

- an entity adopts the accounting policies most appropriate to its particular circumstances for the purpose of giving a true and fair view;
- the accounting policies adopted are reviewed regularly to ensure that they remain appropriate, and are changed when a new policy becomes more appropriate to the entity's particular circumstances;
- sufficient information is disclosed in the financial statements to enable users to understand the accounting policies adopted and how they have been implemented.

FRS 18 states that an entity should judge the appropriateness of accounting policies to its particular circumstances against the objectives of relevance, reliability, comparability and understandability.

Relevance

Financial information is relevant if it has the ability to influence the economic decisions of users and is provided in time to influence those decisions.

Reliability (or prudence)

Financial information is reliable if:

- it reflects the substance of the transactions and other events that have taken place;
- it is free from deliberate or systematic bias (i.e. it is 'neutral');
- it is free from material error;
- it is complete within the bounds of materiality;
- under conditions of uncertainty, it has been prudently prepared (i.e. a degree of caution has been exercised).

The rationale for being 'prudent' is to guard the business against the overestimation of income and underestimation of expenses in financial statements. Although revenues and profits should not be anticipated, losses should be accounted for as soon as they arise or are likely to arise. A good example of the prudence concept will arise when we look at stock (inventory) transactions. A retailer will buy goods to sell at a higher price and thereby make a profit. So how much is the stock worth? It could be argued that its value to the retailer is what it will be sold for, but this assumes it will be sold. What if there is a change of fashion? What if there is a surplus of that type of good and the stock has to be discounted to move it on? Both of these factors will change the future worth of the stock and consequently to avoid such future disappointments the stock will be valued at the cost price in the balance sheet (or, if lower, the future expected selling price).

If in doubt, overstate losses and understate profits!

Comparability

Information increases in value to its users if it can be compared with similar information about the company or with that of other companies. Such comparability may be achieved through a combination of consistency and disclosure.

Consistency means that:

1. similar items within a single set of accounts should be given similar accounting treatment (for example, the percentage depreciation written off from fixed asset values);
2. the same treatment should be applied from one accounting period to the next for similar items so that one year's results are comparable to the next.

Two concepts are highlighted in FRS 18 as playing a key role in financial statements and hence in the selection of accounting policies. These two concepts are 'going concern' and 'accruals'.

Going concern

The information presented in the financial statements is prepared on the basis that the organisation will continue to operate for the foreseeable future. This is because users of the statements will normally want to assess the potential for the entity to generate future cash flows and will not be interested in the breakup value of the assets.

Accruals

The accruals basis of accounting requires the non-cash effects of transactions and other events to be reflected in the financial statements for the accounting period in which they occur and not in the period when the cash is paid or received. For example, if a sale is agreed in 2009 but the terms of the deal are that the cash is not received until 2010, the transaction should be shown in the accounts for 2009.

Other concepts

Some other terms and concepts that underpin the thinking and actions of accountants and the accounts they produce are:

- *Materiality*: this means that only items of significance are included in the financial statements. An item is significant if its omission or misrepresentation could influence the economic decisions of those using the financial statements (for example, the British Triathlon Association would record that it owns some racing bikes but it would not record that it had fifty paper bib numbers left over from an event that it staged).
- The *business entity concept* dictates that a line is drawn between the business and its owner(s): the business and its owner(s) are two separate entities. The financial statements will therefore be drawn up from the perspective of the business and not of its owner(s). You saw how this works in practice when we covered legal identity.
- The *money measurement concept* simply means that only items of monetary value may be recorded in a set of financial statements (for example, the stock that Blacks Leisure Group sells in its stores will be shown but the business skills of its store managers will not). The financial statements of an organisation will show the success of the management team but the skills and intellect cannot be given a monetary value and included in the statements.
- The *dual-aspect concept* recognises that each transaction conducted by a business will affect two items within the business. For example, if the business buys stock it will have an increase in the value of stock. If cash is used to buy the stock then the amount of cash available will decrease. We will examine this particular concept in more detail later.
- The *historical cost concept* dictates that the value of items that a business owns must be based on their original cost and must not be adjusted for any subsequent changes in price or value. Much debate surrounds this concept because certain items such as land and buildings will probably change significantly in value over time and using the historical cost is not necessarily the most accurate way of estimating value. None the less, this is what accounts have to do.
- *The accounting period* ensures that the life of an organisation is divided into distinct accounting periods. For each period, usually one year, accounts are prepared and are made available to all of the organisation's stakeholders. This means that every effort is made to include all transactions that occur in an accounting period and not to exclude any items of income or expenditure.

The RFU have to ensure that they conform to all of the concepts and policies that relate to their business and disclose in their annual report exactly how they have constructed their financial statements. Have a look at Figure 2.4 to see what I mean.

Note

The regulatory framework has changed over the years and will continue to change as new ideas and opinions are discussed. However, the bottom line, for you, is that if you grasp the concepts, principles and guidelines discussed above, which are the building blocks of

Statement of the Management Board's Responsibilities

Statement of the Management Board's Responsibilities in Respect of the Financial Statements

The Friendly and Industrial and Provident Societies Act 1968 requires the Management Board to prepare financial statements for each financial year which give a true and fair view of the affairs of the Rugby Football Union and of its income and expenditure for that period. In preparing these financial statements, the Management Board is required to:

- select suitable accounting policies and apply them consistently;
- make the necessary judgements and estimates which are both reasonable and prudent; and
- prepare the financial statements on a going concern basis, unless it is inappropriate to presume that the Rugby Football Union will continue in business.

The Management Board is responsible for keeping proper books of account with respect to the transactions and assets and liabilities of the Union. Such books must enable a true and fair view to be given of its affairs and explain its transactions. The Management Board has a general responsibility for taking such steps as are reasonably open to it to safeguard the assets of the Union and to prevent fraud and other irregularities.

Figure 2.4 RFU statement of responsibility

Source: From the Rugby Football Union Annual Report 2009.

accountancy, you will be able develop with them. We will regularly see the effects of these concepts throughout the remainder of this book and consequently your knowledge and appreciation of them will grow.

MORE ACCOUNTING TERMINOLOGY

You may have come across one or two terms now that you may not be fully comfortable with; before we move on it is worth reinforcing some of the more regularly used terms so that you can begin to use them when communicating accounting information – we touched on some of these in Chapter 1.

> **KEY TERMS**
>
> ### ASSETS
>
> These are items or resources that have a value to the business and items that are used by the business and for the business. Normally we would classify assets as either fixed or current. The basic difference is that a fixed asset is something that the business intends to keep and use for some time whereas a current asset is held for the business to convert into cash during trading. Some good examples here are business premises and motor vehicles, which are fixed assets, and stock and cash, which are current assets.
>
> ### INTANGIBLE FIXED ASSETS
>
> These have a value but are not tangible. For example, a royalty has a value (people have to pay you) but it is not a physical item.
>
> ### TANGIBLE FIXED ASSETS
>
> These are tangible, i.e. they are physical items (e.g. property, equipment, machines).
>
> ### LIABILITIES
>
> These are amounts owed by the business to people other than the owner. Normally we will see liabilities classified as either payable within one year (e.g. bank overdrafts, supplier accounts) or payable after one year (e.g. longer term bank loans).

KEY TERMS

CAPITAL

Generally considered to be the owners' stake in the business and may also be called equity. To take this a step further it is also the excess of assets over liabilities.

DEBTOR

An entity or person who owes money to the business.

CREDITOR

An entity or person to whom money is owed.

DEPRECIATION

A notional charge made in the accounts to represent the use of an asset. It also serves to reduce the value of an asset in the balance sheet.

THE IMPACT OF THE REGULATORY FRAMEWORK ON SPORT

By now you are probably wondering why you need to know all of this to understand accounts. The answer is simple. In 1997 the Accounting Standards Board (ASB) issued its tenth financial reporting standard or FRS 10. This has since become one of the single most important changes to the world of sport business and in particular professional team sport, as it reclassified the way in which professional clubs could value their players and record them on the balance sheet. In a nutshell, the balance sheet has a section at the top where businesses classify 'Goodwill and intangible assets'. Although the terminology will be meaningless to you at this stage, what we need you to understand is that there should be a way of valuing every item on the balance sheet. This is mainly because it has long been argued that some of the more traditional financial reporting policies didn't allow for a full understanding and consideration of issues relating to professional sports clubs and in particular football clubs. One of the main issues was that clubs operated different systems for the treatment of items such as transfer fees, grants and sponsorship.

FRS 10 and professional team sport

Accounting problems are well documented in the world of professional team sport and although some of the practices are improving through the involvement of professional advisers, greater financial awareness and increased media interest, some questions still remain. Think for a minute about how professional sports clubs should revalue their property assets, for example stadiums, after they have been redeveloped. How do they reduce (depreciate) the value of these assets and, given the loyalty of fans and the power of brand names on a global platform, how can clubs recognise their brand names as accounting assets? However, the most prominent question for clubs in any sport is how to best record the investment made in players.

The introduction of FRS 10 means that there is now consistency in the area of 'Goodwill and intangible assets', which begins to address the questions outlined above. Under the rule, when a club purchases a player through the transfer market they have to include the cost of acquiring the player's registration as an intangible fixed asset on the balance sheet. Each year thereafter, the registration cost has to be written off as an expense (amortised) through the income statement (profit and loss account) until the player's contract expires. Have a look at Figure 2.5 and see how this is done in practice.

Before the rule was introduced there was no way of valuing players on a balance sheet despite the fact that they were important assets. Because of this some clubs began to develop ways of including the costs and purchases of players. However, this was done internally and without direction from the Accounting Standards Board. Consequently the introduction of FRS 10 gives the consistency required for us to confidently compare the financial results of professional sports teams. Such analysis will be examined later in the book. The statement in Figure 2.6 illustrates how FRS 10 is addressed for a football club.

Again these excerpts are here to show you that the regulatory framework and statement of accounting policies and concepts must be used at all times when the financial statements are constructed. While they are based on accounts that were drawn up in 2006 they are a clear example of how FRS 10 is used in practice. Don't worry about all the terminology, as we will cover it later.

INTANGIBLE FIXED ASSETS

The element of each player's transfer fee which relates to his registration is capitalised as an intangible asset and amortised over the period of his contract including any agreed extensions, subject to any provision for impairment. Contingent fees payable, which are dependent upon the number of first team appearances and international debuts made, are capitalised in the period when it is considered probable that the conditions of the contract will be satisfied.

The profit or loss arising out of the disposal of players' registrations represent the difference between the consideration receivable, net of any transaction costs, and the unamortised cost of the intangible asset.

TANGIBLE FIXED ASSETS

Tangible fixed assets are stated at cost net of depreciation and any provision for impairment.

Figure 2.5 An example of an asset statement

Source: From Southampton Leisure Holdings plc Annual Report 2006.

Southampton Leisure Holdings Plc
ANNUAL REPORT AND ACCOUNTS 2006

NOTES TO THE ACCOUNTS CONTINUED
PERIOD ENDED 30 JUNE 2006

11. INTANGIBLE FIXED ASSETS

Group	Goodwill £'000	Player registrations £'000	Total £'000
COST			
At 1 June 2005	1,026	35,393	36,419
Additions	—	2,688	2,688
Disposals	—	(23,975)	(23,975)
AT 30 JUNE 2006	**1,026**	**14,106**	**15,132**
ACCUMULATED AMORTISATION			
At 1 June 2005	128	23,036	23,164
Charge for the period	111	4,574	4,685
Impairment losses	—	734	734
Disposals	—	(17,208)	(17,208)
AT 30 JUNE 2006	**239**	**11,136**	**11,375**
NET BOOK VALUE			
AT 30 JUNE 2006	**787**	**2,970**	**3,757**
At 31 May 2005	898	12,357	13,255

Amortisation of player registrations is normally calculated on a straight-line basis. Where appropriate, adjustments are made to reflect the specific circumstances of individual players. The accounts include additional charges on this basis of £734,000 (2005: £732,000).

Figure 2.6 A breakdown of asset figures applying FRS 10

Source: From Southampton Leisure Holdings plc Annual Report 2006.

CORPORATE GOVERNANCE

Organisations, and their accountants, should behave like good citizens. Laws, ethics and social responsibility should influence their behaviour. However, not all citizens are good. Similarly neither are all organisations, directors, accountants and auditors. Consequently scandals such as Enron and WorldCom and some high-profile companies going bankrupt led to accountants facing the scrutiny and mistrust that are usually reserved for politicians and wayward sports stars!

Accounting bodies, accountants, institutional investors, audit firms and so on responded by promoting 'corporate governance'. The Organisation for Economic Co-operation and Development (OECD) defines corporate governance by stating that the systems by which organisations are directed and controlled involve 'a set of relationships between a company's management, its board, its shareholders and other stakeholders [that provides] a structure through which the objectives of the company are set and the means of attaining those objectives and monitoring performance are determined'.

The major guide to corporate governance in the UK is the '2003 Combined Code'. The code gives guidance on 'best practice' in four categories:

1   boards of directors;
2   executive remuneration;
3   financial reporting and internal control;
4   shareholder relations.

The Combined Code does *not* impose legal requirements: it lays out 'principles'. However, the stock exchange requires that all listed companies *must* include in their financial statements:

- a statement of how they applied the principles of the Combined Code;
- explanations, which give reasons if they did not comply with any of the provisions set out in the Combined Code.

Although corporate governance is generally thought of as being aimed at listed companies the principles should apply to any organisation. Governance is a global issue and many countries have developed their own ideas on corporate governance. In America the system is 'rules based'. The rules are stated in the Sarbanes Oxley Act (2002). Companies and audit firms must comply with the Act if they want to avoid twenty years in prison and huge fines.

Perhaps the best way for you to remember and understand the scope of governance is 'F –TRIADS'. This acronym is based on the seven characteristics of good governance as identified in the King Report from South Africa:

F: fairness

T: transparency

R: responsibility

I: independence

A: accountability

D: discipline

S: social responsibility

Sport organisations, much like any normal business, will have their own governance frameworks. These should conform to the F-TRIADS acronym. The threat of litigation almost forces the organisations that we are concerned with to disclose how they consider corporate governance on an annual basis. Normally statements will be made about how the principles are covered in an organisation's annual report (such as the excerpt shown in Figure 2.7). You should note that providing you are fair, transparent, responsible, independent, accountable, disciplined and show a degree of common sense when working with financial information, you will be fine.

SUMMARY

Do you feel lucky or confused at this point? Although there are a wide variety of accounting concepts, rules and regulations you only have to be aware of them, unlike the poor accountants who have to use them each and every day. The International and UK Accounting Standards bodies provide order for you, which will ultimately make your life much easier when we come to dissect accounts, and begin to understand what they really mean.

The Management Board acknowledges the value of the principles of good governance as set out in the Combined Code

Corporate Governance

One of the objectives in the Union's Strategic Plan is that the RFU will be managed to Plc standards, particularly regarding effective management and corporate governance. The Management Board acknowledges the value of the principles of good governance as set out in the Combined Code, both in terms of ensuring integrity and accountability in the management of the Union's affairs, and also in increasing the effectiveness and efficiency of the Union's business. To that end the Union has adopted certain principles associated with best practice in corporate governance. The following statements describe how these principles have been applied in the period under review.

Management Board

The Management Board's powers are clearly defined in the Rules of the Rugby Football Union, particularly Rule 12. It has clear standing orders and terms of reference, including items that must be referred to the RFU Council for approval, and consists of three executive directors, together with ten other members representing a broad cross section of the game of rugby who do not have executive responsibilities.

> There is a clear division of responsibility between the roles of the non-executive Chairman and the Chief Executive

Other directors or individuals may be present during the meetings to ensure that the relevant knowledge and expertise is brought to bear on decisions. There is a clear division of responsibility between the roles of the non-executive Chairman and the Chief Executive, and all executive directors have agreed job descriptions and limits of authority. The Board meets at least ten times each year and considers matters under its terms of reference, which include the development of the Union's Strategic Plan, allocation of financial resources, reviewing the performance of executive directors, approval of annual budgets, considering the recommendation of the Board's Standing Committees, whose responsibilities relate to policy development, and monitoring of the performance of the Union's subsidiary and associated companies.

In the year the Management Board members were as follows:

Peter Baines
Francis Baron
Jonathan Dance
John Douglas
Nick Eastwood
Ian Metcalfe
Paul Murphy
Martyn Thomas
Rob Udwin
John Vale
Paul Vaughan
Brian Williams

Risk Management

As part of the commitment to adopt relevant aspects of best practice in corporate governance, the Union has implemented the requirements of the Combined Code relating to internal controls (including the provisions relating to risk management). This process is carried out by a formally constituted group, the Risk Management Steering Group. This group is under the overall direction of the Finance Director, assisted by the Union's risk management advisors, and comprises key executives from each of the critical areas of the business. The meetings of the Risk Management Steering Group are reported to the Executive Committee and Management Board and the overall process is supervised and monitored by the Audit and Risk Panel. The RFU's Internal Auditor also completed a review of the RFU's risk management processes during the year.

> the Union has implemented the requirements of the Combined Code relating to internal controls

Key activities completed during the year by the Risk Management Steering Group included a review of the RFU's business interruption insurance programme, a loss control survey of the stadium and an assessment of the Union's risk management framework against the new British Standard, BS31100. The group also monitors the individual risks currently faced by the Union, identifies and implements controls to manage those risks and, assisted by the Union's risk management advisors, identifies and evaluates new risks. These risks are evaluated and monitored against a number of criteria including a risk tolerance level of £5m, which is regularly reviewed. At June 2009 no risks were rated in the 'high' category.

Figure 2.7 Rugby Football Union corporate governance

Source: From the Rugby Football Union Annual Report 2009.

The main principles, however, have been considered and, while the exact number, classification and description of these various principles are subject to debate among accountants and professional bodies what is certain is that it would be most unusual if they did not all sign up to the fundamental principles of accruals, prudence, going concern and consistency. In the next chapter we will begin to examine the dual aspect concept in more depth and begin to apply it so that we can see how most modern accounting systems are governed.

By the end of this book you should understand all the concepts that the examples use and in most cases be able to make any adjustments to the financial statements. At this point all you need is a general awareness of the key issues raised in this chapter. To see if you have formed a general understanding, try the following review questions.

QUESTIONS FOR REVIEW

1. List the accounting concepts and principles that you can remember from this chapter.
2. For the following statements fill in the blanks.

    a. The _____ concept recognises that each transaction conducted by a business will affect two items within the business.
    b. The _____ concept dictates that information presented in the financial statements is prepared on the basis that the organisation will continue to operate for the foreseeable future.
    c. Only items of significance are included in the financial statements because accountants apply the _____ concept.
    d. The _____ concept dictates that a line is drawn between the business and its owner(s): the business and its owner(s) are two separate entities.
    e. The _____ basis of accounting requires the non-cash effects of transactions and other events to be reflected in the financial statements for the accounting period in which they occur and not in the period when the cash is paid or received.
    f. The _____ concept simply means that only items of monetary value can be recorded in a set of financial statements.

3. Identify three of the regulatory bodies that oversee accounting.

    - _____
    - _____
    - _____

4. Are these statements true or false?

    a. Assets are items or resources that have a value to the business and things that are used by the business and for the business.
    b. Liabilities are amounts owed to the business by other people.
    c. Capital is generally considered to be the owners' stake in the business and may also be called equity.
    d. Debtors are an entity or person who owes money to the business.
    e. Creditors are amounts owned by the business that are of value.

REFERENCES AND FURTHER READING

Bill, K. (ed.) (2009) *Sport Management*. Learning Matters, Exeter.
Chadwick, S. and Arthur, D. (2008) *International Cases in the Business of Sport*. Butterworth-Heinemann, Oxford.
Fried, G., Shapiro, S. and DeSchriver, T. (2008) *Sport Finance*, 2nd edn. Human Kinetics, Leeds.
Stewart, B. (2007) *Sport Funding and Finance*. Butterworth-Heinemann, Oxford.
Trenberth, L. (ed.) (2003) *Managing the Business of Sport*. Dunmore Press, Palmerston North.

CHAPTER 3

THE MECHANICS OF FINANCIAL ACCOUNTING

On completion of this chapter you will be able to:

- understand and communicate the process of the accounting system;
- understand the accounting equation and its impact upon financial statements;
- understand and use the principles of double-entry bookkeeping.

INTRODUCTION

You already know that every type of sports organisation, large or small, will produce a set of financial statements. In Chapter 1 I told you that the aim of Part 1 was not to teach you how to be an accountant, so you have probably got another question for me: Why have I included a section on the mechanics of financial accounting? The answer to this is twofold. First, because many of you will have to use financial information and when doing so you may need to trace where certain facts and figures have come from. Second, because many of you studying courses related to sport management and sport business management will be expected to have an understanding of how financial transactions are recorded. Looking beyond academic expectations, we believe it is a useful skill to have and one that will increase your employability. Just imagine how impressive it will be when you attend a job interview and can demonstrate that you have a sound understanding of financial management. The information included in this chapter and Chapters 4, 5 and 6 will help you to understand the technical issues that are fundamental in the learning process and that will facilitate your understanding of financial statements.

In the previous chapter a number of basic principles were outlined, including one called the 'dual aspect concept'. All organisations need to record economic transactions so that they can produce financial statements (such as those illustrated in Chapters 1 and 2), and to do this they require an accounting system. The income statement (P&L) and balance sheet do not write themselves! A series of procedures will be established so that the organisation records every transaction that occurs. For each transaction the amount, the date and a description will be required so that those responsible for the organisation are aware of what has happened, when it happened and the financial consequences.

The basic accounting system is commonly known as double-entry bookkeeping and although most organisations now use computerised programs they derive their 'logic' from the basic system. Consequently it will be good for you to understand the logic that drives such systems. The specific application and style of the accounting system will depend on the type and size of business. Most large organisations will have accountants on their staff but small businesses and organisations are more likely to hire 'external' accountants. It is therefore unlikely that you will have to perform specific accounting duties as part of your future role, but it is a certainty that if you are a manager you will have to talk to the accountants (and on a regular basis).

As a result we only really need to focus on the things that you may have to do (i.e. smaller businesses such as sole traders or partnerships), although the general principles that are used apply to *all* organisations. For this reason the examples used in this chapter will be based on a company called Kitlocker.com, a team and leisurewear provider. This organisation will be used throughout the next few chapters as it provides us with a real-life example to illustrate the basic points. We could use a professional sport club or team or even a large leisure organisation, but the problem with these examples is the level of detail required. You do not need that level of depth, and besides it can become rather confusing. If you want to know more about Kitlocker you can go online and have a look (www.kitlocker.com).

As I have already mentioned, it is unlikely that as a non-accountant you will be involved in the recording of financial accounting data. However, there is a more than even chance of your being presented with information based on such data. In presenting it to you it is assumed that you will have some knowledge of double-entry bookkeeping, much in the same way as when you first learned to swim you were probably thrown into the deep end. The point therefore of these next few chapters is to start you off with some arm bands in the shallow end before moving you up to more intermediate and then advanced techniques. The arm bands will help support you with the basics, which, once mastered, can be removed. That said, the best way to grasp double-entry bookkeeping is to do it yourself, which means that you will need to work through, as opposed to read through, this chapter. The reasons for this are twofold: first, the exercises will help you become familiar with the terminology that was outlined in Chapters 1 and 2; second, an understanding of the methods and logic on which double-entry bookkeeping is based will help you in your job.

CASE STUDY

KITLOCKER.COM: AN INTRODUCTION

Introduction

Business partners Mike Kent and Tom Ward established Kitlocker in May 2005. The principal aim of the business is to provide team kit, leisurewear and branding solutions to university sport teams. However, following a successful launch the company set up a website to cater for a much wider market including colleges, schools and the general public.

A bit of history

The idea of Kitlocker came from Mike and Tom's involvement with club and university volleyball. Having both played the sport for a number of years they noticed that the suppliers of team volleyball kit (including leisure wear) were not meeting the requirements of their customers. The lead time on deliveries and general variety of goods available were not up to standard. After talking to friends who played other sports they soon realised that there was a clear gap in the market to provide kit that was fit for purpose, easily obtainable and at realistic 'student' prices.

Moreover, while involved on a sport management degree programme Mike was given an assignment brief to come up with a business idea and produce a business plan. Having noticed the potential for success in the university sport kit market Mike decided to set up, on paper, Kitlocker. The market research that he conducted supported what he and Tom had discovered while playing volleyball on the British Universities Sports Association (BUSA) circuit. This was enough for them to consider setting up the business for real, so they took their plan to a professional enterprise agency for consideration.

The result

The feedback from the enterprise agency was positive and with relatively low start-up costs Mike and Tom made the decision to go live with the project once Mike had completed his studies. Consequently, Kitlocker was formally established as a business partnership on 28 May 2005. In the beginning they had some important decisions to make: how to source goods, how to sell goods and how to get their company known by their market.

The marketing and sales solution was simple and they set up a website (Kitlocker.com) which was used as their interface with their customers. At first this was fairly straightforward with basic listings by sport. Customers would log on to the site and order what they wanted. However, this did not serve the university teams well, as it relied on team secretaries collating orders, collecting money and arranging delivery. As a result in 2006 they launched a new version of the website which is now linked to individual universities. Customers go to their university link, select their sport and then order bespoke kit related to the team.

The finance

At start-up Mike and Tom invested around £6,000 of personal capital, which was supplemented by a start-up grant for small businesses of £3,500. This gave them the necessary funds to purchase a laser cutting machine to help them design bespoke logos for sport teams and to have a professionally designed e-commerce website created. In addition to this they arranged a leasing agreement for two heat-sealing machines that allowed them to put their designs on to actual kit.

> **Summary**
>
> This provides you with a brief overview of Kitlocker.com, which we will come back to regularly during this chapter and again throughout the book. The Kitlocker partnership will be used to illustrate a number of key financial decisions and help you to put the theory you are learning into practice.

RECORDING BUSINESS TRANSACTIONS

The 'dual aspect concept' (outlined in Chapter 2) means that every transaction will affect two 'items' within the business. Think of it like Newton's law; for every action there must be an equal and opposite reaction. The effect on both items must be recognised so that the transaction is recorded correctly. Every transaction will have either an increasing (+) or a decreasing (−) effect on an item (or account). An increase in one account will mean that another account will decrease but, given that some accounts are for assets and others are for liabilities, they may both increase and decrease. Confused? Good! At least it shows that you are thinking. We will solve this riddle and many more during the course of this chapter.

In recognition of the dual aspect concept the system of recording accounting data was born and we will refer to it as double-entry bookkeeping from now on. The main objective of double-entry bookkeeping is quite straightforward: to record the dual effect of all transactions. The reasons for this are, and hopefully you have guessed it, twofold. First, it will provide valuable information about the effect of each transaction, and second, as every transaction is recorded twice, it provides a check on the accuracy of the recording system or recorder so that it also acts as a quality control method. More about this later.

Before we go any further you need to remember that the business entity concept states that business transactions are recorded from the point of view of the business (not the owner). In other words, the business and its owners are two separate legal identities and as such must be viewed from an accounting perspective as being totally separate bodies. However, they can, and do, carry out transactions with each other. For example, as soon as a business starts up it will need some cash. The owner will lend cash to the business. The business will now have an asset: cash. By the dual aspect concept, something else must happen too. The business will now have a liability: it owes money to the owner. This debt to the owner by the business is part of the 'capital structure' of the business (i.e. how it is financed). The organisation may also be financed (get its cash or acquire assets) by other sources such as a loan from a bank or by taking credit from suppliers. Remember how Kitlocker.com was financed? If you don't, look back at the case study on pp. 42–3. However, in a nutshell we saw that the company was set up with £9,500 in cash, which was made up of £6,000 of personal funds and a grant of £3,500. A rough balance sheet for the organisation is shown in Figure 3.1.

	£	£
Assets		
Non-current assets		
Property, plant and equipment		0
Current assets		
Inventories		
Cash and cash equivalents	9500	
		9500
Total assets		9500
Equity and liabilities		
Equity		9500
Non-current liabilities		
Current liabilities		
Trade and other payables		0
Total equity and liabilities		9500

Figure 3.1 Kitlocker.com and their start-up balance sheet

THE ACCOUNTING EQUATION

The relationship among all the assets, liabilities and capital of an organisation forms what accountants call the 'accounting equation'. This simple relationship governs the recording and presentation of all financial transactions. It must always balance. The equation is as follows:

$$\text{Assets} = \text{Capital} + \text{Liabilities}$$

or if we move it around

$$\text{Assets} - \text{Liabilities} = \text{Capital}$$

This shows that the assets of the organisation must equal the total of the combined value of capital and other liabilities; that is to say, the equation must balance. The equation could be Assets = Liabilities, as 'Capital' is a liability, but it is always better to identify capital separately (capital is the amount of resources provided by the owners of the business). Let us have another look at Kitlocker.com and see how some of their early business decisions affected their accounting equation.

CASE STUDY

KITLOCKER.COM AND THE ACCOUNTING EQUATION

To begin with, Kitlocker.com had £9,500, so their accounting equation would have looked something like this:

$$\text{Assets} = \text{Capital} + \text{Liabilities}$$

$$£9{,}500 \text{ (Asset, Cash)} = £9{,}500 \text{ (Capital)} + £0 \text{ (Liabilities)}$$

Fairly easy? I hope so, because now we are going to work out how the equation changes when business decisions are made and how you can rearrange the equation should you wish to do so. Look back at the case study on pp. 42–3, where you saw what Kitlocker.com did with their start-up capital. The first thing they did was to purchase a laser cutting machine which cost the company £1,800. Do you think that their accounting equation changed to reflect the transaction?

Hopefully, you replied 'No'. Although they have purchased something it is classified as an asset. The company used the asset of cash to get the asset of machinery. If we get technical here, they have traded a current asset for a fixed asset. Have a look at how the accounting equation is now:

$$£9{,}500 \text{ (Assets)} = £9{,}500 \text{ (Capital)} + £0$$

or,

$$£1{,}800 \text{ (Fixed Asset, Machine)} + £7{,}700 \text{ (Current Asset, Cash)} = £9{,}500 \text{ (Capital)} + £0 \text{ (Liabilities)}$$

Once in existence the company began making sales. In doing so they needed to buy things from suppliers and sell them to customers. One of their transactions was to purchase twenty hooded sweatshirts from a local supplier. These hoodies cost the company £200 which they paid immediately. What will the accounting equation look like now? Hopefully, something like this:

$$£1{,}800 \text{ (FA, Machine)} + £7{,}500 \text{ (CA, Cash)} + £200 \text{ (CA, Stock)} = £9{,}500 \text{ (Capital)} + £0 \text{ (Liabilities)}$$

This is all very well but it is also very easy. Consider now that Kitlocker.com purchases 100 rugby jerseys from an Italian supplier for £1,500. Instead of paying for them immediately, the company put them on credit, i.e. they agree to pay for the jerseys at a later date (usually twenty-eight days after the invoice date). What will this do to their accounting equation?

$$£1{,}800 \text{ (FA, Machine)} + £7{,}500 \text{ (CA, Cash)} + £1{,}700 \text{ (CA, Stock)} = £9{,}500 \text{ (Capital)} + £1{,}500 \text{ (Liabilities, Creditors)}$$

Hopefully, you got this but if you didn't it may well be because you've forgotten some of the terminology that you looked at earlier. Remember that if something is purchased and not paid for immediately we call the supplier a trade creditor. Pause for a minute

	£	£
Assets		
Non-current assets		
Property, plant and equipment		1800
Current assets		
Inventories	1700	
Cash and cash equivalents	7500	
		9200
Total assets		11000
Equity and liabilities		
Equity		9500
Non-current liabilities		
Current liabilities		
Trade and other payables		1500
Total equity and liabilities		11000

Figure 3.2 Kitlocker.com balance sheet Mk II

and have a look at their new balance sheet in Figure 3.2. Can you follow how the accounting equation has altered the statement?

In this situation they will be recorded as a liability because when they are paid the business will be worth what it was originally. Let us see what happens when the supplier is paid in full:

£1,800 (FA, Machine) + £6,000 (CA, Cash) + £1,700 (CA, Stock) = £9,500 (Capital) + £0 (Liabilities, Creditors)

Before we move on from this there is one more transaction that it is worth looking at. Kitlocker.com purchased and eventually paid for 100 rugby jerseys in the above example. This was so that they could sell the jerseys to a university rugby team. As the company was established to make a profit a cash sale of the jerseys was made for £2,100. You can probably see that a profit of £600 was made on the original purchase but it is worth illustrating this in the accounting equation:

£1,800 (FA, Machine) + £8,100 (CA, Cash) + £200 (CA, Stock) = £10,100 (Capital) + £0 (Liabilities, Creditors)

In making the sale the stock worth £1,500 was used up and cash of £2,100 received. You should note that the capital amount changes by the amount of profit (£600) generated in making the sale. The company's rough balance sheet is shown in Figure 3.3. We will come back to this later.

Figure 3.3 Kitlocker.com balance sheet Mk III

	£	£
Assets		
Non-current assets		
Property, plant and equipment		1800
Current assets		
Inventories	200	
Cash and cash equivalents	8100	
		8300
Total assets		10100
Equity and liabilities		
Equity		10100
Non-current liabilities		
Current liabilities		
Trade and other payables		0
Total equity and liabilities		10100

THE DOUBLE-ENTRY RULE

This is where, in my opinion, financial accounting gets interesting (and logical!). You already know that accountants need to identify, collect, measure, record, summarise and communicate financial information, but as yet you probably have no idea how they do it. This section will begin to address the issues from 'identification' through to the 'recording' of transactions. Furthermore, we are still not too concerned about numbers: if you can understand the concept at this stage in your studies you will find it easy to become proficient with the numbers when we start to play with some.

The 'double-entry rule' is the method by which financial transactions are recorded. The rule reflects the dual nature of all business transactions. It also provides a way of checking that all transactions have been recorded correctly. This in turn can lead to controls being put in place within the business.

Information is collected and stored in a nominal ledger (generally referred to as 'accounts' which I will show you in a minute). This is an accounting record which summarises the financial affairs of a business, and it will contain details of assets, liabilities, incomes and expenditures. The ledger will normally consist of a large number of different accounts, each having its own purpose or name. Examples of these accounts may include machinery (a fixed asset), stock (current assets), wages and salaries (an expense) and sales (an income). Each transaction will give rise to a *debit* entry and a *credit* entry in the relevant accounts. The manual way of recording information is based on 'T' accounts: one half of the T will be for debits (the left-hand side) and the other half (which is the right-hand side – see how logical this is!) is for credits. The easy way to remember which side is which is: 'cRedit' has the letter 'R' in it and is therefore on the Right. Ledger accounts are just like 'T' accounts: each one has a debit side and a credit side. An example is as follows:

Account name (e.g. Machinery account)

Debit	Credit

At the top of the account will be its name. Underneath the name will be the 'T' format which will be made up of the left-hand *debit* side, and the right-hand *credit* side. One side of each account is for increases and the other for decreases. The problem here for students and managers is normally to decide which is which. The answer will become simple if you understand the 'double-entry rule' which I discuss below.

The double-entry rule:

INCREASES (+) in ASSETS and EXPENSES

DEBIT	CREDIT
HERE	

INCREASES (+) in LIABILITIES and CAPITAL

DEBIT	CREDIT
	HERE

It follows that DECREASES (–) to an account will be the reverse of the above.

DECREASES (–) in ASSETS and EXPENSES

DEBIT	CREDIT
	HERE

DECREASES (–) in LIABILITIES and CAPITAL

DEBIT	CREDIT
HERE	

Observing this rule means that a transaction should *always* be recorded on the debit side of one account and on the credit side of another. This will provide you with an arithmetical check on the accuracy of your records, as the total debits should always equal the total credits.

A tricky one that often causes problems for students is 'sales'. What do you think 'sales' are recorded as? Hopefully you replied 'a credit'. You can think through the logic of this as: if you sell something, in return you will receive cash (or the promise of cash later, i.e. a debtor), the increase in cash is a debit entry (an asset) and therefore, to make things balance, the sale must be a credit entry. Another way of remembering the pattern to underpin the 'rule' is:

- Assets and expenses are debit entries.
- Sales and liabilities are credit entries.

See how easy accounting is? Let's have a look at an example of a business transaction for Kitlocker.com.

In the Case study where we played around with the accounting equation you saw how things changed for Kitlocker.com following the purchase of a laser cutting machine. If we apply the double-entry rule we can see how the 'T' accounts can be constructed.

First, we need to establish what is going on. As the machine was paid for in cash it is fairly easy to see what is happening. There has been an increase in the value of assets (Machines) of £1,800 and a decrease in assets (Cash) of the same amount. Now that we know what the two parts of the transaction are we can safely apply the rule.

INCREASES (+) in ASSETS and EXPENSES

DEBIT	CREDIT
HERE	

And

DECREASES (–) in ASSETS and EXPENSES

DEBIT	CREDIT
	HERE

So,

Machinery A/C

DEBIT	CREDIT
1,800	

And

Cash and bank A/C

DEBIT	CREDIT
	1,800

Hopefully you were able to follow this. Don't worry if you are still unsure though, as we have many more examples to show you below. However, before we go any further it's probably time for another terminology check.

the mechanics of financial accounting

> **KEY TERMS**
>
> ## INCOME
>
> Simply all money that is received or receivable to the business regardless of its source or purpose.
>
> ## EXPENSES
>
> Virtually the reverse of income! All money spent in relation to the company's commercial activities.

CHOICE OF ACCOUNTS

Before you work through the application of the double-entry rule in detail I want to run through how to assign financial transactions to specific accounts. Essentially this is as a result of the lessons I have learned while teaching financial recording to my students and it is one of the main points of confusion. Most transactions are easily assigned to an appropriate account. The number and type of accounts that are used will depend on the nature of the organisation and how the owner wants the information to be summarised. However, in practice there are a number of common accounts that are used (see explanations below) and you should always remember the following rule: If in doubt, open a new account (you can always close it down afterwards).

- *Capital account*: records what the owner has put into the business and therefore shows us what the business owes to him or her.
- *Cash and bank account*: records how much money the organisation keeps in the bank and therefore what cash has been paid to the organisation and what bills the organisation has paid. This will normally be the most frequently used account in any business.
- *Trade creditors*: this type of account will record what the organisation owes to other people. It is often sufficient for small organisations to keep one trade creditor account, although it can also be standard practice to set up a trade creditor account for each creditor (i.e. an account for each person owed).
- *Trade debtors*: in contrast to trade creditors the trade debtor account will record what money is owed to the business by others. Once again there may be one single trade debtor account or several, one for each debtor.
- *Purchases*: the term 'purchase' has a specific meaning in accounting, as it relates purely to those items bought to sell; in other words, stock that the organisation will use for trading. The purchase of assets will be recorded in the appropriate asset account (e.g. motor vehicles, equipment).
- *Stock*: the stock account is used to record the value of goods which have not been sold by the end of an accounting period. In accounting terminology (as will be explained in Chapter 6) stock left over is referred to as closing stock, which will become opening stock at the beginning of the next accounting period.

- *Sales*: this account will, predictably, record the value of goods sold to customers during the accounting period. However, it is worth noting here that we would not use the sales account for recording information relating to the sale of any of the organisation's fixed assets such as motor vehicles or equipment.
- *Drawings*: this account is used to record all of the money that the owner takes out of the business for his or her own use.

APPLYING THE DOUBLE-ENTRY RULE

Dealing with the mechanics of the process (including the numbers) will be a case of practice makes perfect. If you understand the concept and don't get confused by the accounting terminology, the practical implementation of the rule should not cause you any worries. It is also worth including a reference point (an extra column) for each account so that we can cross-reference transactions. To help you get to grips with this, the following questions will take you through some typical transactions for Kitlocker.com and illustrate the way in which the double-entry rule is applied and used.

1. If a printing machine is bought in cash for £1,500, which two items will be affected?

In this question the values for machinery and cash will change. You should also have said that machinery increases while cash decreases. We can summarise this transaction as follows:

- Machinery + £1,500
- Cash – £1,500

We can now apply the double-entry rule to construct the 'T' accounts. To do this we need to record the following:

- £1,500 on the debit (left) side of the machinery account. Remember that machinery is an asset and that these are increasing.
- £1,500 on the credit (right) side of the cash account. Here the asset of cash is decreasing as a result of buying the printing machine.
- If you haven't followed this, take another look at the double-entry rule.

The 'T' accounts will therefore look like this.

Machinery A/C

DEBIT (£)	CREDIT (£)
1,500	

Cash and bank A/C

DEBIT (£)	CREDIT (£)
	1,500

2. The business sells £500 of goods on credit.

Again we need to work out what is going on here. There is a sale and a credit transaction, which means that cash has not yet been received for the goods.

- Sales + £500
- Trade debtors + £500

The transaction will need to be recorded in the company 'T' accounts as follows:

- £500 on the debit (left) side of the trade debtors account. Trade debtors are an asset to the business and are increasing.
- £500 on the credit (right) side of the sales account. Since the income from sales is being increased, so will capital.

The 'T' accounts will therefore look like this.

Trade debtors A/C

DEBIT (£)	CREDIT (£)
500	

Sales A/C

DEBIT (£)	CREDIT (£)
	500

You should note here that the transactions have been recorded on the correct sides of each account in accordance with the double-entry rule so that for each recorded debit we have a corresponding credit. Moreover, you could include a reference column, which, in practice, may be used for recording a date or the name of the other account involved. This will help you when we go back through the books to ensure that everything has been recorded properly.

ACTIVITY

Now it's your turn. See if you can construct the 'T' accounts for the following three transactions before looking at our workings. These are a continuation of the examples illustrated above.

3   The business buys a delivery van for £1,000 and pays for it in cash.

Motors A/C

DEBIT (£)	CREDIT (£)

Cash and bank A/C

DEBIT (£)	CREDIT (£)

Here the asset of cash is being used to purchase the asset of motors. So debit motors (+asset) and credit cash (−asset).

Motors A/C

DEBIT (£)	CREDIT (£)
1,000	

Cash and bank A/C

DEBIT (£)	CREDIT (£)
	1,000

Happy? Try the next one.

4   Goods for resale are purchased on credit from company X for £1,600.

Purchases A/C

DEBIT (£)	CREDIT (£)

Trade creditor X A/C

DEBIT (£)	CREDIT (£)

Hopefully your answer looks something like this:

Purchases A/C

DEBIT (£)	CREDIT (£)
1,600	

Trade creditor X A/C

DEBIT (£)	CREDIT (£)
	1,600

Did you get this right? If not don't worry, as there are some important lessons here. First, it is important that purchases of stock and sales of stock are recorded in separate accounts as one is at cost price and the other is at selling price. This will help us to work out what profit was made on top of the purchase price. If you follow this logic then the account entries can be explained easily.

- Debit (left) side of the purchases account (an expense). Remember that it costs the business something before they can sell stock.
- Credit (right) side of the trade creditor X account as the trade creditors of the business have increased since they have not yet been paid. The business must acknowledge that they have to pay back the trade creditor.

- We can assign individual creditors their own accounts; hence this one is called trade creditor X. This will help you to work through accounts containing lots of transactions.

5   Cash sales are made of £3,600.

Sales A/C

DEBIT (£)	CREDIT (£)

Cash and bank A/C

DEBIT (£)	CREDIT (£)

Hopefully this one was easy. If not check the double-entry rule again.

- Debit the cash and bank account (+ Asset) £3,600.
- Credit the sales account (+ Income and ultimately Capital).

Sales A/C

DEBIT (£)	CREDIT (£)
	3,600

Cash and bank A/C

DEBIT (£)	CREDIT (£)
3,600	

Note: As you have sold goods the stock that you are holding will go down. Therefore there need to be two more entries: credit the purchases account (by the amount the goods cost the business to buy), and debit the 'cost of sales' account).

6   Wages of £200 are paid.

Wages A/C

DEBIT (£)	CREDIT (£)

Cash and bank A/C

DEBIT (£)	CREDIT (£)

Wages A/C ||	Cash and bank A/C	
DEBIT (£)	CREDIT (£)	DEBIT (£)	CREDIT (£)
200			200

This transaction is an example of a bill being paid immediately. If the bill is not paid immediately it will go down on the trade creditor account. In these 'T' accounts we recorded the information in this way because:

- Wages are an expense, so we record £200 on the debit (left) side.
- Cash is a business asset and is used to pay the bill, so the £200 is recorded on the credit (right) side.

Don't panic if you are unable to follow how all of this worked. In the next chapter we will examine the routine policy decisions that managers make and how these are recorded in an organisation's 'T' accounts. However, the basic principles used to work out all the information are relatively straightforward: (1) identify which two accounts are affected; (2) work out how they are affected (e.g. increase/decrease); and (3) apply the double-entry rule.

What you are probably wondering is where all of this is going, and how we can use all this information to develop company accounts. Simply, all of these accounts will need to be collated and checked for accuracy before the figures can be placed into the final accounts. The process for doing this is called a 'trial balance', but don't worry about this now, as we will look at it in Chapter 5.

SUMMARY

During this chapter you have seen the accounting system in practice. This is how accounting information is collected, recorded and summarised in its first stage. The examples from Kitlocker.com have illustrated how to keep 'T' accounts in good order and hopefully given you the basic skills needed to apply your knowledge to live situations. You must make sure that when you see transactions for a business you apply the double-entry rule. If you do you will have a debit and credit entry for everything and will be well on the way to sorting out some final accounts. It is imperative that you understand these basic rules before you move on.

As a non-accountant it is unlikely that you will be asked to become too heavily involved in constructing ledger accounts like the ones we have examined in this chapter. However, you may well be asked to produce financial information that can be used in the accounting system, so it is important that you understand its logic. Moreover, while it is true that medium and large sport organisations will use a computerised system or have an accountant to deal with the information, small organisations and sole traders (when starting out) may well need to construct some basic accounts. In order to appreciate the value of accurate financial data it is important that you can see where it comes from and how it is constructed.

Before moving on from this chapter make sure that you are familiar with the common accounts that are used, the meaning of the terms 'debit' and 'credit' and the method of entering data into 'T' accounts. Why not try answering the following review questions and see how much you can remember?

QUESTIONS FOR REVIEW

1. Complete the 'T' accounts for the following questions:

   a. The owner of the firm introduces capital of £15,000 in cash.

DEBIT (£)	CREDIT (£)

DEBIT (£)	CREDIT (£)

   b. Goods for resale are purchased, by cash, for £6,000.

DEBIT (£)	CREDIT (£)

DEBIT (£)	CREDIT (£)

   c. The rent bill arrives for the gym amounting to £3,500.

DEBIT (£)	CREDIT (£)

DEBIT (£)	CREDIT (£)

d   New machinery costing £10,000 is purchased for cash.

DEBIT (£)	CREDIT (£)

DEBIT (£)	CREDIT (£)

e   Cash sales amount to £21,000.

DEBIT (£)	CREDIT (£)

DEBIT (£)	CREDIT (£)

f   The business buys £5,000 of goods for resale on credit.

DEBIT (£)	CREDIT (£)

DEBIT (£)	CREDIT (£)

g   New vehicles are bought for £30,000. A deposit of £13,000 is paid and the rest is put on credit.

DEBIT (£)	CREDIT (£)

DEBIT (£)	CREDIT (£)

the MECHANICS of financial accounting

2 Which of the following items are shown under the wrong headings?

Assets	Liabilities
Stock	Cash
Amounts due on stocks purchased	Amounts owing to creditors
Trade debtor	Mortgage
Bank overdraft	
Motor vehicle	

3 Complete the gaps in the following table:

	Assets	Liabilities	Capital
	£	£	£
(a)	16,200	8,500	?
(b)	21,000	?	11,075
(c)	?	4,560	18,790
(d)	12,350	?	8,000
(e)	65,800	?	55,000

REFERENCES AND FURTHER READING

CIMA (2009) *Financial Accounting Fundamentals*. BPP Professional Education, London.
Dyson, J.R. (2003) *Accounting for Non-accounting Students*, 6th edn. Financial Times Press, Harlow.
McLaney, E. and Atrill, P. (2005) *Accounting: An Introduction*, 3rd edn. Financial Times Press, Harlow.
Wilson, R. and Joyce, J. (2008) *Finance for Sport and Leisure Managers: An Introduction*. Routledge, London.

CHAPTER 4

ACCOUNTING RECORDS IN SPORT

On completion of this chapter you will be able to:

- understand and communicate the impact of decisions and policies, and their effect on financial statements;
- apply common 'routine' transactions such as loan interest, depreciation, discounts, bad debts, returns and disposal of fixed assets.

INTRODUCTION

In this chapter we begin to bring together some of the principles that were covered in Chapters 2 and 3 where we looked at the basic format and contents of the accounts that are drawn up. The double-entry system provides us with the 'technique' to record business transactions. You saw how it works in the real world when we looked at some typical trading transactions for Kitlocker.com. However, although you may have followed the logic in some of our examples what you have seen so far is not a full view of the type of business transactions that you may come across. Therefore, we will use this chapter to cover some more 'common' transactions, and get you to apply your knowledge to record such transactions.

LOAN INTEREST

Businesses may take out loans to start the business, to finance their operations or to expand. Unless the business has a generous benefactor, interest will have to be paid on the loans. A rate of interest will be agreed with the financier (usually a bank) and this will be charged on outstanding balances until the loan is repaid in full. The interest due will be calculated in reference to the amount borrowed and the rate of interest, and will be recorded in the accounts as an expense. For example, if a business takes out a loan of £10,000 at an interest rate of 6 per cent per year the interest expense for the first year will be £600 (£10,000 × 0.06).

Recording interest paid

Recording the interest paid is easy. All we need to do is open two accounts and follow the double-entry rule. To illustrate, the interest in the example above will be recorded as follows: debit interest payable (+ Expense), credit cash and bank (– Asset).

Cash and bank A/C

DEBIT (£)	CREDIT (£)
600	

DEBIT (£)	CREDIT (£)
	600

You should note here that we have a debit and a credit entry so we have followed the double-entry rule. However, there are a couple of points that you should always remember. First, interest must not be entered on the loan account itself, as the payment of interest does not represent a repayment of the loan (the amount borrowed). Second, interest paid (or payable) for the period will appear on the debit side of the trial balance (which we will look at in Chapter 5), as it is a business expense. However, sometimes you may come across situations where the interest has been incurred but not paid. Can you remember what we do in this situation? If you said that it is an accrual, then well done! Interest due at the end of an accounting period, but not yet paid, must be added to the interest paid account in order to account in full for the interest expense for that period. It must also be recorded as a liability (a trade creditor) because we have not paid the bill. Have a look at the example below to see how this works.

CASE STUDY

INTEREST DUE BUT NOT YET PAID

On the first day of an accounting period a business takes out a loan of £10,000 at an annual interest rate of 5 per cent. The terms of the loan are that repayments will be 'interest only'. This means that the annual amount of interest payable is £500 (£10,000 × 0.05). (*Note:* 'interest only' means that the annual payments will be just for the interest and the capital element of the loan will be paid off at an agreed date with one final payment. In this situation the amount of the loan will always be shown at the full amount until it is paid off.)

First, we need to record the loan amount, so debit cash and bank £10,000 (+ Asset) and credit loans £10,000 (+ Creditors).

During the year, £200 of the interest is paid, so debit interest paid £200 (+ Expense) and credit cash and bank £200 (– Asset).

At the end of the year the outstanding interest must be recorded: it is an expense for that period. In practice the accounts are short of £300 (£500–£200 = £300) of interest, so we need to debit interest paid £300 (+ Expense) and credit trade creditors £300 (+ Creditors). Consequently our 'T' accounts will look like this:

Cash and bank A/C

DEBIT (£)	CREDIT (£)
10,000	200

Interest paid A/C

DEBIT (£)	CREDIT (£)
200	
300	

Loans A/C

DEBIT (£)	CREDIT (£)
	10,000

Trade creditors A/C

DEBIT (£)	CREDIT (£)
	300

When the final accounts are prepared for the year, the expense of 'interest paid' will be listed on the income statement (profit and loss account) as part of the calculation of profit. Loans will be recorded on the balance sheet under 'Non-current liabilities' (i.e. creditors payable after one year). However, the outstanding loan interest for the year will be part of the trade creditors that will be listed under 'Current liabilities' (i.e. creditors payable within one year).

It is important for you to realise that if payments are not made it will impact upon the decisions and activities that the business can (or should!) make in the following accounting period. It is simple things like this that are often the reason for sport and leisure organisations losing control of their finances and facing growing debts.

ACTIVITY

1 What is the amount of interest payable for the year on a loan of £50,000 at an annual rate of interest of 7 per cent?
2 What is the percentage rate of interest per annum on a loan of £25,000 where the interest payable for the year is £1,250?
3 A business takes out a five-year 'interest-only' loan of £250,000 at an interest rate of 4 per cent per annum.

- Calculate the interest payable in the third year of the loan.
- What is the balance on the loan account at the end of the third year?

> **Answers**
>
> 1   £3,500 (£50,000 × 0.07 = £3,500)
> 2   5% (£1,250/25,000 = 0.05, × 100 = 5%)
> 3   £10,000 (£250,000 × 0.04 = £10,000) and £250,000 (the capital will not be paid off until the agreed final date).

The above examples illustrate how to record the transactions for simple 'interest-only' loans. The same pattern should be used when recording the transactions that arise with other loans. In reality, lenders are more likely to want some of the capital sum to be repaid each year. An example of how this would be recorded is given below.

The annual repayments on a five-year £12,000 loan at 10 per cent per annum would be £3,165. The mechanics of the loan would be:

- When taking out the loan, the entries would be the same as before: debit 'bank' (or cash) and credit 'loan' with the capital sum (in this case £12,000).
- Year 1: the interest would be £1,200 (calculated as 10 per cent of £12,000). This means that £1,965 is paid off the capital (£3,165 – £1,200). The financial statements at the end of the year will show 'interest paid' of £1,200 and a loan of £10,035.
- Year 2: the interest would be £1,004 (calculated as 10 per cent of the outstanding loan of £10,035). This means that £2,161 of the loan is paid. The financial statements at the end of the year will show 'interest paid' of £1,004 and a loan of £7,874.
- Years 3, 4 and 5 will follow the same pattern. After the payment at the end of the fifth year the balance on the loan will be zero. Please work through the numbers for years 3, 4 and 5 to prove to yourself that it works (with a small rounding factor!).

DEPRECIATION

Many businesses will purchase fixed assets such as machines and motor vehicles for use within the business. Such fixed assets will normally be used for more than one accounting period. This causes a problem: the asset has been bought and consequently recorded in the accounts of one year but will serve the business for more than one year. It would not be 'fair' to charge the income statement with all of the cost of the asset in the first year of ownership: the business will receive the benefits of owning the asset for future years too. If we charged the full amount in the year that we acquired the asset we would distort the income statement: too much expense would be charged in the first year and the later years would not have any expense. This contravenes the matching concept: income and related expenses must be matched with each other. In addition, it is unrealistic not to charge any expense in any of the years; this would mean that the asset would continue to be valued at its purchase price on the balance sheet (this is not logical: the value will reduce owing to usage, wear and tear, etc.).

For example, at the beginning of Year 1 a business buys a printing machine for £5,000 cash. The business estimate that they will be able to use the asset for five years but then it will have to be replaced and have no scrap value. Therefore we need to charge each of the five years with some of the cost of the machine. The resulting charge is called 'depreciation' and given that it as an 'expense' it must be charged against income for each year and as a reduction in the value of the fixed asset. This follows the 'double-entry rule': we will debit an expense and the opposite credit value will be to an account 'Provision for depreciation'. At the end of the year the balance sheet will show the asset at £5,000 less £1,000 depreciation. The resulting balance of £4,000 is known as the 'net book value' (cost less accumulated depreciation). In the second year, another £1,000 will be charged to the income statement for Year 2 and the balance sheet for that year will show the asset as having a net book value of £3,000. Depreciation is the accounting entry made to share the cost of an asset over its life.

Note: It is very important that you realise what is happening to cash here. Depreciation has got nothing to do with cash flow. If a business buys an asset for cash, the cash will leave the business on the day that the asset is purchased. Alternatively, if a loan is arranged to buy the asset, the cash leaves on the days the repayments are due. Depreciation is not a cash flow. This is one of the reasons why 'profit' is not 'cash': a business may show that it has made a profit in the income statement but it does not mean that it has got cash.

Recording depreciation

If we stay with our printing machines example we can illustrate the recording of depreciation in the 'T' accounts. Most businesses assume that the depreciation will be spread equally over the life of the asset. This makes our job much easier. The method for doing this is called 'Straight-line depreciation' and it is very simple. To work out the depreciation for our machine all we do is divide the value by the number of useful years (£5,000/5). This means that our annual depreciation charge will be £1,000.

The entries in the 'T' accounts are also simple when we use the double-entry rule. First, open the necessary accounts and record the acquisition of the machine. Debit machinery at cost £5,000 (+Asset) and credit cash and bank £5,000 (– Asset): remember you have used one asset to get another. Second, we need to record the depreciation: debit depreciation expense £1,000 (+ Expense) and credit provision for depreciation of machinery £1,000 (+ Provision). This done, our 'T' accounts will look like this:

Cash and bank A/C

DEBIT (£)	CREDIT (£)
	5,000

Machinery at cost A/C

DEBIT (£)	CREDIT (£)
5,000	

Depreciation expense A/C

DEBIT (£)	CREDIT (£)
1,000	

Provision for depreciation of machinery A/C

DEBIT (£)	CREDIT (£)
	1,000

As with the loan interest example, when the final accounts are prepared the depreciation expense will be recorded on the income statement as an expense so that net profit can be calculated. The balances remaining on the machinery at cost account and on the provision of depreciation of machinery account will appear on the balance sheet. In this example our machine will have a net book value of £4,000 (£5,000–£1,000). The balance on the provision account should increase each year so that by the end of Year 5 it is worth £5,000, whereas the machine at cost is £0.

ACTIVITY

Assume Kitlocker.com are expanding and they need to purchase an embroidery machine costing £20,000. They estimate that the machine will have a useful life of eight years, after which time the item will have no scrap value. Kitlocker.com use the straight-line method of depreciation.

1. How much is the depreciation charge per annum?
2. What will be the annual percentage rate of depreciation?
3. What will be the balance on the provision for depreciation of machinery account at the end of Year 4?
4. What will the net book value of the machine be at the end of Year 6?

Answers

1. £2,500 (£20,000/8 = £2,500)
2. 12.5% (£2,500/20,000 = 0.125 × 100 = 12.5%)
3. £10,000 (£2,500 × 4 = £10,000)
4. £5,000 (£20,000 – (£2,500 × 6) = £5,000)

Depreciation adjustments

Generally the recording of depreciation is straightforward and most students will understand how to perform the calculations after some practice. However, one of the areas that seems to cause trouble for students is making depreciation adjustments. Depreciation allocates part of the cost of a fixed asset as an expense to the income statement (in order to match the use of the assets through its estimated useful life). However, in reality estimates are rarely 100 per cent accurate. An asset may well be used beyond the end of its original estimated useful life (for example, if it has been well maintained) and conversely it may become useless before originally expected. To account for the change in the profile of the asset it is necessary to make a one-off adjustment to the depreciation provision to reflect a change of circumstance.

Making the adjustment is itself fairly easy, providing that you understand whether the provision for depreciation account needs to be increased or reduced – this is normally the first troublesome issue for students – and a corresponding entry needs to be made in the depreciation expense account. Can you remember how depreciation was recorded earlier? To remind you, the two entries needed are: debit depreciation expense account (+ Expense) and credit the provision for depreciation account (+ Provision).

Consequently, if we decide that the balance on the provision for depreciation account is too low (i.e. the asset will not be useful for as long as we originally expected), an additional amount must be debited to the depreciation expense account and credited to the provision for depreciation account. Alternatively, if we believe that the asset will be useful for longer than originally expected, we need to raise the balance on the depreciation provision account by recording a credit on the depreciation expense account and a debit on the provision for depreciation account. Get it? Don't worry if you don't; we'll look at an example.

CASE STUDY

DEPRECIATION ADJUSTMENT

Kitlocker.com decide to purchase a new computer for £2,000, to help design kit logos. They expect to be able to use the computer for five years. Therefore, using the straight-line method for depreciation, the depreciation charge will be £400 per year (£2,000/5). At the end of Year 3, the computer will have a net book value of £800. However, during a financial review, it is decided that due to advances in technology the computer will become useless at the end of Year 4. An adjustment needs to be made to the provision for depreciation account as follows.

First, we need to work out what the adjustment is:

- Annual depreciation based on a life of three years (not five) = £500 (£2,000/4)
- Accumulated depreciation to the end of Year 3 = £1,500 (£500 × 3 years)
- Accumulated depreciation already provided = £1,200
- Adjustment or extra depreciation needed = £300 (£1,500−£1,200)

The rest is easy, thanks to the double-entry rule. Our entries will be: debit depreciation expense £300 (+ Expense) and credit provision for depreciation £300 (+ Provision). It is also important to note here that as a result of the extra depreciation profit will decrease by £300. The 'T' accounts will look like this.

Depreciation expense A/C ||	Provision for depreciation of machinery A/C	
DEBIT (£)	CREDIT (£)	DEBIT (£)	CREDIT (£)
1,200			1,200
300			300

DISCOUNTS

If you think back to Chapter 3 where you were introduced to Kitlocker.com and some of their transactions you may have noticed that they purchased and sold stock on credit terms; hence we used the trade creditor and trade debtor accounts regularly. This is a very common situation: many businesses buy and sell goods on credit terms. It may be several weeks before bills are finally settled. This arrangement can be useful to businesses and their customers, since it offers a good incentive to buy and sell. However, as we have mentioned throughout this book, a business is measured on its ability to pay debts as they fall due. Consequently, getting money from customers and paying creditors is very important.

Discounts allowed

In order for Kitlocker.com to collect cash from their customers (debtors) as quickly as possible they may offer a discount for prompt payment. When this situation occurs the business will receive less money than they had originally hoped. The difference, or discount allowed, must be recognised as a business expense. For example, Kitlocker.com sell goods to a regular customer for £500. They tell the customer that they will offer a 5 per cent discount if they receive payment within ten working days. The necessary entries will be as follows. First, ignore the discount and record the sale: debit trade debtors £500 (+Asset) and credit sales (+Income). Next, the debtor pays immediately so we need to record the settlement. Debit cash and bank £475 (£500 – 5 per cent) (+Asset), credit trade debtors £475 (– Asset). Kitlocker.com agree the discount of £25, so debit discount allowed £25 (+Expense) and credit trade debtors (–Asset).

The 'T' accounts are illustrated below but you should also note that the discount allowed reduces the asset of debtors and not the sales income. When the final accounts are prepared the sales figure will go to the income section of the income statement and the discount allowed to the expense section.

Sales A/C	
DEBIT (£)	CREDIT (£)
	500

Cash and bank A/C	
DEBIT (£)	CREDIT (£)
	475

Trade debtors A/C	
DEBIT (£)	CREDIT (£)
500	475
	25

Discount allowed A/C	
DEBIT (£)	CREDIT (£)
25	

Discounts received

While we are talking about discounts it is also worth noting that they can work in favour of Kitlocker.com. Remember that they purchased some of their goods on credit and as such Kitlocker will be recorded as a trade debtor in the books of their suppliers. They will have many suppliers who will want payment as soon as possible and consequently will offer them a discount to pay early. When a business like Kitlocker.com deduct discount from the amount owed to their trade creditors, the cash paid will be lower than the amount being settled. The difference, or discount received, may therefore be treated as income. Again we can have a quick look at an example.

Kitlocker.com purchased 200 rugby jerseys from one of their regular suppliers for £1,000. They will receive an 8 per cent discount if they can make the payment within twenty-one days. The entries will mirror what we did with discount allowed, with two notable exceptions – can you spot them? First, we can ignore the discount and record the purchase of the goods, so debit purchases £1,000 (+Expense) and credit trade creditors £1,000 (+Creditors). Kitlocker.com then pay within the twenty-one days, so we debit trade creditors £920 (£1,000 – 8%) (–Creditors) and credit cash and bank £920 (–Asset). Finally, Kitlocker.com claim the discount and debit trade creditors £80 (–Creditors) and credit discount received £80 (+Income). Discounts received reduce the amount of creditors and not the purchases since, when the final accounts are prepared, the purchases figure is used to calculate the cost of sales figure (which we will look at later). Discount received is treated as income in the income statement.

Before you look at the 'T' accounts illustrated below, did you spot the two differences? If you said that two of the accounts were different, well done. Here we use purchases instead of sales and trade creditors instead of trade debtors.

Purchases A/C

DEBIT (£)	CREDIT (£)
1,000	

Cash and bank A/C

DEBIT (£)	CREDIT (£)
	920

Trade creditors A/C

DEBIT (£)	CREDIT (£)
920	1,000
80	

Discount received A/C

DEBIT (£)	CREDIT (£)
	80

ACTIVITY

One of Kitlocker.com's trade creditors is owed £5,000. The supplier has arranged for a discount of 10 per cent to be deducted if Kitlocker.com pay within fourteen days. Assuming that payment is made within fourteen days, can you answer the following?

1. Will this be 'discount allowed' or 'discount received' in Kitlocker's accounts?
2. What is the amount of the discount?
3. What accounting entries will be required to record the discounted payment (ignore the original purchase)?
4. What impact will the discount have on the profit on the period?

Answers

1. Discount received
2. £500 (£5,000 × 0.1 = £500)
3. Debit trade creditors £4,500, credit cash and bank £4,500, debit trade creditors £500 and credit discount received £500
4. Profit will increase by the £500 discount received.

BAD DEBTS

In the previous section you will have seen one of the strategies businesses use in an attempt to recoup money that is owed to them. For the most part, customers will pay you what they owe but there will be examples where a debt 'goes bad' and is not paid. The offering of credit terms will usually be an incentive for customers to trade with you; however, it must be noted that there is always a risk that some of your debtors may not pay up. You have to recognise that when a debt goes bad it can no longer be viewed as an asset (remember that when a sale is made on credit the trade debtors (assets) of the business go up). Therefore, a bad debt must be recorded as an expense. As usual, an example is the best way to see how this works in practice.

CASE STUDY

RECORDING BAD DEBTS

Assume that Kitlocker.com have recently sold a team volleyball kit to a local team. The sale of £1,500 was made on credit terms. First, they need to recognise the sale so they debit trade debtors £1,500 (+Asset) and credit sales £1,500 (+Income). However, the team are declared bankrupt and cannot pay their debt to the company. If you remember that a bad debt reduces the asset of debtors, not income, the double entry is quite easy. Although Kitlocker.com don't necessarily want to, they are forced to write off the £1,500 as a bad debt. The entries are: debit bad debt expense (+Expense) and credit trade debtors (–Asset). When the final accounts are prepared the sales figure is transferred to the income statement as income and the bad debt expense to expenses. It is also worth noting here that on the balance sheet the trade debtors account must not include any bad debts. The 'T' accounts are shown below.

Sales A/C

DEBIT (£)	CREDIT (£)
	1,500

Trade debtors A/C

DEBIT (£)	CREDIT (£)
1,500	
	1,500

Bad debt A/C

DEBIT (£)	CREDIT (£)
1,500	

As a manager or potential manager, you should note here the dangers of offering credit facilities. Kitlocker.com, as a relatively new business, would need to break into new markets and would therefore offer credit facilities and discounts as incentives to customers. However, you should always seek to establish the credit-worthiness of a business before trading in this way. Furthermore, you should make every effort to recover debts, even if only in part. Writing off transactions as bad debts should be a last resort.

Provision for bad debts

Some businesses will set up a 'Provision for bad debts' just in case anything goes wrong with their debtors. Such provision will be necessary if it is considered that there may be doubtful debts contained in the trade debtors figure (remember that final accounts have to give a true and fair picture). The creation of these provision accounts follows much the same logic as the provision for depreciation. By making the provision of bad debts account we are able to reduce the debtors figure on the balance sheet in accordance with the prudence concept, which states that revenues and profits should only be recognised when they are realised.

For example, if Kitlcoker.com sold various team kits to credit customers for £10,000 they would have debited trade debtors £10,000 and credited sales £10,000. However, if we look back at the previous example we saw that debtors worth £1,500 went bad and were written off by debiting bad debt expense £1,500 and crediting trade debtors £1,500. Following this, Kitlocker.com approached some of their other customers to ask for payment to avoid a similar situation. Consequently, debtors worth £6,000 paid up. Kitlocker.com were then able to debit 'cash and bank' £6,000 and credit 'trade debtors' £6,000. This left them with a balance of £2,500 on their trade debtors account. At the end of the accounting period they evaluated their existing debtors and decided that 5 per cent of the remaining debt might be bad, i.e. £125 (£2,500 × 5%). They decide to make a provision to cover this and debit bad debt expense £125 (+Expense) and credit provision for bad debts £125 (+Provision). Their ledger accounts would look like this:

Sales A/C

DEBIT (£)	CREDIT (£)
	10,000

Trade debtors A/C

DEBIT (£)	CREDIT (£)
10,000	1,500
	6,000

Bad debt expense A/C

DEBIT (£)	CREDIT (£)
1,500	
125	

Cash and bank A/C

DEBIT (£)	CREDIT (£)
6,000	

Provision for bad debt A/C

DEBIT (£)	CREDIT (£)
	125

You should note here that the purpose of having a provision for bad debts account is purely to provide an amount, which will reduce the asset of trade debtors (much like the depreciation exercise) on the balance sheet to net realisable value (in other words, the balance sheet is showing the amount of money that you expect to be paid). This is achieved by subtracting the balance on the provision for bad debts account from the balance on the trade debtors account. If you are required to make any adjustments you can follow the same stages as you did to adjust depreciation. For example, if it is believed that more customers will default on their debts it will be necessary to change the provision for bad debts to a higher percentage. The value of the change would be shown as an extra expense in the income statement and the revised provision would be used to reduce the value of the debtors shown in the balance sheet.

As a manager, you should be careful in your treatment of credit and bad debts. It may well be your responsibility to provide a detailed analysis of customers so that you can decide whether credit options should be given. This information may then be used to decide how to manage the recovery of outstanding debt and to calculate a realistic provision for bad debts.

RETURNS

In business there may be times when goods will have to be returned to a supplier. Consider how many times you have had to take things back to shops. What do you think happens to the goods that you return? If they are just wrong for you, then they may well go back onto the shelf; however, if they are faulty, chances are that they will be sent back to the supplier. You may have noticed that there are actually two things going on here. First, you have the customer return (i.e. the football boots you have returned because the soles came apart); we call this a return of sale or returns inwards. Second, you have the return of goods to the supplier (i.e. the return of the faulty football boots to the manufacturer); we call this a return of purchase or returns outwards.

Returns inwards

If a customer returns goods (for example, football boots back to a shop) the shop accounts must show a decrease in sales and a decrease in cash (if a cash refund is given immediately) or a decrease in trade debtors (if there is no immediate cash refund). Note that these two 'decreases' balance each other off because one is a debit and the other is a credit.

The sale of the boots caused the accounting entries debit 'Cost of sales' and credit 'Inventory'. The return of the boots means that the entries now have to be reversed to cancel out the previous ones (we now credit 'Cost of sales' and debit 'Inventory').

Returns outwards

Just like returns inwards, returns outwards are easy to record. When purchases are returned to a supplier (football boots back to the manufacturer) the accounts must show a decrease in purchases (or inventory) and an increase in cash (providing a cash refund is obtained immediately) or a decrease in trade creditors (if there is no immediate cash refund). Again this is simple to record. If a cash refund is obtained immediately, a company will debit cash and bank (+Asset) and credit purchases (–Expense) and if a cash refund is not obtained immediately they debit trade creditors (–Creditors) and credit purchases (-Expense).

ACTIVITY

Consider the following question for Kitlocker.com.

What accounting entries will the company need if:

1. Customers return goods and obtain a cash refund immediately?
2. The company return goods to one of their suppliers and receive a credit note (i.e. do not obtain a cash refund)?

Answers

1. Debit 'Sales' and credit 'Cash and bank' with the sales value of the goods, and debit 'Inventory' and credit 'Cost of sales' with the price Kitlocker paid for the goods.
2. Debit 'Trade creditors', and credit 'Purchases' or 'Inventory'.

DISPOSAL OF FIXED ASSETS

If you think back to Chapter 2 where you were introduced to assets and in particular fixed assets you may have thought that accounting for bringing them into the business is all very well, but what happens if and when you dispose of them? Indeed, earlier in this chapter when we considered depreciation you may have wondered why a company would keep assets until they were worthless – why not sell them while they still had some value? Here we will deal with those questions and show you how it can be done and how it should be recorded.

You are aware that fixed assets are used by a company so that it can carry out its business (the fixed assets are not for trade – they are used to enable trade to take place). The assets will last for more than one accounting period but their value will depreciate over time. However, before the end of an asset's useful life it may and probably will be sold (the company may need more efficient machinery in order to remain, or become, competitive). Occasionally an asset may be sold for its net book value (cost – depreciation) but given that the depreciation charge is only an estimate, it is more likely that the net book value (NBV) and the sale proceeds are two different figures!

CASE STUDY

ASSET DISPOSAL

When Kitlocker.com were established in 2005 they purchased a van for £1,000. This van has been depreciated by 25 per cent per year on cost, meaning that the NBV of the van at the end of Year 1 is £750. Immediately after the end of the first year Kitlocker decided to get a better van. They sold the old van for £600. Clearly there is a 'loss' of £150 (the business valued the van at £750 but it only realised £600) and it is important that this, and the associated transactions, are dealt with in the income statement for Year 2 so that the accounts show a true and fair view.

In order to make the necessary entries in the company's 'T' accounts a number of stages have to be followed. We will need to open some new accounts that are unfamiliar to you so that we can record the sale of the van (so take your time when reading this and then you will appreciate the logic). First, the company need to identify the original cost of the vehicle being sold (£1,000) and transfer this to the disposal account. To do this they debit the disposal account £1,000 (+Expense) and credit vehicles at cost £1,000 (–Asset).

Second, they need to calculate the accumulated depreciation provided on the asset being sold: in this case it is only one year's worth (£250). This figure is transferred to the disposals account using the following entries: debit provision for depreciation of vehicles account £250 and credit disposals account £250. At this stage the balance on the disposals account represents the NBV of the vehicle, i.e. £750.

Finally, they need to record the sale of the asset. We can assume that the cash is paid immediately so the entries will be: debit cash £600 and credit disposals account £600. The balance on the disposals account will now represent the profit or loss on the disposal. You should also note here that for each stage of the transaction the disposals account is used. Ultimately the 'T' accounts will look like this:

Vehicles at cost A/C

DEBIT (£)	CREDIT (£)
	1,000

Provision for depreciation of vehicles A/C

DEBIT (£)	CREDIT (£)
250	

Disposals A/C

DEBIT (£)	CREDIT (£)
1,000	250
	600

Cash and bank A/C

DEBIT (£)	CREDIT (£)
600	

accounting records in sport

In this example, when we balance off the accounts there will be a debit balance of £150 on the disposals account that will be transferred to the expense section of the income statement which will reduce any profit by £150.

ACTIVITY

Assume that Kitlocker.com purchase a new embroidery machine that will allow them to produce team kit with stitched logos and names. The machine costs the business £15,000 and should have a useful life of ten years. They find out that the industry standard is to depreciate the equipment by 12 per cent per annum on cost.

1. What will be the annual depreciation charge for the machine (assume the straight-line method for depreciation)?
2. What will be the accumulated depreciation by the end of Year 5?
3. What will be the NBV of the machine at the end of Year 5?
4. At the end of Year 6 the company decide to sell the machine for £3,000. What is the profit/loss for the machine?
5. What are the accounting entries for Question 4?

Answers

1. £1,500 (£15,000/10 = £1,500).
2. £7,500 (£1,500 × 5 = £7,500).
3. £7,500 (£15,000–£7,500 = £7,500).
4. Loss on disposal is £3,000 (NBV end of Year 6 = £15,000 – (£1,500 × 6) = £6,000. Therefore loss on disposal = £6,000 – £3,000 = £3,000).
5. Entries are:
   a. Debit disposals a/c £15,000, credit machinery at cost a/c £15,000.
   b. Debit provision for depreciation of machinery £9,000, credit disposals a/c £9,000.
   c. Debit cash and bank £3,000, credit disposals a/c £3,000).

SUMMARY

The aim of this chapter was to introduce you to the common routine decisions and transactions that sport and leisure managers make on a regular basis. It is important that you understand how these actions are recorded in the company accounts so that you can begin to see the consequences of their (and soon *your*) decisions. Obtaining loan finance, giving trade and cash discounts, offering credit facilities, returning goods and disposing of assets will all have an impact upon the running, and finances, of the business.

QUESTIONS FOR REVIEW

1   What is the net book value of an asset?
2   A machine cost £50,000 and was being depreciated at 20 per cent per annum. If the depreciation rate was changed to 25 per cent per year, how much extra cash would leave the company in the second year of the machine's usage?
3   Would 'interest receivable' be shown as an expense?
4   Explain the difference between 'interest payments' and 'capital repayments' on a loan.
5   Would 'discounts allowed' be shown as an expense?

REFERENCES AND FURTHER READING

CIMA (2009) *Financial Accounting Fundamentals*. BPP Professional Education, London.
Dyson, J.R. (2003) *Accounting for Non-accounting Students*, 6th edn. Financial Times Press, Harlow.
McLaney, E. and Atrill, P. (2005) *Accounting: An Introduction*, 3rd edn. Financial Times Press, Harlow.
Wilson, R. and Joyce, J. (2008) *Finance for Sport and Leisure Managers: An Introduction*. Routledge, London.

CHAPTER 5

FROM 'T' ACCOUNTS TO FINANCIAL STATEMENTS

CONSTRUCTING A TRIAL BALANCE

On completion of this chapter you will be able to:

- understand and communicate the interrelationship between 'T' accounts and financial statements;
- determine balances on 'T' accounts and construct a trial balance;
- construct an outline income statement and balance sheet.

INTRODUCTION

By now you should understand the rules that govern how and why ledger accounts are constructed. Hopefully you have now begun to wonder how all of this information will ultimately be recorded in a set of final accounts (like the ones we saw illustrated in Chapters 1 and 2). Remember that the details of all transactions for a business are recorded in the appropriate 'T' accounts as and when they occur. Before we use them to construct the final accounts, however, it is necessary to make sure that they are correct. We can test the arithmetical accuracy of the accounts by constructing a trial balance; this merely involves listing and then totalling, separately, the credit and debit balances (we told you there is no need to be a skilled mathematician to understand accounts). The trial balance is the second step in the production of the final accounts.

KEY TERM

TRIAL BALANCE

This is simply a list of nominal ledger ('T') account balances. It is used primarily as a measure to see if credit balances equal debit balances. Ultimately it will offer some reassurance that the double-entry rule has been applied correctly.

Nearly all the information that you need to draw up an income statement (profit and loss a/c) may be found in the trial balance. All you need to do is pick the right figures. The balance sheet is formulated in a very similar way. However, you will need to make certain adjustments to the basic information held in the trial balance before we can work out profit values etc. Chapter 2 outlined the fundamental rules and now we have to apply them to ensure that when we come out with a set of final figures they represent a true and fair view. Later chapters will cover the key adjustments that you need to be aware of, and show you how to perform the calculations. However, before we do this we need to cover the trial balance.

THE TRIAL BALANCE

It is very important that when recording transactions in the ledgers you have some sort of control system to check the 'accuracy' of what has been done. One of these controls, which also serves as an arithmetical check, is the trial balance. In this section we will outline the guiding principles of constructing one. You will need to apply this knowledge in later chapters (so it is important that you understand what is happening as we go along).

As each transaction involves a debit entry and a credit entry of the same value, it will follow that if we add up all of the debits they should equal the total of all of the credits. The aim therefore of the trial balance is to prove that for every debit entry a balancing credit entry has been made. As one side of each individual 'T' account records increases and the other records decreases, the difference between the two sides will represent the net value, or balance, of that account. For example, if total cash receipts amount to £25,000 and total cash payments total £15,000, the value, or balance, of the cash account will be £10,000. By balancing off the account we can simplify it so that only one figure is carried forward to the final accounts. Below you will see how this balancing-off process works in practice.

1. Leaving a line blank, rule a total box on each side of the account. The total boxes must be level with each other. This is demonstrated by the cash and bank account below.

Cash and bank A/C

	DEBIT	(£)		CREDIT	(£)
1 January	Capital	15,000	2 January	Motors	5,000
6	Sales	6,750	9	Purchases	3,250
18	'T' debtors	3,250	19	Wages	750
			29	'T' creditors	6,000
	(Total box)				

2. Add up the debit side of the account (= £25,000).
3. Add up the credit side of the account (= £15,000).
4. Enter the *greater* value in each total box (= £25,000).
5. Enter the shortfall – the closing balance to be carried down ('c/d') of £10,000 – to the credit side to make both sides equal.
6. The balance must be brought down ('b/d') on the *opposite* side (the debit side), *below* the total box.

Cash and bank A/C

	DEBIT	(£)		CREDIT	(£)
1 January	Capital	15,000	2 January	Motors	5,000
6	Sales	6,750	9	Purchases	3,250
18	'T' debtors	3,250	19	Wages	750
			29	'T' creditors	6,000
			31 January	Balance c/d	10,000
	(Total box)	25,000			25,000
1 February	Balance b/d	10,000			

Please note:

- The balancing-off of the account has netted the total value of all the entries on the account for the period.
- As the debit side exceeded the credit side, the balance of £10,000 is a debit balance, i.e. a net debit.
- The cash transactions for the following period will be entered as debits and credits below the ruled-off total box and the brought-down entry.
- According to the cash and bank account, there is £10,000 available at the end of the period/beginning of the following period, i.e. 31 January/1 February.
- At the end of the year the final 'T' accounts will be balanced off and their values used for the final accounts.

That should have been relatively straightforward. However, let us see if you can put it into practice by answering the following questions. Record each of the 'T' accounts on paper and balance them all off. If it makes it easier, pretend that the transactions relate to Kitlocker.com.

ACTIVITY

Mike sets up a company to sell sports kit to university sport teams. He puts £7,000 of his own money into the business and in the first period of trading the following transactions occurred.

1. Mike introduces £7,000 of cash into the business as capital.
2. The rent for the shop (£3,500) is paid in cash.
3. Clothing for resale costing £5,000 is purchased on credit.
4. The company take out a bank loan for £1,000.
5. Shop fittings are purchased for cash of £2,000.
6. A university team is signed and the company makes sales of £10,000 for cash.
7. More goods are sold, this time on credit, for £2,500.
8. Trade creditors are paid, by cash, £4,250.
9. Trade debtors pay £1,500.
10. Interest on the business loan is paid totalling £100.
11. Administration costs of £100 are paid in cash.
12. Mike makes drawings of £1,500.

Once you have completed the 'T' account entries, balance off each account and record the balances in a trial balance.

Hopefully it should look something like this (don't worry if things are in a different order):

	Debit (£)	Credit (£)
Cash	8,050	
Capital		7,000
Bank loan		1,000
Stock (purchases)	5,000	
Trade creditors		750
Rent	3,500	
Shop fittings	2,000	
Sales		12,500
Trade debtors	1,000	
Loan interest	100	
Administration expenses	100	
Drawings	1,500	
	21,250	21,250

If your calculation is slightly different, or if the debits do not equal the credits, go back through your accounts and check them against the double-entry rule. It may help if you work out the difference first as you may have only made one error. However, before you start your trawl, check the list of common errors below:

1 Is there a complete omission of a transaction?
2 Have you posted something to the wrong account?
3 Have you recorded a credit when you should have recorded a debit?
4 Are there more debits than credits (or vice versa), i.e. have you followed the double-entry rule?

In this example there was actually very little balancing to do. Only the cash account and sales account had some real activity, with the remaining ones having only one or two transactions. If you've really got into a mess have a look at our 'T' accounts, which you can find after the review questions at the end of the chapter.

You shouldn't worry if your trial balance has been prepared in a different order from ours as it is not a published document like the balance sheet and income statement. It is, as the key term above suggests, just a method to test the accuracy of your double-entry bookkeeping.

LIMITATIONS TO THE TRIAL BALANCE

Obviously if the debit column and credit column do not balance you have made an error in your application of the double-entry rule. However, you need to be aware that the trial balance is not a perfect measurement tool. It too has its limitations due to its inability to uncover the following errors:

- An error of omission: if there is a total omission of a transaction the trial balance may still balance (providing there are no other mistakes). For example, in the activity above there would have been no quick way of knowing that you had forgotten to record the details of the rent.
- An error of commission: you may post a transaction to the wrong account while choosing the right type of account. For example, you may post something to the telephone account when you should have posted it to the rent account.
- Compensating errors: these occur when one error is cancelled out by another.
- Errors of principle: transactions are posted to the wrong account; for example, you post something to motor expenses rather than fixed assets.
- Errors of original entry: the wrong amount is debited and credited to the correct accounts. You should probably note that this is also one of the most common yet basic errors in student work!

THE TRIAL BALANCE BALANCES! NOW WHAT?

Now it's time to start thinking about the two major financial statements: the income statement and the balance sheet. These are designed to provide the users of accounting information with a picture of the overall financial position and performance of the business. Providing that the trial balance has been produced and we have been reassured that the double-entry rule has been applied correctly, the next step in preparing the financial statements is to produce a trading income statement and balance sheet. These 'trading' statements are not the final statements that we are looking for but they will give us an early picture of what needs to be completed before we produce them.

The first step you need to take when doing this is to identify which accounts feed into the income statement and which feed into the balance sheet. At this point it is probably worth reminding you what each of the main statements is for, as you need to be able to put the trial balance into context and we shall be using the two statements more regularly from now on.

> **KEY TERMS**
>
> ## THE INCOME STATEMENT (profit and loss account)
>
> A statement showing the profits (or losses) recognised during a period. The profit is calculated by deducting expenditure (including charges for capital maintenance) from income.
>
> ## THE BALANCE SHEET
>
> A list of all the assets owned by a business and all the liabilities owed by a business at a specific point in time. It is often referred to as a 'snapshot' of the financial position of the business at a specific moment in time (the end of the financial year).

With these definitions in mind, we can begin to identify which accounts will feed into which statement. For example, in the activity above, Mike had to pay a rent bill of £3,500. If you accounted for it correctly you will have noticed that it is an expense and will therefore go on the income statement.

> **ACTIVITY**
>
> Go through the trial balance from the previous activity and identify which accounts will be recorded on the income statement.

A brief insight into the trading income statement

For the previous activity you should have been able to identify that the following accounts would be transferred to the trading income statement:

- purchases (stock) £5,000 debit;
- rent £3,500 debit;
- loan interest £100 debit;

- administration expenses £100 debit;
- sales £12,500 credit;
- drawings £1,500 debit (will go in the final income statement but not the 'trading' bit).

Once this has been done we can construct the trading account as shown in Figure 5.1.

Cost of sales is what the cost to the company was for the goods that had been sold. The goods are hopefully sold at a higher price, and that price should also leave a surplus to cover the other expenses of the business. In this example it has been assumed that all of the goods purchased have been sold. In reality that will not be the case: companies hold stock (inventory). Therefore it will be necessary to do a stock-take to see what has not been sold. Stock is valued at its cost price and not at its resale value. Continuing this idea means that at the start of the period there will have been some stock brought forward from the previous period (unless the company has just started trading). Thus to ensure that we have got the correct figure for 'Cost of sales' we use the formula:

$$\text{Cost of sales} = \text{opening stock} + \text{purchases} - \text{closing stock}$$

Don't worry if this is the first time you have seen a statement like this (or that I haven't really discussed it). It is here to serve a purpose and I will come back to it in detail in the next chapter.

	£	£
Sales		12,500
Cost of sales (see below*)		(5,000)
Gross profit		7,500
Expenses		
Rent	3,500	
Loan interest	100	
Administration expenses	100	
		(3,700)
Net profit		3,800

Figure 5.1 Mike: trading income statement

A brief insight into the balance sheet

Identifying the accounts, which feed into this statement, should be really easy. Look back at which ones were not used to construct the income statement and you should find the following: cash, capital, bank loan, trade creditors, shop fittings, trade debtors and drawings. The only point of real note here is that the income statement and balance sheet work together using profit (or loss), so this will also need to be recorded somewhere.

In our example Mike's capital will comprise any cash that he introduced plus any profit that the business makes, minus any drawings. He introduced £7,000 and made drawings of £1,500 while the business made a profit of £3,800. Consequently the owner's capital equals £9,300 (7,000 – 1,500 + 3,800). Understanding this allows us to construct the balance sheet shown in Figure 5.2.

Assets		
Non-current assets		**Figure 5.2** Mike: balance sheet at end of first trading period
Property, plant and equipment	2,000	
Current assets		
Inventories	0	
Trade receivables	1,000	
Cash and cash equivalents	8,050	
Total assets	**11,050**	
Equity and liabilities		
Equity	9,300	
Non-current liabilities	**1,000**	
Current liabilities		
Trade payables	750	
Total equity and liabilities	**11,050**	

Notice that in Figure 5.2 the balance sheet balances. Again, don't worry about this too much at this stage – we'll look at it later. However, the basic point behind all of this is to help with the preparation of the final statements. We can be confident with our trial balance and trading accounts at this stage, since they balance.

SUMMARY

This chapter should have helped you understand why 'T' accounts are constructed in the first place and that each account should be periodically balanced off. All of the individual ledger accounts should be balanced off at the end of the accounting period, be it the end of a month, quarter or year. The debit and credit balances are then listed in two columns in a financial statement called the trial balance. Providing that the sum of the credit balance is the same as the sum of the debit balance we can make the assumption that the records are mathematically correct. However, it is still good practice to check your records against the limitations of the trial balance to ensure that there are no other errors. This trial balance, subject to some more alterations such as cost of sales, mispostings, accruals and prepayments which we cover in the next chapter, will then be used as the basis for drawing up the balance sheet and income statement.

Remember: a trial balance is your way of checking your bookkeeping skills as it helps to perform an arithmetical check. However, there are some notable drawbacks to the trial balance, which should prompt you to be vigilant when applying the double-entry rule and constructing 'T' accounts.

QUESTIONS FOR REVIEW

1   List the five circumstances in which a trial balance might balance, even though some of the balances are incorrect.

- _____
- _____
- _____
- _____
- _____

2 What is the purpose of the trial balance?
3 Indicate where each of the following items will be shown (in the trading income statement or balance sheet):

- trade debtors;
- cash and bank;
- bank loans;
- rent;
- wages;
- loan interest paid;
- trade creditors.

4 Should the cost of equipment we have purchased be shown in the income statement?
5 What effect does profit have on capital?
6 A company takes out a loan to pay for a new van. Is the loan an asset?
7 A company has owned a van worth £10,000 for two years. It depreciates the van by £2,000 each year. What would be in the trial balance at the end of the second year for the van and its depreciation?
8 Does a trial balance list all the transactions made by the business?

REFERENCES AND FURTHER READING

CIMA (2009) *Financial Accounting Fundamentals*. BPP Professional Education, London.
Dyson, J.R. (2003) *Accounting for Non-accounting Students*, 6th edn. Financial Times Press, Harlow.
McLaney, E. and Atrill, P. (2005) *Accounting: An Introduction*, 3rd edn. Financial Times Press, Harlow.
Wilson, R. and Joyce, J. (2008) *Finance for Sport and Leisure Managers: An Introduction*. Routledge, London.

CHAPTER 6

FINAL ADJUSTMENTS IN SPORT

> **On completion of this chapter you will be able to:**
>
> - make routine adjustments to the trial balance (cost of sales, mispostings, accruals and prepayments).

INTRODUCTION

We ended the last chapter with a look at how to construct a trial balance. The trial balance not only helps us to check the arithmetical accuracy of our bookkeeping but enables us to prepare basic accounts (as you saw). The information contained in these basic financial statements can help us answer the three main questions which are commonly asked by owners:

1. What profit has the organisation made?
2. How much money does the organisation owe to others?
3. How much money is owed by others to the organisation?

Consequently, this chapter will bring together the knowledge that you have gained from the earlier chapters so that we can move towards compiling the financial statements in order to answer these questions (and one or two more). However, before you can progress to constructing a set of financial statements you need to go through one final stage. This will involve making certain adjustments so that your accounts conform to the accounting principles that we took you through in Chapter 2. These adjustments are commonly known as 'trial balance adjustments' because they make use of information that was not taken into account when preparing the trial balance and therefore cause it to be adjusted (what a good name to call them!).

Throughout the previous three chapters you should have been asking yourself questions such as: what happens to transactions that occurred during this accounting period but we won't pay (or get paid for) until the next one? How do I deal with stock because when I make a sale the money is not all profit? What happens if I forget to record a transaction in the ledgers? The answers to these questions (and one or two more) will be explained in this chapter. We will examine cost of sales (you were introduced to this at the end of Chapter 5), mispostings, accruals and prepayments. These are the types of things you will encounter when sorting through the books of organisations that you may work for.

The income statement and balance sheet cannot be prepared until all of the accounts have been balanced and a trial balance constructed (see Chapter 5 for details on this). For any business this can be a lengthy exercise so it is probably a good idea to do it periodically. However, no matter how up to date the accounting entries are, there are always a number of transactions that come up at the very end of the financial period. Due to the lateness of some transactions, the trading income statement and balance sheet may have already been drawn up. Clearly there will be a need for some more adjustments to be made before the final statements are drawn up when we consider all of the accounting concepts outlined in Chapter 2 – can you remember what these were?

ACTIVITY

List as many of the accounting concepts as you can.

Hopefully you listed the following: Going concern, Accruals, Materiality, Business entity, Money measurement, Dual aspect and historical cost, Prudence and consistency.

If you have forgotten the meaning of any of these concepts I suggest you have a quick flick through Chapter 2 again as they are fundamental underpinnings for what we are about to do. Once you are happy, we can tackle the four key adjustments.

COST OF SALES

The income statement matches the cost of goods sold against sales income in order to calculate profit. I introduced you to this briefly in the last chapter. The purchases 'T' account allows us to record the costs of any goods the business buys. However, in practice not all of the goods the business buys will be sold by the end of the accounting period, so purchases will not equal cost of sales. We need to take opening and closing stock into consideration to account for the difference. For example, if Kitlocker.com make purchases in January of 100 pairs of swimming trunks at a stock cost of £10 each, sales are made of seventy-five of the units for £20; i.e. at a gross profit of £10 per unit the accounting records for the business will show:

1   Purchases £1,000 (100 × £10)
2   Sales £1,500 (75 × £20)

In order for the income statement to accurately reflect this transaction we need to make an allowance for the twenty-five unsold pairs of swimming trunks, i.e. they must be removed from the cost of sales figure. This is easy when you apply the following formula:

Cost of sales = Opening stock + Purchases − Closing stock
(remember this from Chapter 5?)

For our example the cost of sales figure (assuming that the company started the year with no opening stock) will be:

$$\text{Cost of sales} = £0 + £1{,}000 - £250 \text{ (i.e. 25 pairs worth £10 each)}$$

$$\text{Cost of sales} = £750$$

The cost of sales figure will then be put into the income statement under sales to help calculate gross profit as follows:

	£	£
Sales		1,500
Cost of sales		750
Gross profit		750

KEY TERMS

GROSS PROFIT

Sales income less the direct cost of the goods or services sold.

NET PROFIT

Any profit left over after deducting all costs of supply and overheads, i.e. gross profit minus other costs (expenses).

ACTIVITY

Let us assume that Kitlocker.com get the same answer as us in the above example because they are doing their books correctly. In February they purchase another fifty pairs of swimming trunks at a cost of £10 a pair. They sell forty-five pairs at £20 each.

Complete the cost of sales adjustment for February.

Hopefully you worked it out like this:

$$\text{Cost of sales} = \text{Opening stock} + \text{Purchases} - \text{Closing stock}$$

$$\text{Cost of sales} = £250 \text{ (25 pairs left over from January)} + £500 \text{ (February purchases)} - £250 \text{ (25 remaining pairs)}$$

Did you remember to include the opening stock?

There are a number of lessons you should learn here about why the cost of sales adjustment is made. First, the cost of the units has been matched against the selling price of the units in accordance with the accruals concept. Any profit has only been recognised on the goods sold in accordance with the prudence concept. Closing stocks have been valued at cost, in our example £10 per pair of swimming trunks, because the potential profit of any unsold goods cannot be recognised until they are physically sold – this is again in accordance with the prudence concept.

There is, however, one more connection that you need to recognise: the value of closing stock (at the end of the period) will be used on the balance sheet.

MISPOSTINGS

Let us assume that you are preparing the accounts for your local five-a-side football team and you have successfully balanced the trial balance. At first you will be pleased, but then you will remember that the trial balance is not a perfect tool, as it does not show any transactions that you have missed out entirely (omissions) or whether you have made entries on the correct sides of wrong accounts (mispostings); for example, you purchased five new match balls and recorded them on the purchases account instead of the fixed asset (equipment) account. Remember that you are not going to sell the match balls – you are going to use them.

If and when this type of situation occurs you will need to do something about it. The trial balance has been constructed so we need to make our second type of adjustment: 'mispostings'. These are fairly straightforward to do as they follow the double-entry rule. That is to say, you will need to complete a debit and a credit entry to rectify your mistake. We will continue with our example to illustrate this:

- First, debit the equipment account (this will record your equipment).
- Second, credit purchases (this cancels out the earlier posting if you consider that recording an amount on this side will reduce the value of the account).

That should have been easy. Now have a go at drawing up the 'T' accounts for the following two activity questions and then make the necessary adjustments for misposting.

ACTIVITY

Construct the 'T' accounts for the following.

1   Your five-a-side football team purchased some new goal nets for £100 cash and made the following *incorrect* entries:

- Debit purchases £100
- Credit cash and bank.

2   The telephone bill arrives for £50:

- Debit rent, rates and insurance
- Credit trade creditors.

Now correct the entries.

You should have made the following changes:

1   Debit equipment £100
    Credit purchases £100.

2   Debit telephone £50
    Credit rent, rates and insurance £50.

ACCRUALS

You will have first come across the term 'accruals' in Chapter 2, as it is one of the most important accounting conventions that you need to understand. By now you should have a good understanding of the definition and when and how the concept is applied. Accruals will crop up in a sport and leisure setting, just as they do elsewhere. Because 'business life' is divided up into accounting periods we are faced with an immediate problem: which of the transactions should be included in the accounts for this year? This is due to the fact that the income statement and the balance sheet are drawn up for one year only but the business is a going concern and therefore 'lives' through many periods.

As you should know by now, profit is calculated by matching the income that has been earned during an accounting period with the expenses that have been incurred for that period. This is known as the accruals concept. Consequently, income and expenses should be attached to the accounting period that they relate to even though they may be paid in a different accounting period. The application of the accruals concept is therefore integral to constructing an income statement that offers a true and fair view.

A business will sometimes incur expenses before it has paid for them. A good example of this is electricity. Electricity bills are paid quarterly in arrears but when we are preparing the accounts for a period we need to show the expenses incurred for that period, even if we have yet to be billed for them. How this would be dealt with is explained below.

If the electricity bill arrives and is paid immediately the business will debit light and heat (+Expense) and credit cash and bank (–Asset). If the bill isn't paid immediately the business will deal with it slightly differently and will debit light and heat (+Expense) and credit trade creditors (+Creditors). These entries will be made during normal day-to-day activities, will be recorded in the appropriate 'T' accounts and will ultimately end up in the trial balance.

However, if at the end of an accounting period electricity has been used for which a bill has not yet been received, the expense must be 'accrued' (you will need to estimate what you think you will be charged for the electricity for this period). In this situation the business will debit light and heat (+Expense) and credit trade creditors (+Creditors) with the estimated amount. This will allow the business to recognise the expense as something that they owe when they move into the next accounting period and will ensure that the expenses that have been incurred for the period have been charged in the income statement.

Accrued income can be dealt with in much the same way. If we assume that Kitlocker.com make sales at the end of an accounting period on credit and they do not send the invoice it still needs to show on the income statement. Remember that the income statement must show the total income earned during the period. Consequently, the following entries will be required: debit 'Trade debtors' (+Asset) and credit 'Sales' (+Income). Hopefully this will seem straightforward but you need to understand it, since students often make errors here.

PREPAYMENTS

Prepayments are simply the opposite of accruals: prepayments are expenses that have been paid in advance (i.e. they do not relate to this accounting period). Prepayments are therefore a way for us to show amounts that are paid for expenses incurred in readiness for a future accounting period. An example of this is when you pay for the insurance on your car. Normally it will be paid in full at the start of the coming year. However, if your insurance was due for renewal in August and the accounting period ends in March you will have paid for five-twelfths of the insurance for the next accounting period. If we assume that the insurance cost £240, only £140 relates to the current accounting period. This is the amount that will be included on the income statement with the remaining £100 being recorded in the trade debtor account, as it represents five months' insurance cover that is owed to the business.

SUMMARY

The adjustments to the trial balance that you have been introduced to here represent those that you will be most likely to meet in your future career. You must be aware that making such adjustments will alter the trial balance so that it offers a true and fair view of an organisation before the final accounts are drawn up. Consequently the information will now be ready for the preparation of the final set of financial statements. That is what we will do in the next chapter and then we will look at the good stuff (i.e. interpreting annual reports and using financial information). Putting the accounts together is easy – it is the ability to interpret financial statements that needs real skill.

QUESTIONS FOR REVIEW

1. Explain what is meant by (a) an accrued expense and (b) a prepaid expense.
2. How do accruals and prepayments affect the trial balance?
3. A business paid its annual rent of £12,000 in August. The business has an accounting period that ends in March. Explain the accounting entries that would be needed for the rent.
4. What is gross profit and how is it calculated?
5. What is net profit?

REFERENCES AND FURTHER READING

CIMA (2009) *Financial Accounting Fundamentals*. BPP Professional Education, London.
Dyson, J.R. (2003) *Accounting for Non-accounting Students*, 6th edn. Financial Times Press. Harlow.
McLaney, E. and Atrill, P. (2005). *Accounting: An Introduction*, 3rd edn. Financial Times Press, Harlow.
Wilson, R. and Joyce, J. (2008) *Finance for Sport and Leisure Managers: An Introduction*. Routledge, London.

CHAPTER 7

THE FINANCIAL STATEMENTS

On completion of this chapter you will be able to:

- understand and explain the information needed to construct the financial statements;
- understand the reporting and measurement of financial performance and position;
- understand and explain the accounts of non-trading organisations;
- explain the difference between cash and profit.

INTRODUCTION

By now you should be able to confidently construct and adjust a trial balance and be ready to move on to the final stage in constructing final accounts. In Chapters 1 and 6 you were given some brief information about the income statement and balance sheet, which was necessary to place what you were doing into context. The statements will now, finally, be considered in detail so that you can see what the accountant has to do in practice. Consequently, most of this chapter focuses on the format of an income statement, balance sheet and cash flow statement.

As well as being of interest to management, the financial health of an organisation will be significant to all of the external users of financial information that we examined in Chapter 1. We can use the income statement and balance sheet to examine this concept by measuring financial performance and financial position. The income statement may be used to work out how profitable an organisation has been over a given accounting period, therefore highlighting financial performance; and as the balance sheet summarises what the business owns and owes it may be used to show us its financial position. However, while we examine all of this information we need to be aware of the importance of cash. Cash is different to profit and the cash flow statement needs to be used in conjunction with the income statement and balance sheet to show further details about the organisation and its performance.

You have seen the regulatory framework in action already, so, in addition to the three key statements outlined above, this chapter will begin to show you the real implications of it and start to make you aware of why you really need to know everything I have told you so far. Many general accounting books go into great detail about various systems and procedures, some of which you have not been subjected to so far because you are not training to be accountants. What you have been doing, though, is developing a general awareness of accounting practices and information so that you understand the final accounts.

The basics of what you will be doing in the sport and leisure industry may be based around much of the information so far. However, by virtue of your future qualifications you may become increasingly involved in the detailed financial affairs of organisations through your personal involvement with sport clubs and teams, small leisure organisations and the voluntary sector. Therefore, I also need to show you what these 'non-trading organisations' do when it comes to finance.

At the time of writing there is much debate and soul-searching by accountants in many organisations about the format they should use to publish their financial statements. Should it be the ones recommended in the Companies Act or those recommended by the International Accounting Standards Board? The dilemma is caused by the accountants trying to choose the one that best portrays a 'true and fair view'. However, it should be remembered that it is only listed companies that have this dilemma; other organisations are free to choose whatever format they like (providing it also gives a true and fair view). Besides, if things change too much I'll be able to write a new edition!

International Accounting Standard 1

The Standard states that the set of financial statements should include:

- income statement;
- balance sheet;
- a statement of changes in equity;
- cash flow statement;
- notes giving a summary of the accounting policies used and other explanations.

The statement of changes in equity is beyond the scope of this book and consequently we will not cover it. However, we do need to examine everything else and although we won't get bogged down in telling you how to write statements summarising accounting policies we will give you some examples from actual accounts. The three major statements will now be covered.

THE INCOME STATEMENT: MEASURING FINANCIAL PERFORMANCE

The purpose of an income statement is to show you a history of financial performance (profitability) of the business over the accounting period. It is by definition retrospective because it covers the last accounting period (normally the past year). Businesses exist (in most cases) to generate wealth, or profit, and it is this wealth or profit that most people will be interested in. If you think back to the Manchester United case study in Chapter 2 you will probably remember that the profitability of the football club was the principal reason why Malcolm Glazer bought it.

The measurement of profit first requires the business to calculate the total revenue generated in a particular period. Following this, the business will need to calculate the total expenses relating to the accounting period. The income statement will then deduct the total expenses from the total revenues. The difference will represent either profit (if revenue exceeds expense) or loss (if expenditure exceeds revenue).

> **KEY TERMS**
>
> **REVENUE**
>
> A measure of the inflow of assets to a business. Such assets could take the form of cash or amounts owed by debtors. Some more traditional forms of revenue will be generated by the sale of goods, fees for services, subscriptions and interest received.
>
> **EXPENSE**
>
> A measure of the outflow of assets from a business, which are incurred as a result of generating revenue. Some of the more common types of expenses could be the cost of buying goods that are then sold (cost of sales), wages and salaries, rent and rates, insurance, telecommunications, etc.

Before we see what the income statement will look like you need to take note of a few extra points and issues – just to confuse you even further – IAS1 allows two methods of presentation for the income statement: by the 'function' of the expenses or by the 'nature' of the expenses. The Standard allows organisations to choose the one 'which most fairly represents the elements of the enterprise's performance'. The Standard recognises that analysts will want to be able to compare the performance of several organisations and therefore will want to ensure that they are comparing like with like. To ensure that the necessary information is available, the Standard states that information on the nature of expenses, including depreciation and staff costs, should be disclosed.

IAS 'by function' format

Income statement for the year ended DD/MM/YYYY:

	£m
Revenue	X
Cost of sales	(X)
Gross profit	X
Other operating income	X
Distribution costs	(X)
Administrative expenses	(X)

	£m
Profit from operations	X
Net interest cost	(X)
Profit before tax	X
Income tax expense	(X)
Net profit for period	X

The notes accompanying the statement would disclose the depreciation and staff costs included in the above figures. So that you can appreciate how all of this will actually work in practice, have another look at the Tottenham Hotspur Football Club income statement in Figure 7.1.

You will see from Tottenham Hotspur Football Club's income statement that it conforms to the 'by function format' suggested by the IAS. The statement itself details the key points, i.e. that operating loss is about £20 million and that profit after tax is £23 million. We can, however, get more information on such details as where the revenue came from by looking at the notes to the accounts. For Spurs a selection of such information is highlighted in Figure 7.2.

CONSOLIDATED INCOME STATEMENT
for the year ended 30 June 2009

Continuing operations

	Note	Operations, excluding football trading* £'000	Football trading* £'000	Total £'000	Year ended 30 June 2008 Total (note 3) £'000
Revenue	4	**113,012**	**–**	**113,012**	114,788
Operating expenses	5	(94,622)	(38,099)	(132,721)	(124,298)
Operating profit/(loss)		**18,390**	**(38,099)**	**(19,709)**	(9,510)
Profit on disposal of intangible fixed assets	8	–	56,500	56,500	16,362
Profit from operations	6	**18,390**	**18,401**	**36,791**	6,852
Finance income	9			4,563	1,797
Finance costs	9			(7,956)	(5,662)
Profit on ordinary activities before taxation				**33,398**	2,987
Tax	10			(10,234)	(2,018)
Profit for the period from continuing operations	23			**23,164**	969
Earnings per share from continuing operations – basic	11			**25.0p**	1.0p
Earnings per share from continuing operations – diluted	11			**12.9p**	1.0p

* Football trading represents the amortisation, impairment, and the profit/(loss) on disposal of intangible fixed assets and other football trading related income and expenditure.

There were no other gains or losses in either the current or prior year, accordingly no consolidated statement of recognised income and expense is presented.

Figure 7.1 Tottenham Hotspur income statement

Source: From Tottenham Hotspur plc Annual Report and Financial Statements 2009.

NOTES TO THE CONSOLIDATED ACCOUNTS (continued)

4. Revenue

Revenue, which is almost all derived from the Group's principal activity, is analysed as follows:

	2009 £'000	2008 £'000
Revenue comprises:		
Gate receipts – Premier League	**19,792**	18,274
Gate receipts – Cup competitions	**8,065**	10,341
Sponsorship and corporate hospitality	**27,363**	27,778
Media and broadcasting	**44,811**	40,329
Merchandising	**6,960**	9,723
Other	**6,021**	8,343
	113,012	114,788

All revenue except for £770,000 (2008: £176,000) derives from the Group's principal activity in the United Kingdom and is shown exclusive of VAT.

In addition to the amounts shown, the Group recognised finance income of £4,563,000 in 2009 and £1,797,000 in 2008 as set out in note 9. Consequently total revenue is £117,575,000 (2008: £116,585,000).

Figure 7.2 Tottenham Hotspur notes to the accounts

Source: From Tottenham Hotspur plc Annual Report and Financial Statements 2009.

INTERPRETING THE INCOME STATEMENT

When the income statement is presented to its users (much like the Spurs example), often only the net profit is examined. Granted, this is the primary measure of performance but you must recognise that it is not the only one. In Chapter 9 you will see how we can analyse the figures contained in the income statement and balance sheet, but for the purposes of this chapter you need to recognise the value of the income statement when seen on its own.

In order to evaluate an organisation's performance effectively you will need to find out how the net profit, or 'Profit for the period from continuing operations' in our Spurs example, is derived. The best way to do this is to analyse the level and amount of sales, the nature and amount of expenses, and profit in relation to sales. I will do this in basic terms for the Spurs example so that you can understand what I mean by this.

The sales figure for 2009 may be compared to that of 2008. This shows us that Spurs have been able to generate slightly less revenue (£113,012,000 compared to £114,788,000). In addition, in generating this revenue they have increased their cost of sales (or 'operating expenses') from £124,298,000 in 2008 to £132,721,000 in 2009. This suggests that their profitability is likely to reduce.

Next, we will examine the gross profit figure as both an absolute number and in relation to revenue. In absolute terms Spurs lost an additional £10 million between 2008 and 2009 (£19,709,000 compared with £9,510,000). Relative to revenue, this is a loss of about 17 per cent in 2009 and 8 per cent in 2008. I will explain the reasoning and mechanics of this calculation in Chapter 9; however, it tells us basically that in 2009 for every £1 of revenue that Spurs generated they made a loss of 17 pence, i.e. it cost them money to generate revenue.

However, despite this gross loss, Spurs managed to sell a number of intangible fixed assets which enabled them to make an overall net profit in both 2008 and 2009.

By using this basic analysis and the notes to the accounts (a section of which was illustrated in Figure 7.2) we can begin to build up a fuller picture of the organisation's financial performance. The basic lesson in the Spurs example (without going through all of the notes) is that they are performing quite well but are reliant on the sale of intangible assets in order to make a profit. Before we move on to examine the balance sheet and cash flow statement you need to remember one more thing. The income statement recognises transactions for the period concerned irrespective of when cash changes hands and it therefore shows the profit or loss achieved over an accounting period.

THE BALANCE SHEET: A SNAPSHOT OF THE FINANCIAL POSITION

The balance sheet is the financial statement that reflects the accounting equation – remember what this is? We covered it in detail in Chapter 3. The accounting equation states that the assets of the business will equal the capital and other liabilities (Assets = Capital + Liabilities). The equation, like the balance sheet, must balance. If you think back to when you studied maths at school you will realise that the equation can be rearranged so that Assets – Liabilities = Capital. This equation will help us to recognise the financial position of a business at a given point in time with the help of the balance sheet. We will come back to this in a minute.

If we agree that the balance sheet reflects the accounting equation, then we also agree that the balance sheet shows the financial position of the business because it shows us details of what the business owns and what it owes. It is often referred to as a 'snapshot' or 'picture' as it only shows us what is going on at a specific point in time. Normally the business will prepare its balance sheet at the close of business on the last day of the accounting period. In doing this, however, it has a weakness. A photograph only illustrates a specific moment and cannot show us what has happened before or after. It is the same for the balance sheet, and as such it may not represent a typical trading position, but we won't worry about this for the moment.

The balance sheet should distinguish between non-current assets and current assets. When classifying the assets you need to recognise the guidance provided by IAS1. The Standard stated that current assets are:

- part of the organisation's operations;
- held for trading purposes;
- cash and cash equivalents;
- all other assets will be classified as 'non-current' assets.

Similarly, the liabilities need to be split between 'current' and 'non-current'. Current liabilities are:

- within the normal course of business;
- due to be paid in the next financial year;
- all other liabilities will be shown as 'non-current'; for example:

Balance sheet as at DD/MM/YYYY

	£m	£m
Assets		
Non-current assets		
Property, plant and equipment	X	
Goodwill	X	
Other intangible assets	X	
		X
Current assets		
Inventories	X	
Trade and other receivables	X	
Other current assets	X	
Cash and cash equivalents	X	
		X
Total assets		X
Equity and liabilities		
Equity		
Issued capital	X	
Reserves	X	
Accumulated profits	X	
		X
Non-current liabilities		
Long-term borrowings	X	
Long-term provisions	X	
		X
Current liabilities		
Trade and other payables	X	
Short-term borrowings	X	
Proposed dividends	X	
Tax payable	X	
		X
Total equity and liabilities		X

Again the basic structure is all very well but it is always more useful for your learning to see this in practice, so let's look back again at what Tottenham Hotspur Football Club's balance sheet looked like when they constructed their financial statements at their year end (Figure 7.3).

As was the case with Spurs' income statement, their balance sheet conforms to the guidelines of the IAS. The statement itself details the key issues that arise such as the value of their total assets, total liabilities and total capital (looks like the information required for the accounting equation to me!). You will also notice that there are once more many references to 'notes to the accounts' here. As each individual business transaction will have been recorded in the organisation's ledger accounts a summary is given in the published balance sheet. The additional detail will be held as it was for the income statement. Have a quick look at Figure 7.4 so that you can see what I mean.

CONSOLIDATED BALANCE SHEET
as at 30 June 2009

	Note	30 June 2009 £'000	30 June 2008 £'000
Non-current assets			
Property, plant and equipment	12	**103,338**	74,130
Intangible assets	13	**128,432**	62,423
		231,770	136,553
Current assets			
Inventories	14	**1,172**	1,884
Trade and other receivables	15	**37,738**	41,292
Current tax receivable		**1,104**	2,182
Cash and cash equivalents	16	**19,622**	35,283
		59,636	80,641
Total assets		**291,406**	217,194
Current liabilities			
Trade and other payables	17	**(89,579)**	(77,496)
Interest bearing loans and borrowings	17	**(13,810)**	(7,798)
Provisions	17	**(1,211)**	(5,602)
		(104,600)	(90,896)
Non-current liabilities			
Interest bearing overdrafts and loans	18	**(66,504)**	(57,187)
Trade and other payables	18	**(37,871)**	(14,607)
Deferred grant income	18	**(2,211)**	(2,143)
Deferred tax liabilities	18/19	**(18,157)**	(9,751)
		(124,743)	(83,688)
Total liabilities		**(229,343)**	(174,584)
Net assets		**62,063**	42,610
Equity			
Share capital	21	**4,640**	4,639
Share premium		**11,638**	11,637
Equity component of convertible redeemable preference shares ("CRPS")	22	**3,805**	3,806
Revaluation reserve		**2,240**	2,288
Capital redemption reserve		**595**	595
Retained earnings		**39,145**	19,645
Total equity	23	**62,063**	42,610

These financial statements were approved by the Board of Directors on 9 November 2009.

Figure 7.3 Tottenham Hotspur balance sheet

Source: From Tottenham Hotspur plc Annual Report and Financial Statements 2009.

INTERPRETING THE BALANCE SHEET

Despite the fact that the balance sheet only illustrates an organisation's financial position at a given point in time, it does contain some quite useful information. As with the income statement, we will provide a deeper analysis in Chapter 9 but for now we can see what the balance sheet can tell us in its own right. The balance sheet can provide us with some useful information and insights into the financing and investing activities of a business.

We can for, example, see how much cash the organisation has that it could use, if required, to pay its creditors or purchase new assets. In 2009 Spurs had £19,622,000 in cash compared to £35,283,000 in 2008. This indicates that while their cash amounts had reduced significantly

13. Intangible assets

£'000

Cost of registrations
At 1 July 2008	121,078
Additions	119,336
Disposals	(43,292)
At 30 June 2009	**197,122**

Amortisation and impairment of registrations
At 1 July 2008	58,655
Charged in year – amortisation and impairment	37,288
Disposals	(27,253)
At 30 June 2009	**68,690**

Net book value of registrations
At 30 June 2009	**128,432**
At 30 June 2008	62,423

Intangible assets relate entirely to the carrying value of the playing squad and are being amortised over the remaining length of the players' contracts which are between one and five years.

14. Inventories

	2009 £'000	2008 £'000
Inventories	**1,172**	1,884

Inventories comprise merchandising goods held for resale.

15. Trade and other receivables

	2009 £'000	2008 £'000
Trade receivables due in less than one year	**30,557**	22,309
Trade receivables due in more than one year	**1,180**	6,624
Other receivables	**2,338**	7,246
Prepayments and accrued income	**3,663**	5,113
	37,738	41,292

Trade receivables above include £25,049,000 (2008: £15,601,000) in respect of the disposal of players' registrations.

The Directors consider the carrying amount of trade and other receivables approximates their fair value.

Refer to note 20 for disclosures relating to debtors ageing and other credit risk considerations.

16. Cash and cash equivalents

Cash and cash equivalents comprise cash held by the Group and short-term bank deposits.

	2009 £'000	2008 £'000
Bank balances	**19,606**	35,267
Petty cash	**16**	16
Cash and cash equivalents	**19,622**	35,283

The carrying amount of these assets approximates their fair value.

Figure 7.4 Tottenham Hotspur notes to the accounts

Source: From Tottenham Hotspur plc Annual Report and Financial Statements 2009.

they still had a large amount of cash which will give the organisation some flexibility when it comes to paying its debts.

Next we could examine the mix of business assets. The relationship between fixed and current assets is quite important because businesses with too few current assets could get into financial difficulty if creditors called in their debts. There is no 'golden rule' about the correct mix of fixed and current assets. There are many factors that will impact upon that structure: the type of organisation and how the company is financed are two major ones. If the company has loans, it will need to pay the interest – remember the Southampton Football Club case study in Chapter 1? Spurs had an obvious split between fixed and current assets in 2009 (£231,770,000 fixed assets compared to £59,636,000 current assets). This demonstrates that they must have followed a policy to increase their fixed asset holding and replaced their current asset holding during the course of 2009 – this shouldn't be a problem providing that they don't need to get hold of a large amount of cash quickly.

Heavy borrowing brings with it a commitment to high interest charges and large capital repayments at regular intervals that are legally enforced. Finances raised from the owners of the business will not have the same obligations: there is not a contractual obligation to pay dividends to shareholders. The owners of a business receive their 'rewards' from the residue of profit after all other obligations have been met. For Spurs in 2009 there is a significant level of borrowing which needs to be serviced and their current assets (i.e. those that can be converted into cash quite quickly) only cover about 50 per cent of their current liabilities (£59,636,000 current assets against £104,600,000 current liabilities).

RELATIONSHIP BETWEEN THE INCOME STATEMENT AND BALANCE SHEET

The income statement and balance sheet should not be seen in isolation or as substitutes for one another. Instead you should use them in tandem with each other so that you can build up a stronger idea of an organisation's financial health. You should hopefully have noticed when looking at all the income statement and balance sheet examples in this book that the two statements are actually interlinked. The income statement may be seen as linking the balance sheet at the beginning of an accounting period with the balance sheet at the end of the accounting period.

When a business starts up at the beginning of a financial period a balance sheet may be drawn up to reflect the opening position (i.e. how many assets it owns, how many creditors it owes and how much it is worth (capital)). After an appropriate amount of time has passed an income statement may be constructed to illustrate how much profit or loss has been incurred during that time. A new balance sheet will then be derived to reflect the new financial position at the end of the accounting period and as if by magic we can see how well the business has done!

CASH FLOW STATEMENT

Since being in business is about money, information about cash will be very important. Without sufficient cash an individual or organisation will get into financial difficulty or in some cases be declared bankrupt. With this in mind, although the income statement is vital in helping to discover businesses profitability, it does not give us a clear insight into any problems the business may have with its cash flow. Do you know why? If not, think back to Chapter 2 and the accruals concept.

> **KEY TERM**
>
> **ACCRUALS**
>
> The accruals basis of accounting requires the non-cash effects of transactions and other events to be reflected in the financial statements for the accounting period in which they occur and not in the period when the cash is paid or received. For example, if a sale is agreed in 2009 but the terms of the deal are that the cash is not received until 2010, the transaction should be shown in the accounts for 2010.

Because we base all our double-entry bookkeeping on the accruals concept any cash problems that a business may have can be disguised. Any items of large expenditure will not have an immediate impact upon the income statement but will have a significant impact upon the amount of cash that a business has available to it. If you think about this logically it is quite simple – a business needs cash so that it can operate.

Remember what I said at the end of the income statement section. The income statement recognises transactions when they occur, regardless of when cash changes hands, and therefore shows the profit or loss achieved over an accounting period – so why all the fuss? Well, it's because in business, people and organisations will not normally accept anything other than cash in settlement of activity. A business will have to pay its employees in cash, its suppliers in cash and its customers will have to pay in cash. Consequently if the business does not have enough cash it will probably fail – after all, you can't pay people with profit. This means that when you examine and construct financial statements you need to understand cash flow so that you can appreciate how the business will continue to survive or take advantage of new opportunities.

In 1991, the financial reporting standards people realised this and wrote FRS 1. Because the income statement (or P&L as it was then) and balance sheet were based on accruals and not on liquidity the concept of going concern was compromised. As a result, FRS 1 requires all apart from the very smallest companies to produce and publish a cash flow forecast in their annual report.

The cash flow statement is basically a financial summary of all the cash receipts and payments over an accounting period. All of the payments of a particular type are grouped together to give one figure; for example, all cash payments to creditors will be totalled up and the single figure recorded. Following this, the total payments will be deducted from the total receipts to give a net increase or decrease in cash over the period. We will have a look at the cash flow statement for Spurs so that you can see this in practice in just a minute.

Since 1991 the International Accounting Standards people have joined in and now IAS 1 refers readers to IAS 7 for details of the required presentation needed for the cash flow statement. The statement should separate cash flows into operating, investing and financing activities to show the changes during the year to cash and cash equivalents.

The classifications are defined as:

- *Operating*: these are the main revenue-producing activities of the organisation that are not investing or financing activities. They will include cash received from customers and cash paid to suppliers and employees.
- *Investing*: these activities are the acquisition and disposal of long-term assets and other investments that are not considered to be cash equivalents.
- *Financing*: these activities cover the acquisition and disposal of long-term assets and other investments that are not considered to be cash equivalents.

Hopefully you will have remembered from the earlier chapters, and the previous few paragraphs, that profit and cash are not the same thing. Therefore it is important that the readers of the statements (many of whom will not be financially literate) can readily distinguish between them. The cash flow statement will do this and will also show immediately how much cash the organisation has (i.e. the 'liquidity' of the business), and how much cash is generated by the operating side of the business (as opposed to other activities).

The Standard encourages organisations to use the following format:

	£m
Cash flows from operating activities	
Cash receipts from customers	X
Cash paid to suppliers	(X)
Cash paid to employees	(X)
Cash paid for other operating expenses	(X)
Cash generated from operations	X
Interest paid	(X)
Income taxes paid	(X)
Net cash flow from operating activities	X
Cash flows from investing activities	
Purchase of non-current assets	**(X)**
Proceeds of sales of non-current assets	X
Net cash used in investing activities	X
Cash flows from financing activities	
Proceeds from issue of share capital	X
Proceeds from long-term borrowing	X
Dividend paid	(X)
Net cash used in financing activities	X
Net increase in cash and cash equivalents A+B+C	X
Cash and cash equivalents at start of period	X
Cash and cash equivalents at end of period	X

Note: The three statements are interrelated. For example, consider the impact upon the statements if an organisation sold a delivery van for £4,000 that it had bought for £15,000 and had used for three years, and had charged £9,000 depreciation against it to the accounts during that period.

The income statement (and notes) would show that there had been a loss of £2,000 on the disposal of a non-current asset (proceeds £4,000, initial cost of £15,000 and depreciated by £9,000). The balance sheet (and notes) would show the adjustment to net book value of the non-current assets caused by the disposal of the van (i.e. a reduction of £6,000). The cash flow statement in the 'Cash flows from investing activities' section would show an income of £4,000. Take a look at Figure 7.5 and see what the Tottenham Hotspur Football Club cash flow statement looks like.

Once again, the Spurs example puts the IAS regulation into practice clearly. The cash flow statement tells us how well the business has generated cash during the accountting period and importantly where that cash has gone. Net cash flow for Spurs is strong, although it reduced from £14,627,000 in 2008 to £11,884,000 in 2009. New business assets absorbed

CONSOLIDATED STATEMENT OF CASH FLOWS
for the year ended 30 June 2009

	Note	Year ended 30 June 2009 £'000	Year ended 30 June 2008 £'000
Cash flow from operating activities			
Profit from operations		36,791	6,852
Adjustments for:			
Amortisation and impairment of intangible assets		37,288	35,057
Profit on disposal of intangible assets		(56,500)	(16,362)
(Profit)/loss on disposal of property, plant and equipment		(3)	14
Depreciation of property, plant and equipment		2,842	2,877
Capital grants release		66	58
Foreign exchange loss		2,235	1,319
Decrease/(Increase) in trade and other receivables		12,928	(4,225)
Decrease/(Increase) in inventories		712	(668)
(Decrease)/Increase in trade and other payables		(6,415)	10,327
Cash flow from operations		29,944	35,249
Interest paid		(4,342)	(3,164)
Interest received		1,080	1,094
Income tax paid		(750)	(3,610)
Net cash flow from operating activities		25,932	29,569
Cash flows from investing activities			
Acquisitions of property, plant and equipment, net of proceeds		(32,048)	(25,962)
Acquisitions of intangible assets		(68,609)	(27,456)
Proceeds from sale of intangible assets		47,180	16,222
Net cash flow from investing activities		(53,477)	(37,196)
Cash flows from financing activities			
Dividends paid		(3,712)	(3,733)
Redemption of ordinary shares		–	(841)
Proceeds from borrowings		19,612	20,916
Debt issue costs		–	(275)
Repayments of borrowings		(4,016)	(1,440)
Net cash flow from financing activities		11,884	14,627
Net (decrease)/increase in cash and cash equivalents		(15,661)	7,000
Cash and cash equivalents at start of the period		35,283	28,283
Cash and cash equivalents at end of year	16	19,622	35,283

Figure 7.5 Tottenham Hotspur cash flow statement

Source: From Tottenham Hotspur plc Annual Report and Financial Statements 2009.

quite a substantial amount of cash in 2009 (c. £100 million) but we already know this from our examination of the balance sheet. Overall the net cash flow figure is healthy and the business has room to spend during the next financial period. You should also notice that the final figure on the statement is the same as the one that is recorded on the balance sheet under 'Cash and cash equivalents'.

Because the income statement only shows us details of financial performance and therefore business wealth, it is useful to have an additional statement that highlights cash flows resulting from trading activities. Because cash flows are needed as one of the main financial statements it is important that you understand both how to construct them and how the statement interacts with the income statement and balance sheet.

CASH VERSUS PROFIT

Without meaning to cover the same ground over and over again, I think it is worth while taking a quick pause for thought about the real difference between cash and profit, and for you to be clear that organisations cannot trade on profit terms – they must trade on cash terms. Owners of organisations often try to measure the profit that an organisation has made by deducting the cash held at the end of an accounting period from the cash held at the beginning. It is then assumed that the difference represents profit – but this is not what I, or accountants, mean by the term profit!

Remember that accounting is governed by rules. The realisation rule tells us that we must match the sales revenue against the cost of selling those goods during the same period. It is unlikely that the difference between cash received and cash paid will be the same as income and expenditure. Cash transactions may relate to other periods of time (accruals), and by income we mean something that the organisation has gained during a particular period and by expenditure we mean something that the organisation has lost. This is how you calculate profit – it's a change in the business's worth.

NON-TRADING (OR NOT-FOR-PROFIT) ORGANISATIONS

The previous sections on the income statement, balance sheet and cash flow statement focused on the requirements for organisations of a significant size and status. However, as I have tried to emphasise throughout this book, you are more likely to come into contact with the financial statements of smaller organisations on a more regular basis. With this in mind, it is useful for you to see how things will differ for non-trading or indeed for not-for-profit organisations.

The objectives of non-trading or not-for-profit organisations are to provide services to their members; not to generate profits. Although the financial statements of non-trading or not-for-profit organisations are not covered by the regulations of the Companies Act and the International Accounting Standards Board they will still be prepared using the same principles. Some small clubs and societies may just keep a record of receipts and payments. However, this would not be very informative, and consequently the majority of clubs (especially those with assets), irrespective of their size, will prepare an income statement and a balance sheet.

There may be differences in the objectives of the clubs and societies from those of profit-seeking companies but the fundamental accounting will still be the same. Consequently you should have no trouble in adapting your knowledge of accounting to be able to work in this type of organisation, or indeed adapting your knowledge to apply this to yourself. The language may change: profits and losses become surpluses and deficits, capital becomes the accumulated funds, but the principles are exactly the same.

A swimming club may have several sources of income: subscriptions, sale of kit and fund-raising activities (e.g. a Valentine's Day Dinner and Dance). The income statement would show the net surplus from each one of the activities with separate records being kept to record further details of each sphere of activity. For example, the 'sale of kit' records would show a trading account and balance sheet for that operation but only the resulting surplus would be shown in the club's income statement. Similarly, the Dinner and Dance records would show details of income from ticket sales and the expenses of organising the event and all related transactions but only the surplus would be shown on the income statement. Any assets (kit yet to be sold, Romeos yet to pay for their tickets) and liabilities (unpaid suppliers for the kit and the fee for the thrash metal band that played at the dance) would be shown in the club's balance sheet.

If you grasped the key issues out of this, it will be useful for you to see what the financial statements of non-trading organisations look like. Let us see how the financial statements prepared by the British Triathlon Federation (BTF) (see Figures 7.6 and 7.7) differ from those of the Tottenham Hotspur Football Club statements illustrated earlier in this chapter.

Hopefully you will see how the two sets of financial statements are similar in their standard layout, the notable differences being the amount of information included. This is indicative of what non-trading organisations accounts will look like. Generally speaking, the accounts are much easier to understand and should give you the confidence to prepare something similar, should you need to do so.

ACTIVITY

Using the profit and loss account and the income statement for the BTF illustrated in Figures 7.6 and 7.7, answer the following questions.

1. What is the BTF's financial performance?
2. What is the BTF's financial position?
3. What is the BTF's overall financial health?

Overall, the BTF's financial performance is good, given that the organisation is there to provide a service and not make substantial profits. The income figures show us that the BTF have generated more income (£3,935,351 in 2009 compared to £3,414,149 in 2008). In addition, in generating this income their administrative costs increased from £3,352,788 in 2008 to £3,773,449 in 2009. The gross profit figure (in this case operating surplus) in absolute terms was higher in 2009 than in 2008 (£161,902 compared with £61,361). There is little point in examining the relationship between operating profit and income, as it will be insignificant.

THE BRITISH TRIATHLON FEDERATION
INCOME AND EXPENDITURE ACCOUNT
FOR THE YEAR ENDED 31 MARCH 2009

	2009 £	2008 £
INCOME	3,935,351	3,414,149
Administrative costs	(3,773,449)	(3,352,788)
OPERATING SURPLUS	161,902	61,361
Interest receivable	27,774	11,582
SURPLUS ON ORDINARY ACTIVITIES BEFORE TAXATION	189,676	72,943
Taxation	(5,670)	(2,201)
SURPLUS ON ORDINARY ACTIVITIES AFTER TAXATION	184,006	70,742
Retained surplus brought forward	102,107	31,365
RETAINED SURPLUS CARRIED FORWARD	286,113	102,107

Figure 7.6 British Triathlon Federation income and expenditure account

Source: From British Triathlon Federation Annual Report and Financial Statements 2009.

Finally the retained profit carried forward figures, in absolute terms, demonstrate that the BTF are doing quite well. The company has more than doubled in value from £102,107 in 2008 to £286,113 in 2009.

In terms of financial position the BTF are well balanced. There is plenty of cash in the organisation's account (£704,525 in 2009) and it covers approximately two-thirds of the organisation's creditors falling due within one year (£768,336). The mixture of fixed and current assets is very good for an organisation of the Federation's size as the BTF had only £1,321 tied up in tangible fixed assets in 2009. If the creditors called in their debts the BTF could convert their liquid assets into cash to pay their creditors very quickly. The organisation has no long-term liabilities and therefore is supported solely by its members' funds. This is a great position to be in as it allows the board of directors to control the organisation easily and without external pressures from creditors.

In summary, the financial health of the BTF is good. The organisation is not stretching itself and has sufficient funds to cover all of its responsibilities. Hopefully your answers were similar to mine. If not, can you see where mine have come from and, more importantly, do you

THE BRITISH TRIATHLON FEDERATION
BALANCE SHEET
AS AT 31 MARCH 2009

	2009 £	2008 £
Tangible fixed assets	1,321	12,766
Current assets		
Stock	0	78,671
Debtors	384,093	157,802
Cash at bank and in hand	704,525	500,737
	1,088,618	737,210
Creditors: amounts falling due within one year	768,366	612,409
Net current assets	321,573	137,567
Reserves		
Members' special reserve	35,460	35,460
Income and expenditure account	286,113	102,107
Members' funds	321,573	137,567

Figure 7.7 British Triathlon Federation balance sheet

Source: From British Triathlon Federation Annual Report and Financial Statements 2009.

agree? Remember that organisations such as the BTF are quite easy to manage financially as they are based on members' subscriptions. This means that they can only use the money they have for the day-to-day running of the business and do not have the financial pressures of other trading companies. Incidentally these figures are better across the board than those I found in the 2006 accounts when I wrote *Finance for Sport and Leisure Managers: An Introduction* with John Joyce, which suggests that the Federation is going from strength to strength, something that we don't always see with national governing bodies.

SUMMARY

This chapter has taken you on a fairly long journey through the meaning, preparation and publication of the three main financial statements so that you can be confident when reading them. You have seen the impact of the regulatory framework in practice through the examples drawn from Tottenham Hotspur Football Club and more recently the British Triathlon Federation. These examples have demonstrated how sport organisations, no matter what their size and sector, conform to the standards set out by the IAS.

The three statements work in unison to develop a picture of the financial health of an organisation. The income statement may specifically be used to measure financial performance or profitability, while the balance sheet is used to examine an organisation's financial position. However, the impact of each of the three statements is important to understand; in isolation they are not as useful.

You will have performed some basic analysis on the income statement and balance sheet, which should have highlighted their usefulness – the statements are worth much more than just the figures that are shown. Furthermore, to obtain valuable details you will need to delve deeper into an annual report and examine the notes, and this is where I think finance becomes truly interesting and meaningful. These notes explain how certain figures are calculated and under which accounting conventions they are derived. The next chapter will take this analysis much further and show how we can make good use of an annual report.

QUESTIONS FOR REVIEW

1. What does the income statement report?
2. What does the balance sheet show?
3. Are cash and profit the same thing?

REFERENCES AND FURTHER READING

CIMA (2009) *Financial Accounting Fundamentals*. BPP Professional Education, London.
Dyson, J.R. (2003) *Accounting for Non-accounting Students*, 6th edn. Financial Times Press, Harlow.
McLaney, E. and Atrill, P. (2005) *Accounting: An Introduction*, 3rd edn. Financial Times Press, Harlow.
Wilson, R. and Joyce, J. (2008) *Finance for Sport and Leisure Managers: An Introduction*. Routledge, London.

CHAPTER 8

ANNUAL REPORTS

On completion of this chapter you will be able to:

- identify and explain the main sections of an annual report;
- understand the need for the chairman's statement, auditor's report and directors' report;
- locate major components of the annual report including how to use the notes to the accounts.

INTRODUCTION

Providing that you have been through the previous seven chapters you will by now understand that the production of an annual report is a legal requirement. Contained within it will be the main financial statements that we covered in Chapter 7 alongside a plethora of other information. Consequently, this short chapter will outline what the annual report is, what it contains and how to use it in its basic form. Once you are comfortable with picking up an annual report and reading it you will be able to confidently analyse its contents using the tools outlined in Chapter 9.

An annual report from a major multinational company can be off-putting, especially to those who have had no financial training. Indeed shareholders may find them difficult to dissect, so expecting middle management to use them can be a serious task. It is not uncommon for an annual report to be more than 100 pages long, be full of text and numbers and include various reports from people in an organisation. In this chapter you will find some basic guidance about the contents of the annual report so that, as managers and potential investors of the future, you will be able to find your way around them relatively easily. There is of course a caveat to this guidance as not all annual reports will follow the same format. In such cases you should apply some logic and common sense as you work your way through them.

CONTENTS OF AN ANNUAL REPORT

Any annual report should include four main sections: introductory material, including a contents page and a financial summary; operational review and reports from the key people who compiled the report; the accounts; and any shareholder information. To illustrate the contents of an annual report Figure 8.1 shows the contents page of the JJB Sports plc report which we examine in more detail in Chapter 9.

As soon as you open an annual report you will be confronted by a series of reports and financial summaries. Small reports may contain only one or two, perhaps one from the managing director and one from the auditor; however, larger annual reports could contain several. In the JJB Sports example that we examine in Chapter 9 there are five, including those from the Board of Directors, the Chairman and the Auditors. The various reports are often accompanied by numerous pages detailing the organisation's operating activities and as such will include information on marketing, production, market pressures and staffing. Despite their length the key reports and summaries place into context the financial statements so that the numbers have some substance. As a result this is the best place to start when undertaking an annual report review.

It is not uncommon for people to view these reports as something of a public relations exercise. However, the reports will also include information on market developments, the use of new technology, staff cuts or growth, and is often used in the organisation's business plan when they need to attract additional finance. A cursory look at the JJB report outlines that they made some poor business decisions, have replaced the Board of Directors and are streamlining the business (see Chapter 9).

You will probably find that the most interesting report is the one by the organisation's chairman, as it will highlight the key financial information that may be of interest to you for any future analysis. The chairperson is free to include what information he or she wishes, there is no statutory or professional requirement to prepare one and there is no specified format.

Overview		Financial statements	
Key points for 2008/2009	01	Consolidated income statement	35
Post Balance sheet events	01	Consolidated statement of recognised income and expense	36
Chairman's statement	02	Consolidated reconciliation of movements in equity	36
Business review		Consolidated Balance sheet	37
Operating review	04	Consolidated cash flow statement	38
Corporate responsibility	10	Company Balance sheet	39
Governance		Company cash flow statement	40
Board of Directors	12	Statement of accounting policies	41
Board Committees	14	Notes to the Financial statements	49
Corporate Governance report	15	Five year summary	96
Directors' report	22	**Corporate information**	
Directors' Remuneration report	25	Shareholder information	98
Statement of Directors' Responsibilities	32	Retail store locations	100
Independent auditors' report	33		

Figure 8.1 JJB Annual Report contents

Source: From JJB Sports plc Annual Report and Financial Statements 2009.

A typical chairman's report will generally be found within the first few pages of the annual report, normally after the contents page, introduction and overview. It should include the results for the year, give some details about the dividends that were payable to shareholders (if applicable), highlight any major changes in the organisation's activities for the year and comment on the achievements of the organisation's employees. Remember to read such reports objectively, however, as the report will have been written mindful of the fact that it could have implications for the organisation's share price. Consequently, the chairman needs to be careful not to be too damning in judgements or too optimistic about any future prospects. Take a look at Figure 8.2 which is the opening to the Chairman's report for the 2009 JJB Sports plc annual report.

Directly following the reports will be the financial statements themselves. If you cast your mind back to previous chapters you will remember that the main statements include the income statement (or profit and loss account), the balance sheet and the cash flow forecast. These reports contain the numbers and will outline the financial performance and position of the organisation. Many of these numbers will be meaningless, however, without a quick read of the main discursive reports at the beginning. It is also worth noting that despite the pages that will have been taken up with the discursive reports the main reason for an annual report is to publish the financial performance of the organisation for those who want to use such information.

Overview
Chairman's statement

> The year to 25 January 2009 has been an exceedingly difficult one for JJB Sports plc. A series of bad business decisions taken by former members of the executive management team and the worsening economic environment brought the Company dangerously close to insolvency.

Figure 8.2 The opening to the Chairman's report

Source: From JJB Sports plc Annual Report and Financial Statements 2009.

The accounts form the main section of the report and contain the statutory and professionally required information. As you will have picked up from Chapter 7, the information contained in this section of the report is both detailed and complex. It includes the main financial statements, which include the income statement (profit and loss account), a statement of recognised gains and losses, the balance sheet, a cash flow statement and any notes to the accounts (which provide more numerical detail); and a statement of accounting policies, which will help you understand which accounting policies have been used when compiling the accounts.

While the financial statements are complex you should find it relatively straightforward to extract the information you need once you have been through Part 1 of this book. When reading such information you need to be aware of the fact that organisations do have slightly different ways of presenting the information required. Indeed, it is often the case that when examining large organisations' reports you will find two versions of the income statement and balance sheet, one titled 'Group' and the other titled 'Company'. The group relates to the idea that large organisations often include other trading arms or organisations; consequently the figures will be much larger than those of the company. Other books may go into more detail about this but for the purposes of this text this is as much as you really need to worry about. More detail on the main financial statements is covered in Chapters 7 and 9, so any further interrogation is unnecessary here.

The statement of recognised gains and losses is normally presented immediately after the income statement (profit and loss account). It should include all the gains and losses that the organisation has made during the year and not those that are just listed in the income statement. Given the nature of accounting practice it is possible for some gains and losses (e.g. surpluses or deficits arising from the revaluation of fixed assets) to be taken straight from a balance sheet account. As a result they will never appear on the income statement. An example of a statement of gains and losses may be seen in Figure 8.3.

Accounting policies are an important consideration when extracting information from the financial statements. As you already know, accounting policies govern how accounts are drawn up but as these may be implemented differently from organisation to organisation you do need to be sure about the basis on which the accounts have been drawn up. The section will state which policies have been adopted in preparing the accounts as well as the methods used in dealing with more complex issues, including the definition of turnover and that used for depreciation of fixed assets. An example of such a statement is given in Figure 8.4.

NOTES TO THE ACCOUNTS

The notes to the accounts are often the most underused part of an annual report. This is principally because people don't know how to use and interpret them, but also because people tend not to appreciate their relevance and get concerned about how many notes there may be; in the case of the JJB report there are around forty-five pages of notes! I have lost count of the number of times my students have uttered the words, 'but the notes to the accounts just say the same as the financial statements', so I am giving up trying to emphasise how important they are and have provided this one last attempt.

Financial statements
Consolidated statement of recognised income and expense
For the 52 weeks to 25 January 2009

	52 weeks to 25 January 2009 £'000	52 weeks to 27 January 2008 £'000
(Losses) gains on revaluation of available-for-sale investment taken to equity	(1,555)	1,555
Taxation effect on item taken directly to equity	435	(435)
Exchange differences on translation of foreign operations	1,549	(1,398)
Net income (expense) recognised directly in equity	429	(278)
(Loss) profit after taxation for the period	(167,556)	9,630
Recognised (expense) income for the period	(167,127)	9,352

Consolidated reconciliation of movements in equity
For the 52 weeks to 25 January 2009

	52 weeks to 25 January 2009 £'000	52 weeks to 27 January 2008 £'000
Opening total equity	365,055	377,026
Recognised income and expense for the period	(167,127)	9,352
Share issues	3,405	1,899
Share based payment reserve	(45)	383
Dividends paid	(16,657)	(23,605)
Closing total equity	**184,631**	**365,055**

Figure 8.3 Statement of gains and losses

Source: From JJB Sports plc Annual Report and Financial Statements 2009.

Financial statements
Statement of accounting policies
For the 52 weeks to 25 January 2009

Accounting period
Every accounting period ends on the Sunday which falls on or before, but closest to 31 January, resulting in accounting periods of either 52 or 53 weeks.

Adoption of new and revised Standards
In the current year, two interpretations issued by the International Financial Reporting Interpretations Committee are effective for the current period. These are: IFRIC 11 IFRS 2 – Group and Treasury Share Transactions and IFRIC 14 IAS 19 – The Limit on a Defined Benefit Asset, Minimum Funding Requirements and their Interaction. The adoption of these Interpretations has not led to any changes in the Group's accounting policies.

Basis of preparation
The Financial statements have been prepared in accordance with International Financial Reporting Standards ("IFRS"s). The Financial statements have also been prepared in accordance with IFRSs adopted by the European Union and therefore the Group Financial statements comply with Article 4 of the EU IAS Regulation.

Going concern
As part of the Group's restructuring and refinancing, the CVA proposal (as described in note 45) was implemented on 29 May 2009 and the Company subsequently moved to new financing arrangements (see note 25) on 3 June 2009. BoS has provided a £25,000,000 revolving working capital facility which terminates on 30 September 2010 and Barclays has provided a £25,000,000 short term loan, which will be repaid progressively as the deferred consideration proceeds from the disposal of the fitness clubs business are received and must be repaid in full by 31 August 2009.

Figure 8.4 Statement of accounting policies

Source: From JJB Sports plc Annual Report and Financial Statements 2009.

All of the main financial statements – the income statement, balance sheet and cash flow statement – are supported by a great deal of information which is more commonly known as the 'notes to the accounts'. These notes will have been supplied to provide two main uses. First, they enable the accountant to refrain from using too much information in the financial statements themselves, and second, they make it easier to provide supplementary information. This confirms to me their importance as part of the annual report because it gives us more information about what the figures are and how they are calculated. A good example of how notes are used is when considering revenue. Instead of listing all of the different, key elements that make up turnover, the financial statements will simply include one figure. The notes to the accounts are then used to provide more detailed information. An example of this is given in Figure 8.5.

This more detailed information can then be analysed to establish whether a particular part of the organisation is failing. In our example of revenue we can see clearly that the two major sources of revenue – revenue from retail operations and income from sales of goods – are both down from the previous year. This in turn will ensure that unless additional income is generated elsewhere (which it isn't) the organisation will struggle to match performance from the previous year. We would not have been able to draw these conclusions simply by

3. Revenue

An analysis of revenue is as follows:

	52 weeks to 25 January 2009 £'000	52 weeks to 27 January 2008 £'000
Continuing operations		
Revenue from retail operations	645,577	745,474
Revenue from fitness clubs	72,704	66,280
Income from sales of goods	718,281	811,754
Other operating income	5,676	3,314
Investment income	10,239	11,551
Total revenue	**734,196**	**826,619**

Figure 8.5 Notes to the accounts: revenue

Source: From JJB Sports plc Annual Report and Financial Statements 2009.

Financial statements
Consolidated income statement
For the 52 weeks to 25 January 2009

	Note	52 weeks to 25 January 2009 £'000	52 weeks to 27 January 2008 £'000
Continuing operations			
Revenue	3	718,281	811,754
Cost of sales		(353,696)	(405,642)

Figure 8.6 Lack of detail in the financial statements

Source: From JJB Sports plc Annual Report and Financial Statements 2009.

examining the financial statements as the information is not there (see Figure 8.6). Instead we are just offered a note to follow up with, in this case note 3.

Another example where it is vital that we get more information is that of any liabilities or creditors that the organisation owes. It is not uncommon for an organisation to simply list totals for current liabilities and non-current liabilities on their balance sheet. If they do this it makes the job of securing finance more difficult as potential creditors will not want to risk investment or lending. In the case of JJB there is at least a breakdown of the major themes for credit but it is still not as detailed as we might like it to be. Another cursory glance at the notes is required if we are to appreciate the full picture; this is shown in Figure 8.7 (an example for note 25) and in Figure 8.8.

25. Borrowings

	Group 25 January 2009 £'000	Group 27 January 2008 £'000	Company 25 January 2009 £'000	Company 27 January 2008 £'000
Loan notes	168,117	168,117	168,117	168,117
Bank loans	75,000	56,355	75,000	56,355
	243,117	224,472	243,117	224,472
Total borrowings				
Amount due for settlement within 12 months	243,117	168,117	243,117	168,117
Amount due for settlement after 12 months	–	56,355	–	56,355

All Group and Company bank overdrafts, bank loans and loan notes are based in sterling.

Loan notes were issued to the vendors of Blane Leisure Ltd (Sports Division) in September 1998, as part of the consideration for the acquisition of that Company and its subsidiaries, under an instrument which provided that the Loan notes were redeemable on any quarterly interest payment dates after 11 June 1999. By a Deed of Variation dated 26 February 2001, the maturity date up to which the Loan notes can be redeemed was extended to 28 April 2011.

Interest is payable on the Loan notes at a rate of 65.63 bps below LIBOR and the Loan notes are secured by an identical amount held in a bank account and shown under Current assets as "Current asset investments", as described in note 22.

The Group's working capital was provided through a 5 year £60 million revolving bank credit facility from Barclays Bank PLC ("Barclays") which commenced in June 2005, a 6 year term loan of £18 million from Bank of Scotland plc ("BoS") which commenced in June 2006 to finance the acquisition of the Glasgow Rangers FC licensing agreement and a further term loan of £20 million from Kaupthing, Singer & Friedlander Ltd (in administration) ("KSF") initially drawn on 6 October 2008 and repayable in full on 14 December 2008.

Pursuant to breaches in the half year loan agreement covenants in relation to consolidated net worth, fixed charge cover and cash flow cover, the Group entered into a standstill agreement with Barclays, BoS and KSF (the "Lenders") on 10 December 2008 (the "Standstill Agreement") whereby £20 million of facilities were cancelled as follows; £13.2 million from the revolving bank credit facility, £2.9 million from the 6 year term loan and £3.9 million from the further term loan drawn on 6 October 2008 and the Lenders agreed to maintain the remaining facilities until 30 January 2009 subject to the Group meeting certain conditions prescribed by the Standstill Agreement.

The Standstill Agreement provided for the interest rate on the revolving bank facility to be increased from 45bps to 400bps above LIBOR and the 6 year term loan from 40bps to 400bps above LIBOR. The term loan entered into on 6 October 2008 carries an interest rate of 400bps above LIBOR.

The Standstill Agreement provided, amongst other matters, for the deferral of the final repayment date in respect of the KSF and BoS facilities and allowed the Company to continue to draw down under the Barclays revolving working capital facility, in each case, to 30 January 2009. In consideration, the Company agreed to a margin uplift for each of the Barclays and BoS facilities as described above and to pay fees of approximately £8.3 million in aggregate to the Lenders, with payment of the fees due in February and April 2009 (or on such earlier date upon the occurrence of certain events, such as on the date of completion of the disposal of the fitness clubs business).

Events after the Balance sheet date
Revision of Bank Facilities

As noted above, the Company entered into the Standstill Agreement with the Lenders in respect of the period to 30 January 2009.

The Group entered into a series of further extensions to the Standstill Agreement with its Lenders after the year end.

Figure 8.7 Notes to the accounts: revenue

Source: From JJB Sports plc Annual Report and Financial Statements 2009.

Total assets		615,342	789,548
Current liabilities			
Trade and other payables	24	(101,334)	(110,874)
Current tax liability		(1,494)	–
Bank loans	25	(75,000)	–
Loan notes	25	(168,117)	(168,117)
Provisions	26	(32,404)	(22,656)
		(378,349)	(301,647)
Net current (liabilities) assets		(56,807)	70,701
Non-current liabilities			

Figure 8.8 Lack of detail in the financial statements (2)

Source: From JJB Sports plc Annual Report and Financial Statements 2009.

ACTIVITY

Find a full copy of an annual report and use it to outline the financial performance and position of the organisation. Once you have done this, break down some of the key figures such as turnover, profit, assets and liabilities so that you can see how the figures are compiled.

Once again these figures illustrate how much detail there is behind the figures that are actually included in the financial statements. Such information may prove vital when making long-term decisions about future financial performance so the notes should be used to help inform such decision-making. The notes to the accounts are an integral part of the accounts and should be used wherever possible.

SUMMARY

While this chapter is the shortest in the book it covers an important topic and one which will come up in any manager's life. Interpreting the information is a fundamental skill and is covered in Chapters 7 and 9. However, a basic understanding of the mechanics of the annual report and its make-up will provide you with useful background knowledge.

You should now be happy with the structure of an annual report and be able to identify the key sections of it, namely introductory material, directors' reports, financial statements and notes to the accounts. The amount of time you will need to spend reading annual reports will vary from job to job and will depend on the size and nature of the organisation. However, having completed this chapter you should feel confident that you can extract the information you need relatively quickly now that you know where to look for it.

QUESTIONS FOR REVIEW

1. Name the three main financial statements.
2. What are the four key sections of the annual report?
3. Why are the notes to the accounts useful?

REFERENCES AND FURTHER READING

CIMA (2009) *Financial Accounting Fundamentals*. BPP Professional Education, London.
Dyson, J.R. (2003) *Accounting for Non-accounting Students*, 6th edn. Financial Times Press, Harlow.
McLaney, E. and Atrill, P. (2005) *Accounting: An Introduction*, 3rd edn. Financial Times Press, Harlow.
Wilson, R. and Joyce, J. (2008) *Finance for Sport and Leisure Managers: An Introduction*. Routledge, London.

CHAPTER 9

INTERPRETING ANNUAL REPORTS

On completion of this chapter you will be able to:

- explain the purpose of analysing financial statements;
- understand how to calculate the basic ratios for accounts analysis;
- appraise an organisation's financial position and performance through the application of ratio analysis and interpretation of the annual report.

INTRODUCTION

So far your studies through most of this book have focused on the preparation of accounts. However, as I have told you all along, the purpose is not to teach you how to become an accountant but to give you the knowledge, understanding and confidence to read a set of financial reports and, if you ever get the urge, to talk to and understand an accountant. Chapter 7 illustrated how all of the stages in the accounting process are managed and ultimately why the major statements are constructed – they even demonstrated how you could basically analyse the main financial statements. However, constructing accurate financial statements, although a brilliant skill in its own right, is only half the story. One of the real purposes of this book is to show you and help you understand what all the numbers actually mean.

The activities of the public, private and voluntary sector sport organisations affect most of us regularly. Most of us will buy the goods and services that they provide and some of us will even work for them and lend money to them. As you found out in Chapter 8, many of these organisations, large and small, have to produce an annual report and financial statements. This document contains a significant amount of information about an organisation and, by definition, its future prospects. In spite of the influence of such organisations very few people can understand an annual report and financial statements. For example, what does it really mean if a company has a gross profit of £10 million? What else do you need to know? What are the financial strengths and weaknesses of a business? How does one organisation compare to another in the same industry? The way in which we can answer these questions, and very many more, is by starting to dissect annual reports.

In this chapter we will see how different financial ratios can help provide the scaffolding to analyse and interpret financial information, and ultimately give you the skills to evaluate the performance, position, solvency and efficiency of a business. This will help you assess how well a company is performing and will add to the basic analysis that you undertook on the income and expenditure account of the British Triathlon Federation at the end of Chapter 7. I will show you how all of this works by applying 'theory' to JJB Sports plc which makes for interesting reading given the results that were reported in my first book. This will give you a tangible example to work with and come back to when you have to do your own ratio analysis in the future.

WHY ANALYSE ANNUAL REPORTS?

The answer to this question is twofold. First, it is because I think that this is where finance gets interesting and meaningful to those of you who wish to manage, and second, and more seriously, it is because when used in isolation the figures tell only half the story and as a result can be rather misleading. Much like the fact that there is a difference between profit and cash, the owner of an organisation could be misled by the apparent trends in profits, by their current liquidity (amount of easily accessible cash) and by the level of assets and borrowings. We need to put everything into context; both in terms of the organisational context and also the industry context. Think about it in simple terms: if a sport club managed to secure a sponsorship package worth £50 million over five years it may seem to be a good result. However, it may only be a few percentage points more than the previous deal when the economy was depressed or the club wasn't performing very well. In addition, the club's competitors may have been able to secure larger deals over the same time period. It is therefore important to measure an organisation's financial performance and position using reference points or benchmarks to give a stronger sense of relative financial health. Given the obvious financial climate that we have been in for the past two years, it is this second point of context that can provide us with more guidance.

It is one thing to compile a few accounts, keep on top of income and expenditure, manage creditors and ensure that you pay your debts as they fall due. It is another thing, however, to understand and calculate measures of an organisation's performance over time.

Casting our minds back to our list of user groups in Chapter 1 we also need to analyse annual reports to satisfy the needs of each of the groups. While financial accounts have their limitations over their sister management accounts they do provide some useful information if analysed correctly. If you are asked to undertake some analysis on a set of accounts you should first understand the reason for doing so. If, for example, you need to appraise an organisation's financial health with a view to investing in it then you will need to do a pretty thorough job; if, on the other hand, you are a creditor and just want to know if you will be paid your dues then the level of analysis will be much more concise and specific to your needs.

You need to be systematic in the way you approach this analysis. I like to think about the analysis of an organisation's accounts as a three-stage process which has a number of different stop-off points depending on your specific needs. Have a quick look at Figure 9.1 to see what I mean, and feel free to adopt this model as and when appropriate.

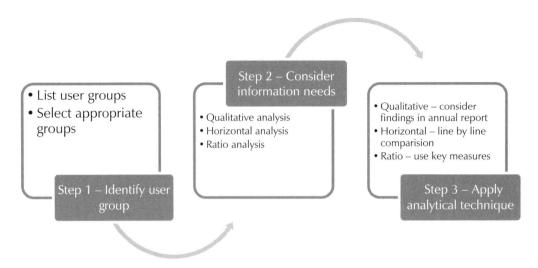

Figure 9.1 Process diagram for considering financial health analysis requirements

It is desirable to look at an organisation's performance over a number of years, especially for investment decisions. However, as a general rule, although at least three years' worth of data are advisable, you can normally get away with one annual report as it will provide the results of the current and previous year. Once you have thought about the user groups, you will be able to determine the level of analysis that is required. Users who have low information needs may be able to get away with a superficial analysis of the annual report (i.e. you can use the summarised findings like those we used in Chapter 1 for Tottenham Hotspur Football Club). Those with medium-level needs can add some horizontal analysis to your package and do some basic comparisons on how much figures have changed over the past twelve months, as we did in Chapter 7. Finally, if the information requirements are significant you will need to add some ratio analysis to the mix as well.

- Superficial analysis makes use of the key written reports in an annual report. These normally come from the chairman, directors and auditors. You can also use the summarised financial data and have a cursory look at the main financial statements (i.e. income statement and balance sheet).
- Horizontal analysis involves making line-by-line comparisons of the accounts for a set number of years. You can do this in absolute terms (i.e. calculate the numerical difference between this year and last year) and/or you can do this relatively (i.e. work out the percentage change).
- Ratio analysis involves much more sophisticated, yet relatively simple, formulas to relate one item to another. Normally we would apply ratio analysis to four key areas: profitability, liquidity, defensive position and, if applicable, investment ratios.

You should note here that the process diagram in Figure 9.1 is only intended to be used as a guide and to help you identify the steps you should go through. You will need to tailor your analysis to the task which may mean using every tool that is at your disposal. On other occasions you may be able to use all the tools on some of the data or some of the tools on all of the data. What you do is simply governed by your needs.

DISSECTING ANNUAL REPORTS

Before any calculations are made you will be pleased to know that some of the first things that you should look for when working out how well a company is doing will be found at the very beginning of an annual report. Normally an annual report will contain four key items of information that you can use. These are the accounts, the key reports (chairman, chief executive and directors), the auditor's report and any other important information. Therefore, the key reports are a great place to start. They will give you information about general performance, the major events that have taken place across the year, changes to the organisation in terms of staffing, accounting practice, exceptional items and so on, and the wider industry situation. This will help you place everything into context. For example, when ITV digital collapsed most of the Football League teams will have shown a drop in revenue and potential poor annual accounts. We therefore have a good reason to explain the situation.

It is important that you begin to see how all of this works in practice; so, as I mentioned in the introduction to this chapter, there is an example that we will use throughout which is based on the annual report of JJB Sports plc. This is therefore a good place to introduce you to the organisation and explain in general terms their annual report findings.

CASE STUDY

DISSECTING ANNUAL REPORTS: JJB SPORTS PLC

In 2006 JJB Sports plc was the UK's leading quoted sports retailer whose main aims were to supply high-quality, branded sports and leisure clothing, footwear and accessories at competitive prices and to expand on their portfolio of successful health clubs. The company started in 1971 by acquiring a single sports store and by 1994 their portfolio had grown to 120 stores, at which point the company was floated on the London stock exchange. In 2006 JJB traded from over 430 stores across the UK and had a chain of combined health club/superstores. However, by 2009, the company was in real trouble. The founder Dave Whelan had left the company, taking the fitness part of the business with him, and JJB, through a series of bad decisions and market problems, found themselves facing insolvency.

In addition, JJB were forced to close 124 stand-alone stores and saw a reduction in sales of 13.4 per cent, yet protected their gross margin, appointed three new directors and negotiated the availability of a £50 million banking facility which ultimately kept them going. This snapshot gives us the context behind the company, and Figure 9.2 highlights their basic operating results.

This operating review illustrates the extent of the market problems that JJB Sports face, resulting in an operating loss of some £178,663,000 following revenue of £645 million and a gross profit of nearly £300 million. It seems that JJB's main problem originates in their high operating expenses of £281 million and the payment of exceptional operating items totalling around £171 million. An analysis of these exceptional operating items is not entirely necessary for the purposes of this case study but is outlined in Figure 9.3.

Business review
Operating review

	52 weeks to 25 January 2009			52 weeks to 27 January 2008		
	Retail operations £'000	Fitness clubs £'000	Total £'000	Retail operations £'000	Fitness Clubs £'000	Total £'000
Revenue	645,577	72,704	718,281	745,474	66,280	811,754
Gross profit	**294,302**	**70,283**	**364,585**	342,403	63,709	406,112
Location net operating expenses before exceptional operating items	(281,272)	(54,351)	(335,623)	(292,968)	(46,597)	(339,565)
Operating profit before central costs and exceptional operating items	**13,030**	**15,932**	**28,962**	49,435	17,112	66,547
Central administration costs			(35,927)			(32,278)
Operating (loss) profit before exceptional operating items			**(6,965)**			34,269
Exceptional operating items			(171,698)			(22,974)
Operating (loss) profit			**(178,663)**			11,295

Figure 9.2 JJB Sports operating results

Source: From JJB Sports plc Annual Report and Financial Statements 2009.

Exceptional operating items
Due to the materiality of the exceptional operating items totalling £171.7 million, these are listed individually as follows:

> *Restructuring/vacant store provisions of £29.5 million, of which £20.7 million represents an increase to the prior year restructuring provision, which, in light of changes in the retail property market in the period, was considered to be inadequate* – This provision is derived from the independent review of each lease prior to the commencement of the Company Voluntary Arrangement referred to later in this review, and following successful implementation, the provision not utilised will result in an exceptional credit to the income statement.

> *Goodwill impairment of £82.3 million* – The principal element is £79.5 million relating to Blane Leisure and has arisen following an impairment review of the present value of the retail operating units for which goodwill has been allocated. This was found to be less than the carrying value in the Balance sheet.

> *Impairment of the fitness club fixed assets of £49.3 million* – Following a value in use calculation, in light of the sale of the fitness clubs for £83.4 million, the carrying value of the fixed assets was higher than the disposal proceeds of the sale resulting in an impairment of the tangible fixed assets within that segment.

> *Impairment of businesses in administration of £8.7 million* – This is a result of the write down of stock and fixed assets preceding the decision to place both Original Shoe Company and Qubefootwear into administration on 19 February 2009.

> *Impairment of investment in associate of £4.9 million* – This mainly relates to the poor performance of the KooGa operations and the decision to cease the current arrangements.

> *Other exceptional items* – There are a number of other exceptional items that are disclosed on the face of the income statement. These refer mainly to the profit/loss on disposals of assets and additional re-organisational costs, mainly advisory fees. Full details are shown on the face of the Consolidated income statement.

Figure 9.3 JJB Sports explanation of exceptional operating expenses

Source: From JJB Sports plc Annual Report and Financial Statements 2009.

It is also useful at this point to consider some of the analysis that was covered in Chapter 7; namely how we can interpret the basics of the income statement and balance sheet (these are shown in Figures 9.4 and 9.5). In terms of financial performance, and ignoring

35 JJB Sports plc Annual Report and Accounts 2009

Financial statements
Consolidated income statement
For the 52 weeks to 25 January 2009

	Note	52 weeks to 25 January 2009 £'000	52 weeks to 27 January 2008 £'000
Continuing operations			
Revenue	3	718,281	811,754
Cost of sales		(353,696)	(405,642)
Gross profit		364,585	406,112
Other operating income	3	5,676	3,314
Distribution expenses		(29,542)	(28,619)
Administration expenses		(37,716)	(35,413)
Selling expenses		(481,666)	(334,099)
Operating (loss) profit		(178,663)	11,295
Operating (loss) profit is stated after (charging) crediting			
Provision for restructuring of retail store chain		(20,742)	(24,970)
Other vacant store provision		(8,770)	–
		(29,512)	(24,970)
Goodwill impairment		(82,275)	–
Impairment of fitness club fixed assets		(49,260)	–
Impairment of businesses in administration		(8,695)	–
Re-organisation costs		(3,175)	–
Net loss on disposal of intangibles		(339)	–
Net gain on disposal of property, plant and equipment		8,745	1,996
Impairment of intangible assets		(2,150)	–
Impairment of loan and investment in associated undertaking		(4,923)	–
Loss on sale of assets held for resale		(114)	–
	5	(171,698)	(22,974)
Investment income	8	10,239	11,551
Other gains and losses	9	1,989	–
Finance costs	10	(22,704)	(12,442)
Finance costs are stated after charging			
Exceptional bank arrangement fees and charges	10	(10,974)	–
Share of results of associated undertaking		(103)	396
(Loss) profit before taxation		(189,242)	10,800
Taxation	11	21,686	(1,170)
(Loss) profit after taxation for the period attributable to equity holders of the parent company		(167,556)	9,630
Basic (loss) earnings per ordinary share	Pence 14	(69.19)	4.07
Diluted (loss) earnings per ordinary share	Pence 14	(69.19)	4.07
Adjusted basic (loss) earnings per ordinary share	Pence 14	(3.53)	10.89

Figure 9.4 JJB Sports income statement

Source: From JJB Sports plc Annual Report and Financial Statements 2009.

interpreting annual reports

Financial statements
Consolidated balance sheet
As at 25 January 2009

	Note	As at 25 January 2009 £'000	As at 27 January 2008 £'000
Non-current assets			
Goodwill	15	106,406	187,834
Other intangible assets	16	24,600	25,417
Property, plant and equipment	17	162,044	198,272
Investment in associated undertaking	19	750	1,677
Loan to associated undertaking	19	–	4,000
		293,800	417,200
Current assets			
Inventories	20	70,569	114,984
Trade and other receivables	21	38,381	45,412
Current asset investments	22	171,954	196,217
Cash and cash equivalents	23	40,638	14,199
Current tax receivable		–	1,536
		321,542	372,348
Total assets		615,342	789,548
Current liabilities			
Trade and other payables	24	(101,334)	(110,874)
Current tax liability		(1,494)	–
Bank loans	25	(75,000)	–
Loan notes	25	(168,117)	(168,117)
Provisions	26	(32,404)	(22,656)
		(378,349)	(301,647)
Net current (liabilities) assets		(56,807)	70,701
Non-current liabilities			
Bank loans	25	–	(56,355)
Deferred tax liabilities	27	(2,682)	(24,237)
Deferred lease incentives	28	(43,894)	(39,950)
Provisions	26	(5,786)	(2,304)
		(52,362)	(122,846)
Total liabilities		(430,711)	(424,493)
Net assets		184,631	365,055
Equity			
Share capital	29	12,542	11,944
Share premium account	31	174,055	171,248
Capital redemption reserve	32	1,069	1,069
Investment in own shares	33	(3,083)	(3,083)
Share based payment reserve	34	635	680
Foreign currency translation reserve	35	338	(1,211)
Retained earnings	36	(925)	184,408
Equity attributable to shareholders of the parent		184,631	365,055

Figure 9.5 JJB Sports plc balance sheet

Source: From JJB Sports plc Annual Report and Financial Statements 2009.

the exceptional items, JJB are doing all right, even though their overall gross profit margin reduced from 45.9 per cent in 2008 to 45.6 per cent in 2009. Its financial position is also all right. While they have a fairly even split between fixed and current assets they also have a significant number of liabilities, in addition to a £75 million bank loan. Consequently you could not make a confident statement that JJB was financially healthy!

We will come back to a lot of the information contained in these two financial statements throughout this chapter. However, if you would like to learn a little more about the company and see the annual report for yourself why not download it from the internet? It may be found at www.jjbcorporate.co.uk/.

INTRODUCING RATIO ANALYSIS

The purpose of financial statement analysis is to help you with your decision-making process. Such analysis can help both you and other interested users of financial information (see Chapter 1 for details) decide on questions such as whether to lend the business money, offer credit facilities, invest in the business and buy goods. Most analysis is conducted by way of applying recognised techniques such as key ratios, which describe the relationship between values. Financial ratios provide a quick and relatively simple way of examining the financial health of an organisation. A ratio will express the relationship of one figure that appears on the financial statements with another (e.g. gross profit to sales) or with another of the organisation's resources (e.g. the number of employees to sales). Once a ratio has been calculated it may then be compared with budgets, previous information, other businesses and industry benchmarks.

It is the relationship among the various items on a balance sheet and income statement that holds the key to understanding their message. The first skill in ratio analysis is the ability to calculate them; hence I will take you through them step by step and illustrate where I have taken the figures from, while the second step is to interpret or analyse their meaning, something which I do after each calculation.

KEY TERM

RATIO ANALYSIS

The calculation of ratios from a set of financial statements, which may be used to compare a business with its performance from previous years or similar businesses to provide information for decision-making.

It is probably worth pointing out here that ratio analysis is not regulated in the same way as accounting practices (see Chapter 2). Therefore, when comparing ratios you should always check the definitions that have been used – unfortunately there may be quite a few – in order to fully understand the information. Ratios cannot and should not be compared unless they are calculated on the same basis. It is therefore a good idea to state the definitions and working concepts when you do your analysis. To make things a little more straightforward for you this book will focus on the most common types of ratios that are calculated in the sport industry.

Some of the most effective ratio analysis is relatively simple to do and is based on year-on-year changes (i.e. horizontal analysis). There are four other key areas to look at when assessing the financial performance and health of a company: profitability, liquidity, defensive position (or gearing) and investment ratios. Don't worry too much about the terminology here, as it will be explained systematically throughout the remainder of this chapter. Ultimately, however, the choice of ratios that are best to calculate will depend on the type of business and the availability of data; for example, if we are looking at a non-trading organisation such as the British Triathlon Federation we will have no need to do any investment ratios, as there are no such figures!

THE STEPS OF FINANCIAL RATIO ANALYSIS

Before you cover any of the key ratios included in this chapter it is important to recognise that they are all calculated through a series of steps. I know this will sound a bit silly but, believe me, it will make your life much easier and certainly less confusing if you approach all of the analysis progressively. The first of these steps will be to identify the key indicators and relationships that require some examination. It is likely that this will come out of the basic analysis that we explained in Chapter 7; for example, you may wish to examine profitability.

In order to carry out the analysis you must then consider who the target users of the analysis will be and why they need the information. As you witnessed way back in Chapter 1, there are many different users who will have varied needs. For example, long-term lenders of finance may be interested in the profitability and gearing of an organisation as they have a long-term interest in business viability. Suppliers, on the other hand (short-term creditors), will be more interested in the liquidity of a business as they will want to know if they are going to get their money sooner rather than later. Don't worry if you don't understand the terminology just yet as the remainder of this chapter will explain everything.

Once you are happy with the users of the analysis it will be time to do the calculations and finally the interpretations. After all, the figures will be meaningless to the untrained eye. Consequently you will need to be able to explain what everything means in the context of both the organisation and the wider industry. It is worth noting here that the calculation of the figures can be very easy. Once they have been mastered you can simply get a computer spreadsheet to do the calculations for you. The devil is in the detail though, and it is where you can really impress future employers and senior management!

To help you through all of this the following sections are systematically broken down into the 'steps' we talked about earlier. You will be shown the theory behind the ratio, given the formula and then taken through the practice. For the purposes of this chapter you will find that JJB Sports is our chosen organisation but there will be plenty of opportunity for you to replicate the analysis on an organisation of your choice or even those covered so far in the book, such as Tottenham Hotspur Football Club or the British Triathlon Federation.

GROWTH

The growth of a business is vital if it is to continue, develop, succeed and meet the ever-changing demands of consumers in the marketplace. Indeed, failure to grow might result in a loss of competitiveness, a decline in demand, and in some cases eventual closure. Growth enables past trends to be examined and predictions of performance to be made in the future. Just think for a moment about how important it is in the sport and leisure industry. In English football, for example, growth will be essential. A club as a whole must grow in terms of membership and fan base in order to generate increased income through ticket and merchandise sales so that it can become more competitive in the field of play. However, if a team does not grow it will not have the resources to match the larger teams in terms of player wages and squad sizes.

The best way to calculate growth is by examining year-on-year changes so that we can analyse how the organisations have progressed over a period of time. We can then link the analysis with other factors that appear in the annual report of an organisation such as commercial activities, sponsorship, television deals and revenue. Year-on-year change can be calculated with a simple formula that may be applied to the entire income statement and balance sheet. This formula is shown below and if you have a look at Figures 9.6 and 9.7 you can see what JJB Sports plc has achieved in terms of growth between 2008 and 2009. For purposes of this analysis I have reproduced the JJB Sports plc financial statements in a spreadsheet.

$$((\text{This Year} - \text{Last Year}) / \text{Last Year}) \times 100$$

It is now a straightforward job of interpreting the year-on-year analysis for the income statement. You will notice that there are two additional columns: first, the year-on-year change which is the absolute difference between the two years; and second, the year-on-year analysis which represents the percentage change. First, we need to pick out the key figures. This may sound simple but it is important not to be misled by some of the large numbers; for example, you should note the increases in goodwill impairment and the like but as the previous year had no value the percentage increase looks unrealistic. Consequently we tend to focus on three areas as key assets: growth in turnover, growth in profit and growth in fixed assets. In our case these have already been noted in the basic analysis that we conducted at the beginning of this chapter; both revenue (12%) and gross profits (10%) have fallen, while distribution costs (3%), administration costs (7%) and selling expenses (44%) have increased, resulting in an operating loss.

Overall JJB is showing a cause for financial concern over the previous year in line with the chairman's comments, which were outlined in the JJB case study introduction. Further analysis of the income statement may be performed on the notes to the accounts and in the wider context of the industry.

The company is showing a size reduction of almost 50 per cent of its total worth, though that is unsurprising given that it has sold 124 stores. The value of fixed assets has reduced across the board; again this is not a surprise, given that the stores have been sold, as has the fitness business and a number of other fixed assets. Something that is very important to note is the clear reduction in inventory (39%) which should be alarming, given that the organisation's principal objective is to sell goods (i.e. stock). If they have less stock to sell it might suggest that creditors do not want to trade with them. Overall this balance sheet reflects the comments

JJB Sports plc
Consolidated income statement Reproduction
For the 52 weeks to 25 January 2009

	52 weeks to 25 January 2009	52 weeks to 27 January 2008	Year on Year Analysis
Continuing operations	£'000	£'000	
Revenue	718,281	811,754	−12%
Cost of sales	(353,696)	(405,642)	−13%
Gross profit	**364,585**	**406,112**	**−10%**
Other operating income	5,676	3,314	71%
Distribution expenses	(29,542)	(28,619)	3%
Administration expenses	(37,716)	(35,413)	7%
Selling expenses	(481,666)	(334,099)	44%
Operating profit	**(178,663)**	**11,295**	**−1,682%**
Operating (loss) profit is stated after (charging) crediting			
Provision for restructuring of retail store chain	(20,742)	(24,970)	−17%
Other vacant store provision	(8,770)	–	
	(29,512)	(24,970)	18%
Goodwill impairment	(82,275)	–	
Impairment of fitness club fixed assets	(49,260)	–	
Impairment of businesses in administration	(8,695)	–	
Re-organisation costs	(3,175)	–	
Net loss on disposal of intangibles	(339)	–	
Net gain on disposal of property, plant and equipment	8,745	1,996	338%
Impairment of intangible assets	(2,150)	–	
Impairment of loan and investment in associated undertaking	(4,923)	–	
Loss on sale of assets held for resale	(114)	–	
	(171,698)	(22,974)	647%
Investment income	10,239	11,551	−11%
Other gains and losses	1,989	–	
Finance costs	(22,704)	(12,442)	82%
Finance costs are stated after charging			
Exceptional bank arrangement fees and charges	(10,974)		
Share of results of associated undertaking	(103)	396	−126%
(Loss) profit before taxation	**(189,242)**	**10,800**	**−1,852%**
Taxation	21,686	(1,170)	−1,954%
(Loss) profit after taxation for the period attributable to equity holders of the parent company	(167,556)	9,630	−1,840%
Basic (loss) earnings per share Pence	(69.19)	4.07	−1,800%
Diluted (loss) earnings per share Pence	(69.19)	4.07	−1,800%
Adjusted basic (loss) earnings per ordiary share Pence	(3.53)	10.89	−132%

Figure 9.6 JJB Sports income statement growth analysis

Source: Adapted from JJB Sports plc Annual Report and Financial Statements 2009.

made in the main written reports and makes rather grim reading for any potential investor, employee or creditor.

This further work has supported some of the basic analysis that had already been undertaken and has highlighted some areas that warrant further attention. The remainder of this chapter will therefore explore these issues in more detail. However, before you move on to the profitability section have a go at this activity and try things out for yourself.

JJB Sports plc
Consolidated balance sheet Reproduction
As at 25 January 2009

	As at 25 January 2009 £'000	As at 27 January 2008 £'000	Year on Year Analysis
Non-current assets			
Goodwill	106,406	187,834	−43%
Other tangible assets	24,600	25,417	−3%
Property, plant and equipment	162,044	198,272	−18%
Investment in associated undertaking	750	1,677	−55%
Loan to associated undertaking	-	4,000	−100%
	293,800	417,200	−30%
Current assets			
Inventories	70,569	114,984	−39%
Trade and other receivables	38,381	45,412	−15%
Current asset investment	171,954	196,217	−12%
Cash and cash equivalents	40,638	14,199	186%
Current tax receivable	-	1,536	−100%
	321,542	372,348	−14%
Total assets	615,342	789,548	−22%
Current liabilities			
Trade and other payables	(101,334)	(110,874)	−9%
Current tax liabilities	(1,494)	-	
Bank loans	(75,000)	-	
Loan notes	(168,117)	(168,117)	0%
Provisions	(32,404)	(22,656)	43%
	(378,349)	(301,647)	25%
Net-current (liabilities) assets	(56,807)	70,701	−180%
Non-current liabilities			
Bank loan	-	(56,335)	−100%
Deferred tax liabilities	(2,682)	(24,237)	−89%
Deferred lease incentives	(43,894)	(39,950)	
Provisions	(5,786)	(2,304)	151%
	(52,362)	(122,846)	−57%
Total liabilities	(430,711)	(424,492)	1%
Net assets	184,631	365,055	−49%
Equity			
Share capital	12,542	11,944	5%
Share premium account	174,055	171,248	2%
Capital redemption reserve	1,069	1,069	0%
Investment in own shares	(3,083)	(3,083)	0%
Share based payment reserve	635	680	−7%
Foreign currency translation reserve	338	(1,211)	−128%
Retained earnings	(925)	184,408	−101%
Equity attributable to equity holders of the parent	184,631	365,055	−49%

Figure 9.7 JJB Sports balance sheet growth analysis

Source: Adapted from JJB Sports plc Annual Report and Financial Statements 2009.

ACTIVITY

Go online and find the annual report of a sport/leisure organisation of your choice – you could use the *Financial Times* link from Chapter 6. This could be a Premier League rugby union club or your local cycling club. Once you have obtained the necessary information examine the directors' and auditor's comments to begin to work out how well the organisation is performing.

Once this has been done, copy the accounts into a spreadsheet and conduct the year-on-year analysis as we have done for JJB. This may seem like a long-drawn-out process but the practice will help you understand the figures in much more detail. Once you have done all of that you can move on to the next section of this chapter.

PROFITABILITY RATIOS

Profitability ratios are used to review the operating performance of the business. We will look at some of the key measures here including the gross profit ratio, net profit ratio and return on capital employed, and glance back at the year-on-year figures outlined above. Profitability is essentially a measure of the company's ability to make a profit in relation to other factors (e.g. turnover). In order to create a meaningful assessment of how profitable a company is, the profit made should be considered in relation to the size of the business. We need to look at 'in relation to' because absolute figures can give a false impression. For example, which would you prefer to own: a company that made a profit of £100 million or one that earned £110 million? The immediate thought is 'I would prefer the one that earned £110 million'. However, this will change if you are told that using assets worth £200 million generated the profit of £110 million, whereas the company that generated the £100 million did so with assets worth £80 million.

To make a profit, a company has to ensure that it sells goods and/or services at a higher price than the cost of producing them. However, in the sport industry there will be exceptions when determining the internal capability to generate profits due to the presence of grants, television revenue and sponsorship agreements. Remember that you can do what you like – it is you who is trying to interpret the accounts and you are doing it for own specific reasons. Consequently you must think of the best ways to find and compare the specific facts and trends that will best suit your purpose. However, there are some ratios that are in common use.

All of the ratio sections that follow are based on the accounts of JJB Sports plc as illustrated in Figures 9.6 and 9.7. In a valiant attempt to make the calculations easier to follow, you will find that each section begins with an introduction to the particular ratio. This is then followed by the formula, an excerpt from the accounts to show you where to find the figures and then a table identifying the results of the calculation. Finally there is some analysis to explain what the values mean.

Gross profit ratio

The gross profit ratio indicates to us the amount of profit the company makes on its cost of sales (or costs of goods sold). Quite simply it shows us how much gross profit the business makes per £1 of turnover. Remember here that turnover equals sales. The gross profit (calculated as sales minus cost of sales) is therefore all of the profit that is made before other business costs have been deducted. The calculation that we shall use is:

$$\text{Gross profit ratio} = \frac{\text{Gross Profit}}{\text{Turnover}} \times 100\%$$

The turnover of a business will show in absolute terms the size of the business but it does not give an indication of the efficiency and effectiveness of the business. The profitability ratios will help to do that.

JJB gross profit ratio

We can get these figures from the first section of the income statement (Figure 9.8).

	Note	52 weeks to 25 January 2009 £'000	52 weeks to 27 January 2008 £'000
Continuing operations			
Revenue	3	**718,281**	811,754
Cost of sales		(353,696)	(405,642)
Gross profit		**364,586**	406,112

Figure 9.8 Gross profit ratio figure selection

Source: From JJB Sports plc Annual Report and Financial Statements 2009.

	2009	2008
Turnover £'000	718,281	811,754
Gross profit £'000	364,585	406,112
Gross profit	51%	50%

The gross profit percentage for JJB for 2009 was 51 per cent. In simple terms this means that for every £1 JJB take in sales, 51 pence of it is gross profit. However, there is little to be gained by looking at this figure in isolation. It may be seen that although the turnover decreased between 2008 and 2009 the gross profit fell. The reasons for this may be found in the chairman's statement in the 2009 report with references to strong competitive pressure in the clothing sector and the clearance of excess clothing ranges and fragmented stocks. This makes sense of the ratio: JJB had to keep prices low owing to competition and also had to discount some stock to get rid of it. Both of these factors will reduce the gross profit.

Operating profit ratio

The operating profit ratio tells us the amount of operating profit per £1 of turnover that a business has been able to earn during an accounting period. This will be after all of the other business expenses such as administration and distribution costs have been deducted; it will therefore be much lower than the gross profit figure. It is advisable to use the profit figure before interest and tax are deducted. This is so that the figure that is used is a 'true' measure of operating performance and is not influenced by financing decisions (e.g. interest on loans) and externalities (tax). As with the gross profit ratio, we need to relate it to the turnover figure so that comparisons can be made (it is difficult to get a true feeling from absolute figures). Operating profit will be the profit before interest and taxation (PBIT).

$$\text{Operating profit ratio} = \frac{PBIT}{Turnover} \times 100\%$$

JJB operating profit ratio

Again we can use the income statement but this time we need the profit figure from the bottom section as well as the revenue figure from the top (Figure 9.9).

	Note	52 weeks to 25 January 2009 £'000	52 weeks to 27 January 2008 £'000
Continuing operations			
Revenue	3	718,281	811,754
Cost of sales		(353,696)	(405,642)
Share of results of associated undertaking		(103)	396
(Loss) profit before taxation		(189,242)	10,800

Figure 9.9 Operating profit ratio figure selection
Source: From JJB Sports plc Annual Report and Financial Statements 2009.

	2009	2008
Turnover £'000	718,281	811,754
PBIT £'000	(189,242)	10,800
Operating profit	−26%	1%

We will see immediately that there are some serious problems here. However, you need to remember that you have to be careful to ensure that you are comparing like with like. This is illustrated in this case: JJB disposed of a part of their fitness club business in 2009. Consequently it is necessary to adjust the accounts to take out the discontinued business so that the remaining figures may be compared with future years.

However, that said, there is a significant decrease in the operating profit percentage from 2008 to an operating loss in 2009. Again the reasons for this may be found in the chief executive's statement. The 2009 statement explains that the drop was due to the impact of disposing of the fitness business and the two acquisitions sanctioned by a previous chairman which resulted in significant losses.

Return on capital employed (ROCE)

This can be really tricky, principally because there are many different views of what is meant by 'Return on capital employed'. The last time I checked there were seven alternatives. As a result you need to be careful how you define 'capital employed' and what 'return' it has earned. The most logical place for us to start is to remember that if the organisation has been formed to generate profits then everything that is used in the business should be viewed as working towards that objective. This would mean that everything is viewed as being 'capital employed' and therefore the shareholders' 'capital' and non-current liabilities (i.e. long-term loans) should be added together to give the total capital employed. Alternatively, you can calculate the 'capital employed' by adding the non-current and current assets and subtracting the current liabilities (this will give you exactly the same figure as previously calculated). My personal view is that this is the fairest and most transparent way of calculating the figure.

Following on logically, the return we should use will be the profits generated by the total capital. These profits will be before deductions for interest (this is the charge for using the loan capital and therefore should not be used to reduce the profit the capital has returned), dividends (this may be viewed as being the charge for using the owners' capital) and tax. This will be the operating profit.

Sometimes ROCE is referred to as the 'prime ratio'. This signifies its importance, as it provides an immediate summary of management's effectiveness in generating revenue and controlling costs. The ROCE ratio should be used as a benchmark, taking into account interest rates, risks and alternative uses, and to establish whether the organisation has generated a sufficient return. For example, if the current interest rate on a deposit account at a bank is 6 per cent and a company has a ROCE ratio value of 5 per cent, investors in the company would not be happy: they are getting a lower return but taking a bigger risk than bank depositors.

Return on capital employed is calculated as follows:

$$\text{ROCE} = \frac{\text{PBIT}}{\text{CE}} \times 100\%$$

JJB ROCE

From the income statement (i.e. PBIT).

Share of results of associated undertaking		(103)	396
(Loss) profit before taxation		**(189,242)**	**10,800**

In order to calculate capital employed we need to use the balance sheet (Figure 9.10).

Provisions		26	(5,786)	(2,304)
			(52,362)	(122,846)
Total liabilities			(430,711)	(424,493)
Net assets			184,631	365,055
Equity				
Share capital		29	12,542	11,944
Share premium account		31	174,055	171,248
Capital redemption reserve		32	1,069	1,069
Investment in own shares		33	(3,083)	(3,083)
Share based payment reserve		34	635	680
Foreign currency translation reserve		35	338	(1,211)
Retained earnings		36	(925)	184,408
Equity attributable to shareholders of the parent			**184,631**	**365,055**

Figure 9.10 ROCE ratio figure selection

Source: From JJB Sports plc Annual Report and Financial Statements 2009.

	2009	2008
PBIT £'000	(189,242)	10,800
Capital employed £'000	236,993	487,901
ROCE	−80%	2%

There was a substantial drop in ROCE from 2008 to 2009. This is as expected, given that the organisation posted significant losses in 2009. What is more interesting is that the value of the organisation's capital employed has more than halved since 2008. This will be as a direct result of the organisation disposing of stores and complementary businesses. Remember also that JJB has taken out a large bank loan to facilitate its ongoing trade. This position will make it increasingly difficult for JJB Sports plc to generate additional capital from investments by others in shares in the business.

A cautionary note: we have calculated the ROCE using the value of the capital employed in the balance sheet. As you will recall from your earlier readings, the balance sheet is a snapshot of the company at the end of the year. If the company had acquired new assets on the day before the balance sheet was compiled it would not have had time for the assets to generate a return. Obviously this can give a false view of the ROCE. Ways to overcome this problem are to reconstruct the capital employed or to take the average of the capital at the beginning and end of the year. However, looking at the long-run trend of the ratio can lessen the distortion.

ACTIVITY

Providing that you now have a company report of your choice in a spreadsheet, apply the profitability ratios we have just been through so that you can confirm some of your earlier analysis. You can use the JJB example as a model if you like but take your time and see what the figures mean in relation to the profitability of your example.

Turnover: capital employed

Owing to the problems with definitions in calculating ROCE we can use a supplementary ratio to work out how 'hard' the business has been working in relation to the size of the assets used (as measured by the capital employed).

JJB turnover: capital employed

From the income statement – turnover.

	Note	52 weeks to 25 January 2009 £'000	52 weeks to 27 January 2008 £'000
Continuing operations			
Revenue	3	718,281	811,754
Cost of sales		(353,696)	(405,642)

And from the balance sheet – capital employed.

Provisions	26	**(5,786)**	(2,304)
		(52,362)	(122,846)
Total liabilities		**(430,711)**	(424,493)
Net assets		**184,631**	365,055
Equity			
Share capital	29	**12,542**	11,944
Share premium account	31	**174,055**	171,248
Capital redemption reserve	32	**1,069**	1,069
Investment in own shares	33	**(3,083)**	(3,083)
Share based payment reserve	34	**635**	680
Foreign currency translation reserve	35	**338**	(1,211)
Retained earnings	36	**(925)**	184,408
Equity attributable to shareholders of the parent		**184,631**	365,055

Figure 9.11 Turnover: capital employed ratio figure selection
Source: From JJB Sports plc Annual Report and Financial Statements 2009.

	2009	2008
Turnover £'000	718,281	811,754
Capital employed £'000	236,993	487,901
T/CE	3.0:1	1.7:1

Secondary analysis: a deeper analysis!

Hopefully you will have realised that we have used some figures several times. What can we gain by an analysis based on just a few figures? Hopefully quite a lot! The analysis we have undertaken so far could enable you to spot a company's strategy or how its operations differ from those of its competitors. We said that ROCE was often referred to as the prime ratio; as such the 'prime' can be split into secondary elements. Here is the formula for ROCE again:

$$ROCE = \frac{PBIT}{CE} \times 100\%$$

Mathematical dexterity will allow us to play about with that equation to show that:

$$\frac{PBIT}{CE} = \frac{PBIT}{Turnover} \times \frac{Turnover}{CE}$$

Therefore we will see that:

$$ROCE = \frac{PBIT}{Turnover} \times \frac{Turnover}{CE}$$

Thus we can see that the return a business generates is a function of its profit margin and how hard it works its assets. Two companies could each have a ROCE of 8 per cent but one could generate it by 4 × 2 and the other could get there by 2 × 4. This would imply two different strategies: one company operates with a high margin but low utilisation of its assets but the other company has lower margins but generates them more often.

LIQUIDITY RATIOS

As you should have picked up from the cash flow forecast section in the previous chapter, cash is the lifeblood of any business. A business must pay its debts as they fall due or risk financial failure (remember the Southampton Football Club case study?). The liquidity ratios are a tool for measuring the solvency and financial stability of a business so that we can assess how effectively it has managed its working capital. Liquidity is therefore about the ability of a business to generate sufficient cash to meet its liabilities as they fall due. You should also note that much like the fact that profit is different to cash, profitability should not be confused with liquidity here. A company could be very profitable but not liquid and will therefore not be able to meet its immediate obligations. There are two principal ratios that you will need to be aware of here for the purposes of the sport industry: the current ratio and quick ratio. Liquidity ratios are normally expressed as real ratios (i.e. χ:1 rather than z%).

> **KEY TERM**
>
> **LIQUIDITY**
>
> Measures the ability of a company to access enough cash to meet its liabilities as they fall due.

The current ratio

The current ratio compares current assets with current liabilities. This will help us to discover whether the company has enough resource to meet its immediate financial requirements. Remember that organisations need to pay their debts as they fall due. Many analysts recommend that a company should have a ratio of at least 1:1, indicating that it has £1 of resource to cover £1 of liability. However, I think that this is too general: it is like saying that every football team should play in a 4-4-2 formation. The industry and many other factors will determine the liquidity profile of a company. For example, a supermarket will have the ability to generate cash a lot quicker than a clothing manufacturer: the supermarket has shelves full of goods that will become cash as soon as a shopper takes them to the checkout, whereas the clothing manufacturer will have to wait for its debtor to pay on credit terms. Thus again we need to place the measure into the context of the organisation that we are examining.

You may think that it is good to have a lot of current assets but you should also consider the fact that you can have too many! It is not good management if you have too much stock and cash floating about in the business: they should be working, not floating.

$$\text{Current Ratio} = \frac{\text{Current Assets}}{\text{Current Liabilities}}$$

JJB current ratio

We can get all of this information from the top section of the balance sheet (Figure 9.12).

Current assets			
Inventories	20	70,569	114,984
Trade and other receivables	21	38,381	45,412
Current asset investments	22	171,954	196,217
Cash and cash equivalents	23	40,638	14,199
Current tax receivable		–	1,536
		321,542	**372,348**
Total assets		615,342	789,548
Current liabilities			
Trade and other payables	24	(101,334)	(110,874)
Current tax liability		(1,494)	–
Bank loans	25	(75,000)	–
Loan notes	25	(168,117)	(168,117)
Provisions	26	(32,404)	(22,656)
		(378,349)	**(301,647)**
Net current (liabilities) assets		(56,807)	70,701

Figure 9.12 Current ratio figure selection

Source: From JJB Sports plc Annual Report and Financial Statements 2009.

	2009	2008
Current assets £'000	321,542	372,348
Current liabilities £'000	378,349	301,647
Current ratio	0.8:1	1.2:1

The ratio shows that JJB did not have sufficient current assets to cover their current liabilities in 2009 in stark contrast to the position that they were in the year before (2008). The table shows that the ratio fluctuates. What could be the reason for this? The first thing to consider is the fact that JJB is a retailer: have there been changes in the amount of inventory (stock) they hold? Have they opened more shops and therefore need to have goods in those shops or indeed have they closed shops and therefore need less stock? Have they got inventory that they cannot sell? What about the liabilities: have JJB stopped paying their creditors and therefore the amounts they owe have escalated? When you are doing your own analysis you may find answers to these questions in the annual report. If not, you will have to think! In the case of JJB the increase in liabilities was due to a long-term loan becoming payable within the following period.

The quick ratio (acid test)

The quick ratio (or acid test) is similar to the current ratio with the exception that inventory (stock) is excluded from the current assets because the inventory may not be 'liquid'. In other words, the inventory is excluded because it may take a while before the inventory can be sold and then there may be a further wait until it is paid for. The circumstances will depend on the type of company: the trading cycle for a supermarket is very different to that of a leisure centre, for example. However, because most sport and leisure organisations exist to provide a service to the public and not to sell stock, it is probable that very little stock will be held.

The quick ratio is therefore a stringent way of testing whether the organisation has the ability to pay its debtors if they demand their cash immediately. Again, it is more insightful to look for trends and examine the particular circumstances of an organisation than to look for a golden number. Obviously an organisation with a quick ratio of less than 1:1 would have to stall for time if the boys with the baseball bats call around to demand that the current liabilities be paid immediately.

$$\text{Quick Ratio} = \frac{\text{Current Assets} - \text{Inventory}}{\text{Current Liabilities}}$$

Quick ratio for JJB

Again we use the top section of the balance sheet; the difference this time is that we deduct inventories from the current assets figure (Figure 9.13).

Current assets			
Inventories	20	70,569	114,984
Trade and other receivables	21	38,381	45,412
Current asset investments	22	171,954	196,217
Cash and cash equivalents	23	40,638	14,199
Current tax receivable		–	1,536
		321,542	372,348
Total assets		615,342	789,548
Current liabilities			
Trade and other payables	24	(101,334)	(110,874)
Current tax liability		(1,494)	–
Bank loans	25	(75,000)	–
Loan notes	25	(168,117)	(168,117)
Provisions	26	(32,404)	(22,656)
		(378,349)	(301,647)
Net current (liabilities) assets		(56,807)	70,701

Figure 9.13 Quick ratio figure selection

Source: From JJB Sports plc Annual Report and Financial Statements 2009.

	2009	2008
Current assets £'000	321,542	372,348
Current liabilities £'000	378,349	301,647
Current ratio	0.7:1	0.9:1

JJB are obviously happy to operate with a quick ratio of less than 1:1. This is not surprising: they are a retailer and the vast majority of their sales will be cash. What is also interesting from the figures and the annual report is that the level of stock (inventory) has reduced markedly. While this will be partially explained by the store closures (i.e. they have fewer stores so need less stock), it is also probable that creditors have reduced the amount of stock that they are prepared to place on credit terms through fear of the organisation becoming insolvent and unable to pay their dues.

It is important for any financial manager to track these ratios as any unexplained movements from one annual report to the next can encourage observers to draw their conclusions about the liquidity position and creditworthiness of the company.

> **ACTIVITY**
>
> For your company apply the liquidity ratios we have just covered. Again you can use the JJB example as a model if you like but take your time and work out what the figures mean.

DEFENSIVE POSITION RATIOS (LONG-TERM SOLVENCY)

For professional team sports these ratios may be two of the most useful methods in deciding how well a company is performing because they measure the relationship between capital (equity) and long-term debt. Again think back to the Southampton Football Club case study – it is fair to say that they had a great deal of long-term debt and that this landed them in a poor financial situation. These ratios allow us to examine the company's financial structure. Investors and other users of accounting information can use defensive position ratios to assess the level of financial risk – they can estimate when (or if) they are likely to get their money back. Consequently these ratios are a more long-term financial measure of the risk taken by an organisation with regard to the amount of money it is has borrowed. In general the lower the level of borrowings the business has, the healthier the position they are in to withstand poor trading conditions. Interest payments on loans and overdrafts have to be paid irrespective of turnover and ticket sales. The two key ratios we use here are the debt ratio and the gearing ratio.

The debt ratio

The debt ratio shows the extent to which creditors have power over an organisation. A high ratio indicates that the creditors are funding most of the firm's assets. Consequently, if the creditors decide that they want repaying, the organisation may have to sell off some of its assets to raise the cash needed to pay off the creditors. In terms of the sport and leisure industry this may mean, for example, a football club having to sell some of its players to pay creditors when they demand their cash. A debt ratio of 50 per cent is considered a safe limit whereas a debt ratio exceeding 75 per cent is a cause for concern. However, the specific context of the organisation must be taken into account. The debt ratio is calculated using the following formula:

$$\text{Debt Ratio} = \frac{\text{Total Debt}}{\text{Total Assets}} \times 100\%$$

The total debt will be equal to current liabilities plus long-term liabilities (loans).

JJB debt ratio

This time we need to use two figures from the balance sheet: total liabilities and total assets (Figure 9.14).

Non-current assets			
Goodwill	15	106,406	187,834
Other intangible assets	16	24,600	25,417
Property, plant and equipment	17	162,044	198,272
Investment in associated undertaking	19	750	1,677
Loan to associated undertaking	19	–	4,000
		293,800	417,200
Current assets			
Inventories	20	70,569	114,984
Trade and other receivables	21	38,381	45,412
Current asset investments	22	171,954	196,217
Cash and cash equivalents	23	40,638	14,199
Current tax receivable		–	1,536
		321,542	372,348
Total assets		**615,342**	**789,548**
Current liabilities			
Trade and other payables	24	(101,334)	(110,874)
Current tax liability		(1,494)	–
Bank loans	25	(75,000)	–
Loan notes	25	(168,117)	(168,117)
Provisions	26	(32,404)	(22,656)
		(378,349)	(301,647)
Net current (liabilities) assets		(56,807)	70,701
Non-current liabilities			
Bank loans	25	–	(56,355)
Deferred tax liabilities	27	(2,682)	(24,237)
Deferred lease incentives	28	(43,894)	(39,950)
Provisions	26	(5,786)	(2,304)
		(52,362)	(122,846)
Total liabilities		**(430,711)**	**(424,493)**
Net assets		184,631	365,055

Figure 9.14 Debt ratio figure selection

Source: From JJB Sports plc Annual Report and Financial Statements 2009

	2009	2008
Total liabilities	430,711	424,493
Total assets £'000	615,342	789,548
Debt ratio	79%	69%

Although JJB have changed the profile of their debts (i.e. they no longer have a long-term loan on their balance sheet), the overall structure means that the debt ratio is now 79 per cent. This makes further borrowing difficult, as creditors may be a little nervous about lending to an organisation that shows an imbalance between its assets and liabilities. Indeed, suppliers have already reduced the amount of stock that they are happy to let the organisation hold due to the financial constraints in which JJB are operating, as it means that they may not be able to settle their debt.

The gearing ratio

You may well have heard of the gearing ratio before, as it is a widely used term in the sport industry, especially by media commentators in relation to professional team sports. The gearing ratio may be used to measure how the organisation is financed. Gearing refers to how much of the capital is made up of debt finance or interest-bearing creditors. The financial structure is a very important aspect of financial management: get it right and there are many benefits but getting it wrong can be disastrous. Debt finance is attractive to organisations because it can be cheap and there are tax benefits (interest payments are allowable tax expenses) but the interest payments (and the capital of the loan) are contractual obligations. Interest and the loan itself have to be paid irrespective of how well the organisation is performing. If there is a downturn in the fortunes of the company it will still have to meet these obligations. Shareholders' dividend payments are not contractual: they are paid if there is a profit after all other obligations have been met. In a company that has a lot of debt finance, shareholders are risking that there will still be enough profit left after the associated loan payments to pay them a dividend. The same principle applies to other investors: if a highly geared company is trying to raise additional capital, new investors may view it as a bad risk.

An organisation that is heavily geared (i.e. it borrows heavily from interest-bearing creditors) is often considered to be in a bad financial position, especially when demand falls. You can apply the principle of gearing to real-life situations and mortgages. Just as a building society borrower needs to pay for his house whether or not he is earning, so a business has to pay interest on borrowed money regardless of profitability (we will follow this concept up when considering debt finance in Chapter 14). Simply put, gearing shows us how much of an organisation is financed by loans.

The formula for the gearing ratio is as follows:

$$\text{Gearing Ratio} = \frac{\text{Interest-bearing creditors}}{\text{Equity}} \times 100\%$$

KEY TERMS

SHARES

Parts of the business that are issued to people in return for cash. It is only when the shares are initially issued that the company receives any cash. Any other sale of the shares is between private individuals (or institutions).

SHAREHOLDER

One of the owners of the shares in a company. Collectively the shareholders own the whole company.

DIVIDENDS

Amounts of money paid to shareholders from profits earned by a company. It is usual for the total payment to be paid in two instalments: an interim payment partway through the year and then the final payments at the year end. Dividend payments are discretionary: they do not have to be paid.

JJB gearing ratio

Again we use the balance sheet; however, we need to identify the interest-bearing creditors and divide the sum of them by equity (Figure 9.15).

Current liabilities			
Trade and other payables	24	(101,334)	(110,874)
Current tax liability		(1,494)	–
Bank loans	25	(75,000)	–
Loan notes	25	(168,117)	(168,117)
Provisions	26	(32,404)	(22,656)
		(378,349)	(301,647)
Net current (liabilities) assets		(56,807)	70,701
Non-current liabilities			
Bank loans	25	–	(56,355)
Deferred tax liabilities	27	(2,682)	(24,237)
Deferred lease incentives	28	(43,894)	(39,950)
Provisions	26	(5,786)	(2,304)
		(52,362)	(122,846)
Total liabilities		(430,711)	(424,493)
Net assets		184,631	365,055
Equity			
Share capital	29	12,542	11,944
Share premium account	31	174,055	171,248
Capital redemption reserve	32	1,069	1,069
Investment in own shares	33	(3,083)	(3,083)
Share based payment reserve	34	635	680
Foreign currency translation reserve	35	338	(1,211)
Retained earnings	36	(925)	184,408
Equity attributable to shareholders of the parent		184,631	365,055

Figure 9.15 Gearing ratio figure selection

Source: From JJB Sports plc Annual Report and Financial Statements 2009.

	2009	2008
Interest bearing liabilities £'000	287,011	264,402
Equity £'000	184,631	365,055
Gearing ratio	155%	72%

These figures show that JJB is very highly geared and has limited capacity for any more debt finance. The amount of interest-bearing creditors has increased only marginally but due to the significant reduction in equity the business is now increasingly vulnerable to any further downturn in trade. However, the problem here for JJB's interest-bearing creditors is that if they call in their loans the company will fold, meaning that they will never see the real value of their lending.

INVESTMENT RATIOS

Existing and potential investors will want to see what the benefits are, or will be, for investing in a company (i.e. becoming a shareholder). Some of the ratios that you have used so far will have given you an insight into the profitability, liquidity and defensive position of a business and these should enable you to gain an insight into the effectiveness of the organisation's management. However, investment ratios allow us to quickly obtain an overview of the results of the organisation from the perspective of an investment (i.e. the rewards due to the shareholders). Existing and potential shareholders will want to see if they are achieving a good return on their investment. Obviously shareholder ratios can only be applied to organisations that have shareholders. Remember: some organisations may be not-for-profit, or they may be clubs and societies.

Investor ratios are calculated for many organisations on a daily basis. You can easily access them by looking at the financial pages of upmarket newspapers. They are usually found towards the back of the paper: after Page 3 but before the sport!

Earnings per share

This, as the name implies, shows the earnings that are attributable to each share. The earnings that each share is entitled to will be the net profit (i.e. profit after all deductions, including payments to preference shareholders) divided by the number of 'ordinary' shares.

The 'earnings per share' figure when viewed in isolation is totally meaningless to any investor. If the earning per share for Company A is 25p and for Company B it is 80p, what is the significance of that information? Answer: absolutely none! In fact the answer provides the reason: they are absolute values. To get any meaning from them we need to compare them to something, and that something is the price of the share. This is done by the 'price/earnings' ratio.

Price/earnings ratio

The price/earnings ratio (P/E) relates the earnings per share to the price of the share: it therefore looks at the size of the investment (as measured by the current trading price of a share in the company) and the reward paid to the holder of that share. A high P/E signals that investors have a high expectation of the future prospects of the company. This is because they are willing to pay a high price for the share. The ratio tells us how many years it will take (based on today's trading price for a share) for a shareholder's return from the company to equal the price paid for the share.

What is an acceptable level of return? The only possible answer to that question is: 'It depends'. There are many factors to consider before anyone can offer their opinion (and it can only ever be their own personal opinion!) about what is an acceptable level of return. Factors for consideration are: the risk associated with that specific organisation, the risk associated with the business sector in which the organisation operates, alternative investments available, personal preference and beliefs, and personal attitude to risk. Do we all support the same football team? Does everyone bet on the same horse in a race? Why not? Do all investors buy the same shares? Does the price of shares stay at the same price? Why not?

The reward for taking a bigger risk is a higher return. That is why some finance companies will lend money to struggling companies: they will charge them a high rate of interest! The quantification of risk (can it ever be quantified if there is so much personal belief involved?) is a 'science' in its own right but the marketplace will always find a seller when the buyer's needs are big enough!

This is probably the most important investment ratio, since it works out the average amount of profits earned per ordinary share issued. Any profit retained in the company to help it grow will still belong to the shareholders, and as such any dividend they receive will only be part of the return on their investment.

Dividend per share

This shows the amount of profit allocated to pay dividends. Many companies will only make a certain amount of money available to shareholders by way of a dividend, as they will want to use some of the profits for other things such as reinvestment in equipment and relocations. Therefore the dividend per share gives you a feel for the short-term return on an investment.

Overall return

The long-term return will include the annual dividend payments and 'capital' growth. For example, if you bought a share today for £2 and the company paid dividends of 15p and 23p in the next two years and at the end of the second year the share price was £2.40, your total gain would be 40p plus 15p plus 23p. That would give you a total gain of 78p (and total growth of 39 per cent on your initial investment over two years). However, the 40p capital gain would only be realised if you sold the share. Therefore you must constantly review the prospects for the company and ask: 'Do I want to continue my investment or can I get a better return elsewhere?'

The dividend policy of an organisation can have an impact on the type of investor it attracts. Some investors may want regular substantial cash flows and will therefore like a company that pays high dividends, while other investors may be in for the long haul and prefer the company to retain profits (as opposed to paying them out in dividends) and use them to fund expansion and future growth.

Wealth warning

Investing can seriously damage your wealth. Investments can go down. Before you invest in anything make sure you have done the preparatory research. In addition, remember that many people have got small fortunes by investing in football clubs; unfortunately they had large fortunes before they invested!

ACTIVITY

1. If you haven't done so already, follow the investment ratios and apply them to your company. What do the results tell you?
2. Having done all of the analysis, what is your assessment of the organisation's current financial position and performance? Remember to couple your analysis with the directors' report and the general figures contained in the income statement and balance sheet.

RATIO ANALYSIS AND ITS LIMITS

As with any measurement tool there will be limitations. Ratio analysis is no different. If we agree that the level and choice of analysis depends on the user and the availability of useful data then we agree that there will be differences in the findings. For example, with an organisation such as the British Triathlon Association not all of the ratios would be applicable. However, there are one or two more limitations to ratio analysis of which you should be aware. We have alluded to some of these already but it is worth recapping:

- There are no universally agreed definitions for the formulas and terminology used. Ratios based on alternative meanings should not be compared. Consequently, always state the definitions you are using whenever you prepare any analysis.
- Some data may not be available, so you may have to use less precise material.
- Ideally you should do some trend analysis but again this information may not always be available or comparable.
- Comparisons with other companies in the industry may be difficult if their data are not published – how do you really know how well you are doing?
- The sport and leisure industry is always in a period of rapid change and therefore some analysis is out of date before it is completed owing to the changes in the operating environment.
- Non-financial factors are not considered in ratio analysis (this is why you should always refer to the directors' reports).

Notwithstanding such limitations, ratio analysis – when used in conjunction with a full range of material – is a very useful management tool and one that I believe you should be competent in. You should be aware that ratios should not just be viewed as 'facts' but as a method of indicating where further research may be required. The real reasons for financial position and performance need to be communicated by you (as managers) in order to make effective business decisions.

SUMMARY

This chapter has shown you how to dissect and interpret annual reports in a meaningful and trustworthy manner. Ratio analysis is fundamental to your own personal development as managers and will help inform you of problems, potential issues and successful ideas. However, access to the appropriate data is integral to calculating the right things, and the results can be widely used by a variety of user groups (as outlined in Chapter 1). I have only shown you the common ratios that are used in the context of sport and leisure organisations, so if you gain employment outside this sector you should familiarise yourself with the specific industry requirements.

In order to make meaningful comparisons you need to interpret the industry trends and examine the directors' report. This will enable you to make a well-rounded response to questions from an organisation. Despite the drawbacks outlined in the final section of this chapter you should realise what an important tool ratios are.

Although annual reports can be very useful to us as users of financial statements their main problem is the sheer volume of information contained within them – if you accessed the JJB report as suggested you will know exactly what I mean here. In order to make sensible use of the figures you need to organise them in a logical way. Several of the techniques covered in this chapter go way beyond the basic analysis we covered in Chapter 7; however, in ratio analysis we have a framework that we can apply to reach some meaningful conclusions about the financial health of an organisation.

QUESTIONS FOR REVIEW

1. What is the purpose of ratio analysis?
2. What are the five key measures for a business?
3. What is ROCE?
4. What is liquidity and how can it be measured?
5. List and explain three limitations of ratio analysis.

REFERENCES AND FURTHER READING

CIMA (2009) *Financial Accounting Fundamentals*. BPP Professional Education, London.
Dyson, J.R. (2003) *Accounting for Non-accounting Students*, 6th edn. Financial Times Press, Harlow.
McLaney, E. and Atrill, P. (2005) *Accounting: An Introduction*, 3rd edn. Financial Times Press, Harlow.
Wilson, R. and Joyce, J. (2008) *Finance for Sport and Leisure Managers: An Introduction*. Routledge, London.

PART 2
FINANCIAL MANAGEMENT

CHAPTER 10

UNDERSTANDING THE NATURE OF COST IN SPORT

On completion of this chapter you will be able to:

- identify and describe the rationale for managing money (finance);
- understand the relationship between cost and management accounting;
- explain the meaning and purpose of cost accounting;
- understand and communicate basic costing terminology.

INTRODUCTION

After reading Part 1 of this book you will have no doubt recognised that the profitability of an organisation depends on the revenues generated and the costs incurred. Expenses will be classified in different ways, depending on the nature of the products and services used in generating the said revenues. These expenses (or costs) will range from the purchase of stock (as we saw with Kitlocker.com), to the provision of services (such as lifeguards so that you can use your local swimming pool) to the provision of miscellaneous items (for example, security for Sir Alex Ferguson on match days at Old Trafford). In financial accounting these expenses are all aggregated up and classified by generic type for reporting purposes. However, there is often a need to classify costs in a much more sophisticated manner to ensure that management can plan, make decisions and control an organisation more effectively – this is where management accounting comes in and is the focus of Part 2.

While not all employment in the sport industry will require practitioners to construct financial statements, most employees will be expected to work with money, and therefore, by definition, manage finance. Operations concerning money may include activities such as applying for major funding from governing bodies, managing membership subscriptions for a local sport club or increasing profit margins for a commercial operation. Consequently, the aim of Part 2 is to provide you with a range of skills to tackle these problems and build your confidence in managing sport finance. This chapter will explore the rationale for managing money and will provide you with a framework to address the variety of requirements that will be placed on you by an organisation. Moreover, we will examine the nature of cost and the relationship between cost and management accounting.

The survival of any organisation, as you should now be aware, depends on its ability to pay its debts as they fall due and on having products (or services) that generate revenues which are higher than the costs incurred in producing and selling them. These ideas are based on the concepts we discussed in Chapter 9: liquidity and profitability. Furthermore, we have already seen that financial reporting may be used to analyse such measures and to examine past performance. However, accounting is multidisciplinary and encompasses more than just financial reporting. Indeed, while it is important to look back to see 'how you did', I would argue that as twenty-first-century managers you will need to look to the future and see 'what you could do'. Broadening your range of skills to consider how to plan, make decisions and control an organisation will be essential. Hence understanding the nature of cost and management accounting will help you become more effective in your chosen career.

COST

Information on the cost incurred in producing and selling individual products and services is not available through financial reports, nor is it a statutory requirement to publish them. Consider for a moment how difficult it would be for you to make a decision on price if you did not know the cost or the capacity of the production. Without such information you cannot make sensible decisions about (1) controlling costs or (2) maximising profitability. Cost accounting provides us with the tools to make decisions by giving us a mechanism to record the cost of resources used by an individual product or service. It also assists us in managing costs by offering various tools for the control and reduction of different types of cost incurred by an organisation. It can also help us to make the most efficient use of our available resources.

Everything that we do, either as private individuals or when acting for our organisations, has a cost (this book has one: my time, my employer's time, the publishing company, the copyeditor, the editor, the marketing of the book, the point of sale). What is difficult to establish is what we really mean by cost. Usually it is used to denote, in monetary terms, the resources needed to obtain a specified object, state, product or service. However, to avoid any possible misunderstandings we need to define the term 'cost' more specifically. For example, what is the cost of 1 kg of material that your organisation has in stock? Is it the price that you paid to the supplier? Is it the price of replacing it? Is it free? Depending on the circumstances and the specific interpretation of 'cost', it is possible that any of the answers (and others) could be correct. To communicate effectively, managers (and not just accountants) must fully understand the differences between various types of cost, their computation and their usage. Consequently it is essential that management have the following information about their costs to carry out their role more effectively:

- costs incurred and controlled by departments;
- costs related to different products or services;
- costs related to actual quantities.

The effective management of cost is, and will continue to be, a major challenge for any sport organisation. The benefits are obvious in that a reduction in costs will lead to an increase in profit, providing that the selling price remains the same. In turn this will lead to a better set of profitability ratios and an improved return on capital employed. However, for many sport organisations including major professional teams, the need for cost controls is only realised when costs have already started spiralling out of control or when revenues fall as a result of intense competition or recession; at the time of writing a cursory look at Portsmouth Football Club confirms this. What is important therefore is that we now consider how routine performance can be monitored and controlled by establishing a thorough understanding of cost (or management) accounting.

WHAT IS COST ACCOUNTING?

Cost accounting is used extensively in a variety of organisations and is especially useful in sport when you consider the complexity and scope of the products and services on offer. In essence the cost accounting system is the basis of an internal financial information system that can assist managers in their role of planning, decision-making and control. Obviously the type and nature of the decision will vary significantly from organisation to organisation, but may include:

- whether to increase the levels of service provided;
- whether to provide a new product or service;
- how to adjust selling prices;
- whether to make or buy a new product.

In today's increasingly competitive and ever-expanding sport market (see Sport Industry Research Centre, 2009) an organisation without effective cost accounting will struggle to maintain its competitive advantage and ultimately compromise survival. The ability to determine the costs of products using product costing techniques (Chapter 11), planning and controlling innovation using budgeting (Chapter 12) and making effective organisational decisions using appraisal tools (Chapter 13) is paramount. If you cast your mind back to the Kitlocker.com examples that we covered in Part 1, you will see how important these tools can be. They can help the managing directors decide on what assets to buy and how much to pay, determine the selling price of their products and determine the types of contracts to use in appointing staff and how much to pay them.

Unlike financial accounting there is no law which governs how cost accounting is carried out or how it is reported. Indeed, it does not even have to undertaken. This means that cost, or management, accounts will vary from organisation to organisation, meaning that you will have much more flexibility to use the tools that best fit your circumstances.

Thus as a potential answer to the question 'What is cost accounting?' one could argue that it is a form of accounting that accumulates historical costs and charges these costs to units of output or departments in order to establish stock valuations, profits and balance sheet items. In a nutshell, we can describe all of the functions of management and cost accounting in three key areas: planning, decision-making and control.

Management accounting is concerned with 'the provision of information to assist management with planning, decision-making and control'. In order to do this effectively you will need 'sufficiently accurate and detailed information'.

Cost accounting therefore is 'a management information system which analyses past, present and future data to provide the basis for managerial action' (CIMA, 2009).

Financial accounting and management accounting record the same basic data for income and expenditure; however, these data can be analysed differently. Financial accounts are prepared for individuals *external* to the organisation, for example shareholders, suppliers, etc.

Management accounts, however, are prepared for the *internal* managers of an organisation. It is important here that you appreciate that the data used for both financial and management accounting are the same (see Table 10.1). It is the way in which we manipulate and analyse the data which is different and it is these skills which you will develop over the next few chapters.

COST CONTROL

As you saw in Part 1, like any other discipline, finance is based on terminology. In order for you to clearly understand the tools and techniques in the following chapters it is important that we make our way through the key terms before applying them to real situations. You will be familiar with the typical financial accounting classification used in the income statement where we compare revenue (income) with expenses (expenditure) for a particular accounting period in order to determine profit or loss. Examples of such expenses could include wages and salaries, utilities and rent. However, cost accounting can classify expenses in a different way as it aims to show that part of the business where the expenditure is incurred. By way of an example we can look at the wages and salaries of a professional cricket team. For the purposes of financial accounting the income statement would detail one figure for 'wages and salaries'. By contrast, cost accounting would attempt to redistribute such a cost to the various parts of the business where the expenditure was incurred (e.g. the first team, the management team, the administrative team, cleaning, security). Once this is achieved it then categorises the costs using other terminology to provide management with more useful information on which to base decisions. Such information could be used to determine whether a particular department is overspending or where there is capacity to spend more.

Table 10.1 The relationship between financial and management accounting

Financial accounts	*Management accounts*
Detail the performance of an organisation over a defined period of time, and state the affairs at the end of that period.	Aid management to record, plan and control the organisation's activities and to help in the decision-making process.
Limited companies must by law prepare financial accounts.	No legal requirement.
Format of the accounts is determined by law and regulating bodies. Different companies should be able to compare their accounts to other's on a reasonably comparable basis.	Format is entirely at the management accountants' discretion. No strict rules apply.
Concentration is on the business as a whole, aggregating revenues and costs from different operations and is an end in itself.	May focus on specific areas of an organisation. Information is produced to aid in a decision and is not the end-product of one.
Displays information of a monetary nature.	Incorporates non-monetary measures.
Present a historical picture of the past.	Current historical record and future planning tool.

KEY TERMS

DIRECT COSTS

A fundamental method in cost classification is to establish which costs are direct and which costs are indirect. Direct costs can be easily identified (or traced) in full to a product, service or department. A good sport example for a direct cost might be the cost of fuel, tyres and engine components for a formula one racing car.

INDIRECT COSTS

By contrast, an indirect cost that is incurred in the course of making a product or delivering a service cannot be traced in full to that product or service. Indirect costs are often termed overheads. Using our F1 example an indirect cost might be the wages of the garage mechanics.

FIXED COSTS

A cost that is incurred for a particular period of time which within certain activity levels is unaffected by changes in the levels of activity. A good example of this would be rent, staff salaries, or (if you cast your minds back to Part 1) straight-line depreciation. If we were to illustrate this on a graph to show the relationship between cost and output we would find that the line moves in a horizontal direction – remember that irrespective of how many units are produced we still have to pay for the fixed cost; on the other hand, if we examine the relationship between the fixed costs and their allocation per unit the graph will look quite different.

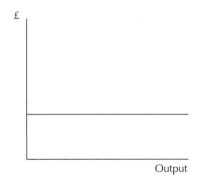
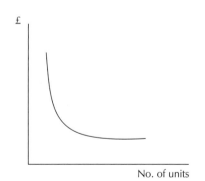

VARIABLE COSTS

These are costs that tend to vary according to the level of activity; for example, direct materials and most utilities. These costs are incurred when you make a product or deliver a service. Unlike fixed costs, if we illustrate a variable cost on a graph showing the relationship between cost and output we can see how cost rises in line with output.

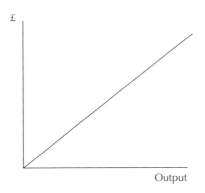
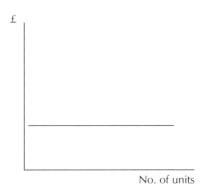

SEMI-VARIABLE COSTS

In reality few costs are ever completely fixed or variable. Many will have fixed elements to them or fixed charges that need to be paid before you can access better deals. Semi-variable costs therefore have a fixed and variable element to them. Such costs are affected by output and we can use the example of mobile telephone contracts to see how this works in practice. Contracts will have a standing charge, say £25 per month, and if you go over your inclusive allowance or use your phone abroad you will incur additional (variable) charges based on usage. On the graph, notice how the line begins above the 00 on the axis (i.e. 0 on the Number of units axis and 0 on the £ axis); this represents the fixed element, while the line represents the variable part.

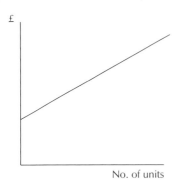

STEPPED COSTS

These are fixed over a certain range of output but will increase as capacity is reached. For example, your salary may stay constant irrespective of what you have to do in your job until an additional shift is added or more staff are recruited, as would be the case with a casual pool attendant. Predictably, stepped costs look like steps on the graph!

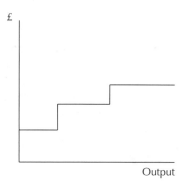

TOTAL COST

Fixed costs + variable costs. When placed on a graph you can see that, by output, the total cost line starts some way up the vertical axis to represent the fixed costs and then moves up to include variable costs. The second graph details total cost per unit which starts high (due to the amount of fixed cost that would be payable if only one unit was produced) and then curves downwards to a plateau.

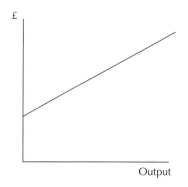
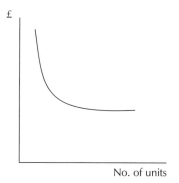

COST BEHAVIOUR

All of the costs outlined above will, and do, behave in different ways. Cost behaviour is the study of the way costs fluctuate and the rationale for such variation. If we strip this back to basics then the basic principle of cost behaviour is that as activity rises, costs will normally rise too.

The principal advantage of classifying these costs is for the purpose of controlling them and making individual people and departments accountable for them. The size and scale of an organisation will have a part to play here; if it is a large organisation there will need to be a number of manageable units, whereas a small organisation will find it easier to hold individuals responsible. The only way, however, that any of this can be achieved is through a structure which forms command and helps communication. The relationship between cost control and organisational structure is very important. If a department takes responsibility for particular activities then it may be held accountable for these activities.

MONITORING ROUTINE PERFORMANCE

The essential requirement for effective budgetary control procedures (examined in Chapter 12) is a system for analysing costs incurred in the organisation. This will normally involve breaking the organisation down into areas of responsibility known as budget or cost centres. Completing this exercise as a manager will mean that you can assign responsibility to individuals for the management of sales and costs in those areas. Typically sport organisations will use two types of budget centre:

1. Cost centre: when businesses reach a certain size it is usual for them to divide into smaller, logical parts to facilitate the charging of costs. A cost centre therefore is a place where costs can be recorded for a particular division of the business. The real advantage of cost centres is that they clearly identify costs with individuals, equipment or work units, thereby facilitating the relationship between cost and individual responsibility.
2. Profit centre: a part of an organisation that is accountable for both costs and revenues (i.e. that part of the organisation which has the direct responsibility to make money).

Operationalising such 'centres' will help to identify how various parts of the organisation are underperforming. This will in turn enable you to make quick decisions to protect the profitability of the organisation.

KEY TERMS

COST ACCOUNTING

The process of collecting, processing and presenting financial data to ascertain the cost of the cost centres and cost units.

COST CENTRE

A designated location, function, activity or item for which costs are collected (e.g. the marketing department).

PROFIT CENTRE

A designated location, function, activity or item for which costs and revenues are collected (e.g. trading activities (sales)).

ACTIVITY

Consider the following sport organisations and identify appropriate cost and profit centres for each:

1. a local authority swimming pool
2. a private health and fitness club
3. a professional sport team (e.g. Manchester United Football Club)
4. a local sport club with which you are familiar.

You may have found that some of these organisations were more difficult than others, particularly if you are not familiar with the industries. However, you may have identified some of the following types of cost centre:

1. A local authority swimming pool may well only have two cost centres: swimming and vending. However, we could split this further still on the swimming side by establishing a cost centre for public swimming and another for swimming lessons.
2. A private health and fitness club will have many more cost centres based on the size of the facility. For example, it would have cost centres for wet side, dry side, café/bar, health and beauty, and crèche. Again we could split these still further; for example, the café/bar might have two cost centres, one for food and the other for drinks.
3. A professional sport team like Manchester United may well have a number of tiers to their cost centre structure. In basic terms, however, the structure may include cost centres for match day, club shop, conferencing, hotel, financial products and catering.

4   A local sport club such as a swimming club would probably split their cost centres by section (e.g. swimming, diving, water polo and synchronised swimming).

We can illustrate a cost centre structure on a hierarchical model to make it clearer for management to understand. If we use the private sector health and fitness club by way of an example we can see how this works in practice (this example is not exhaustive; see Figure 10.1).

SUMMARY

The sole intention of this chapter has been to introduce you to the nature and classification of cost, and to highlight that the management of cost is essential in any sport organisation and should be carried out as a routine exercise rather than in times of difficulty. While the tools of management accounting are saved for Chapters 11, 12 and 13, you should have noted that keeping a lid on cost is one way that an organisation can protect its profit margin and maintain its competitive advantage. Such routine control can be effectively achieved through the establishment of cost and profit centres which assign areas of accountability that we can use to measure the performance of not only the particular department but also the manager and staff who work in it.

The classification of costs involves differentiating between direct and indirect costs, variable and fixed costs, the nature of costs and the function of costs. Cost per unit of production may be calculated by identifying the different elements of cost (i.e. the direct costs and any indirect costs that may be apportioned). This understanding will help you make more effective, evidenced-based decisions on setting selling prices and managing future revenues.

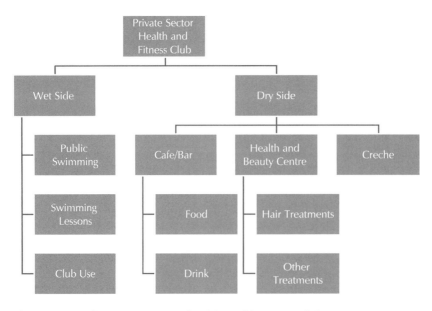

Figure 10.1 The private sector health and business club

QUESTIONS FOR REVIEW

1. What is the purpose of cost accounting?
2. How are cost and financial accounting different?
3. Define a variable cost and give two examples.
4. What is a direct cost and what differentiates it from an indirect cost?
5. What is the difference between a cost centre and a cost unit?

REFERENCES AND FURTHER READING

Bill, K. (ed.) (2009) *Sport Management*. Learning Matters, Exeter.
CIMA (2009) *Financial Accounting Fundamentals*. BPP Professional Education, London.
Collins, J. and Hussey, R. (2007) *Business Accounting: An Introduction to Financial and Management Accounting*. Palgrave Macmillan, Basingstoke.
Knott, G. (2004) *Financial Management*, 4th edn. Palgrave Macmillan, Basingstoke.
Russell, D., Patel, A. and Wilkinson-Riddle, G. (2002) *Cost Accounting: An Essential Guide*. Financial Times Press, Harlow.
Sport Industry Research Centre (2009) *Sport Market Forecasts*. Sheffield Hallam University, Sheffield.

CHAPTER 11

SHORT-TERM DECISION-MAKING

> **On completion of this chapter you will be able to:**
> - describe the main purposes of marginal costing;
> - understand how marginal costing can be an effective tool in making short-term decisions;
> - understand the significance of contribution in short-term decision-making;
> - construct a marginal costing statement;
> - conduct breakeven analysis.

INTRODUCTION

Marginal costing is a widely used technique in the sport industry due to its being relatively simple to understand and easy to apply. Decision-making normally involves a choice between alternatives and will relate to a future period. As a manager you will be expected to make decisions that will affect future performance on a regular basis and you need a technique that will help you appraise projects quickly and will enable you to choose the most profitable path. Marginal costing recognises that costs behave differently as activity changes, so in this chapter we will examine how to construct a marginal costing statement (a tool that you can use to make a quick decision), calculate contribution, and identify the breakeven point in both units and sales (I will explain these terms later).

Examining past costs may be useful for budgeting purposes but they only provide a guide for the future. When making short-term decisions you will need to consider many more factors, and while profitability may be your number one target you will also need to consider the impact of the decision upon existing customers, working capital, quality and labour costs. You will need to develop (or appreciate at least) an understanding of the types of decisions where marginal costing may be beneficial, specifically in the context of short-term decision-making where the best use must be made of your resources. If you use existing capacity, your fixed costs will remain constant and you will be able to make decisions based on contribution rather than profit.

CLASSIFYING COSTS BY BEHAVIOUR

Before we start getting to grips with marginal costing it is worth repeating some of the key components of the previous chapter principally so that you can see how subtle changes in the terminology affect the decision-making process. Marginal costing will meet the need for detailed information about costs in a business where production (or service) levels fluctuate. You will notice that many of the examples we consider over the next few chapters will be based on production – this is by design, since I believe they are easier to understand. You can then apply the framework to the service industry as and when appropriate. This costing method requires the expenditure of revenue to be classified into either fixed or variable costs according to their behaviour when the level of production or sales activity changes. The variable cost incurred in producing one unit is known as the marginal cost.

The variable costs per unit will usually be seen as the direct costs plus any additional overheads and are assumed to remain constant in the short term; for example, the cost of the hooded sweatshirt in our Kitlocker.com activities earlier in the book stayed the same. By definition therefore, if a variable cost is incurred at a constant rate then if output doubles so will the direct costs of materials. It follows here that direct costs will always be variable costs and indirect costs will be fixed costs.

> **KEY TERMS**
>
> ### MARGINAL COSTS
>
> The extra cost of making one more unit in a given period of time (often referred to as the variable cost per unit of production).
>
> ### VARIABLE COSTS
>
> An item of revenue expenditure that will vary with the level of production or sales activity.
>
> ### FIXED COSTS
>
> An item of revenue expenditure that will be unaffected by changes in the level of production or sales activity in the short term.

WHAT IS MARGINAL COSTING?

The term marginal costing really just means the additional cost of making one more in a set period of time. Just imagine that a business produces high-energy carbohydrate 'power bars' and nothing else. Each week the business budgets to make 5,000 of these bars. The workforce is paid by the week, not by the unit produced (i.e. per power bar). Direct labour costs per week total £1,700 (i.e. the wages of the people actually making the power bar rather than the management team and the administrators). The direct material costs of 5,000 power bars are £3,100 (i.e. the cost of the ingredients for the power bar and its packaging). One week's overheads total £2,000 (i.e. administrative staff wages, rent, rates, etc.).

Therefore, one week's costs may be budgeted to equate to:

	£
Direct labour	1,700
Direct materials	3,100
Overheads	2,000
Total costs	6,800

ACTIVITY

If in reality 5,100 power bars are made (owing to a good production run), how much will the 100 extra bars cost? I find it best to first work out the cost of one bar.

If you think this through carefully, and use some of the terminology from the previous chapter, we can make sense of the answer. Direct labour costs will not increase, since the workforce are not paid by the number of power bars they produce. Similarly, overheads will not increase, since there will not be any additional rent to pay just because we have made an extra 100 bars. However, direct material costs will go up as we will have used the ingredients and packaging to produce the extra 100 bars. If £3,100 is spent on 5,000 bars then we can work out the cost of one bar:

$$3,100/5,000 = £0.62$$

Thus each bar will cost 62 pence and 100 bars will cost £62.00.

$$100 \times 0.62 = £62.00$$

In this example the marginal cost of a power bar is 62 pence. It is obvious that you cannot make any more products without additional extra components. However, even though in this example the only marginal cost is direct materials, it is quite possible for elements of direct labour and overheads to be included in it as well. For example, if the workforce were paid a shared bonus of 10p for each bar produced, the marginal cost per bar would be 72p (62 + 10). In our activity the direct labour and overheads are fixed costs, and as such are not normally sensitive to output changes.

So what do we know about this example so far?

1. Some costs will be volume-of-output sensitive. They will increase or decrease as output increases or decreases (variable costs).
2. Some costs will be incurred regardless of the output volume (fixed costs).

MARGINAL COSTING THEORY

Marginal costing theory assumes that every cost can be placed in one of the two categories identified above. Please note here that marginal and variable costs are interchangeable. Fixed costs can be a rather misleading term as they can actually alter. In the marginal costing sense 'fixed' does not mean 'unchanging' but 'will not alter as a direct result of making one or more item'. Rent and rates, for example, can and do go up! However, they do not go up as a result of making one or more product, but as a result (in the case of rates) of the local authority spending more of our money for us than before.

The company's total costs for making the 5,000 power bars in one week may be split into the two categories shown above, i.e. the volume sensitive (variable costs) and the costs incurred regardless of how many units are produced (fixed costs).

Therefore in our example the following may be deduced:

	£
Variable costs	3,100
Fixed costs	3,700
Total costs	6,800

Remember that this is only one way in which we can classify costs and while it is the one that I think is best to use in the sport industry you may come across others. However, now that we have covered the basics it is time to consider how we can put this into practice. The marginal costing framework is straightforward and may be motorised on a spreadsheet for ease of use. That said, the remainder of this chapter will outline how to use it.

REVENUE STATEMENTS IN MARGINAL COSTING FORMAT

The flowing examples illustrate how the marginal costing framework may be applied in real life. I find this method the most straightforward of any that I have seen and it uses simple logic. You don't need to be a mathematician or a genius to work it out. It is a simple case of adding, subtracting, dividing and multiplying. In the early examples I will include the symbols so that you can see where the numbers come from but I will drop them later on once you have grasped them. Rather than try to explain this any further, let us look at an example.

If the business sells the power bars for £2 each, we need to be able to calculate the profit (or loss) that will be incurred.

	Quantity	× Unit price	= Revenue
Revenue	5,000	2	10,000
Less			
Total costs			6,800
Profit			3,200

If we use a marginal costing layout it is normal to expand this statement into 'contribution format'.

	Quantity	× Unit price	= Revenue
Revenue	5,000	2	10,000
Less			
Variable costs		0.62	3,100
Equals			
Contribution		1.38	6,900
Less			
Fixed costs			3,700
Equals			
Profit			3,200

The costs are taken from the revenue in two stages. First, the marginal (variable) cost is subtracted. This leaves the amount of revenue left over after the variable costs have been paid for. The amount left over is called contribution. Following this the fixed costs are taken away to leave us with a profit or loss. Marginal costing theory assumes that the revenue earned from the 5,000 power bars is first used to pay the variable costs (which is sensible). Whatever is left after this determines the amount of contribution. Students in particular get confused by contribution but, put simply, it means 'what remains out of the revenue when the variable costs have been paid'. Consequently, contribution is all that is left to pay the fixed costs.

THE ROLE OF CONTRIBUTION

It is essential that you understand the nature of contribution in order to grasp more advanced calculations within the marginal costing framework.

Earlier we saw that 5,000 power bars were sold for £2 each; total contribution was £6,900; after fixed costs had been paid, a profit of £3,200 remained. If we go back to our opening example where we produced an additional 100 bars and consider that 5,100 power bars had been sold that week, then the revenue, variable costs and most importantly contribution would change.

If we use the marginal costing framework we can work out quite quickly what the new profit figure would be after sales of 5,100 power bars:

	Quantity	× Unit price	= Revenue
Revenue	5,100	2	10,200
Less			
Variable costs		0.62	3,162

	Quantity	× Unit price	= Revenue
Equals			
Contribution		1.38	7,038
Less			
Fixed costs			3,700
Equals			————
Profit			3,338

This illustrates that the new profit figure is £3,338, reflecting an increase of £138 (£3,338–£3,200). Fixed costs have not changed, since the power bars have been made and sold in the same week. Profit therefore increases by the same amount as contribution. Because the fixed element does not change as revenue alters, contribution and profit move up and down by equal amounts (i.e. extra contribution = extra profit).

If we look at this on a unit-by-unit basis, the profit-and-contribution relationship is useful for making quick calculations of the profit effects as output changes and has the potential to make you look very smart in front of your boss. The profit difference if 100 more items are sold will be the contribution gained by selling those extra 100 units. Therefore, if we know the contribution per unit, the extra profit can be calculated from this and the number of items sold (i.e. unit contribution × extra sales = extra profit).

KEY TERM

CONTRIBUTION

The sales value less the variable costs, based on the assumption that the sales value and the variable costs will remain constant.

CONTRIBUTION/SALES RATIO

Before we move on to the uses for you as managers of marginal costing, there is one more concept which you have to grasp. In the sections above we looked at the relationship between contribution and profit, and saw how the two were inextricably linked. There is, however, one more relationship that we need to consider and that is the one between contribution and sales. Many people forget about this relationship, but as we saw in Chapters 8 and 9 it is always worth identifying both the absolute numbers and the percentage relationships, as they often paint conflicting pictures. Understanding this in the context of your role will help you choose the most appropriate reporting method. Consider the following example and note that we have now included an additional column called '% Relationship'. This column details the relationship between sales (always 100) and contribution (in this example 40%). The addition of the variable cost relationship is always a good inclusion, since it provides us with an arithmetical check on our workings (in the example contribution, 40%, plus variable cost, 60%, equals sales, 100%).

	Quantity	Unit price	Revenue	% Relationship
Revenue	100	10	1,000	100
Less				
Variable costs		6	600	60
Equals			_____	
Contribution		4	400	40

Let us look at the effect that an increase in sales has on both contribution, in absolute terms, and the contribution/sales relationship. Imagine that the business sells twenty more items: revenue will increase to £1,200 and the variable costs will increase by the same proportion (i.e. 1/5).

	Quantity	Unit price	Revenue	% Relationship
Revenue	120	10	1,200	100
Less				
Variable costs		6	720	60
Equals			_____	
Contribution		4	480	40

Although the revenue has changed, the proportion of the revenue that is left over as contribution remains the same (i.e. 40%). We call this relationship 'the contribution/sales ratio'. This contribution/sales ratio (C/S ratio) simply means 'the percentage of sales revenue that is left over from contribution'. In the example this is 40 per cent.

Examine the relationship for the original power bar business example above. What is the C/S ratio for our power bar business?

	Quantity	Unit price	Revenue	% Relationship
Revenue	5,000	2	10,000	100
Less				
Variable costs		0.62	3,100	31
Equals			_____	
Contribution		1.38	6,900	69

The C/S ratio is 69 per cent. This relationship holds true for any output level, providing that the unit prices and variable costs do not change. Therefore, one of the uses for this ratio is to calculate the extra contribution resulting from extra sales. For example, if 100 more power bars are sold, the extra contribution will be £138 (as we established earlier).

Extra revenue of 100 bars @ £2 = 200

Extra contribution therefore = 200 × 0.69 = £138. This of course is *profit*.

> **KEY TERM**
>
> ## CONTRIBUTION SALES RATIO
>
> The relationship between contribution and sales revenue. It also means the percentage of sales revenue that is left over as contribution.

BREAKEVEN ANALYSIS

From my point of view this is one of the most important uses of marginal costing which we shall deal with and represents a term that is used widely in all organisations, let alone sporting ones. As we well know, all businesses try to make a profit. However, as we also know, this does not always happen and some companies make substantial losses. By the breakeven (B/E) point we basically mean 'the point at which the firm is no longer in danger of making a loss'. This is therefore an important point to reach. All managers should know where it is and when they have reached it.

Before we get going on this you will need to remember how marginal costing theory works. Revenue first pays for variable costs; this leaves an amount of revenue which we call contribution; next the contribution pays for the fixed costs; and, if any revenue remains, it is profit.

It is often at this point that people ask the question, 'What if contribution only just covers fixed costs?' Under these circumstances all of the costs have been paid, since variable costs are deducted before contribution is derived. The business will therefore make no profit (or loss) – it will have in fact broken even. Consequently, at B/E point *Total revenue = Total costs*. Let us have a look at an example so that you can see how this works in practice:

	£
Revenue	100
Less	
Variable costs	60
Equals	
Contribution	40
Less	
Fixed costs	40
Equals	
Profit (or loss)	0

VC (60) + FC (40) = TC (100), TR = 100   Therefore we have B/E.

If you have followed this you will see that it also stands that at breakeven contribution = fixed costs.

Once you have grasped this concept you can calculate breakeven points relatively easily from marginal costing data. Depending on your responsibilities, it is worth mentioning here that the B/E point may be expressed as:

- the number of items needed to be sold to breakeven, or
- the total sales required to breakeven.

KEY TERM

BREAKEVEN POINT

The level of activity at which there is neither a profit nor a loss. It may be measured in terms of units of production or sales revenue.

ESTABLISHING THE BREAKEVEN POINT IN UNITS

Remember that breakeven occurs when contribution is just enough to cover fixed costs, with nothing left over for profit. So, providing that we know what fixed costs are, the contribution needed for breakeven is known.

ACTIVITY

Imagine that Kitlocker.com sell pairs of running shoes for £25. The marginal cost per unit (i.e. per pair of shoes) is £15. *Remember that marginal cost is another term for variable cost.*

First, what is the contribution per unit?

	£
Unit price	25
Less	
Unit variable cost	15
Equals	
Unit contribution	10

Now assume that the fixed costs are £3,600 for one month's trading. What is the breakeven point in units needed to be sold?

	Quantity	Unit price	Revenue	% Relationship
Revenue	360	25	9,000	100
Less				
Variable cost		15	5,400	60
Equals				
Contribution		10	3,600	40
Less				
Fixed cost			3,600	
Equals				
Profit			0	

If you answered 360 units then you are correct. The following steps were probably used to calculate this figure:

- Fixed costs for one month are £3,600.
- Therefore we need £3,600 in contribution in order to breakeven.
- Therefore when there are enough unit contributions to pay for fixed costs (£3,600) breakeven point occurs.
- Unit contribution = £10.
- So, £3,600/10 = the number of units needed to breakeven = 360.
- One unit contribution can only come from one unit being sold.
- Therefore, if 360 unit contributions are needed to B/E, 360 sales are needed to B/E (i.e. the B/E point is 360 units sold).

This information may also be summarised in a formula:

Breakeven point in units = Fixed costs/Unit contribution

ACTIVITY

Now consider that for the next month a new type of running shoe begins production, replacing the old.

- Fixed costs are £4,800.
- Sale price is £35.
- Variable costs are £21 per unit.

What is the breakeven point in units? First, work out the unit contribution.

	£
Unit price	35
Less	
Unit variable cost	21
Equals	
Unit contribution	14

Now put that information into the marginal costing framework:

	Quantity	Unit price	Revenue	% Relationship
Revenue	343	35	12,000	100
Less				
Variable cost		21	7,200	60
Equals				
Contribution		14	4,800	40
Less				
Fixed cost			4,800	
Equals				
Profit			0	

ESTABLISHING BREAKEVEN POINTS IN REVENUE

As we have already established, there are two ways of calculating the breakeven point: in units or in sales. Your circumstances and level of responsibility will determine which method you need to use but given that you need marginal costing data to calculate them both, it is worth seeing the whole picture. Obviously if the unit selling price is known, together with the number of units needed to be sold to breakeven, it is relatively easy to calculate the breakeven revenue. We saw earlier that, in the running shoes example, the breakeven point was £9,000 per month. That is to say, the company needed to sell 360 pairs of running shoes for £25 per unit to breakeven.

We can express this calculation as a formula:

$$\text{Breakeven revenue} = \text{Breakeven units} \times \text{Unit selling price}$$

In practical business you will usually, if not always, know what the unit selling prices are. However, on the rare occasion that you do not have this information we can use a different method. Consider the following for a business selling bottled water to health and fitness centres. For the next six months, projected costs and revenues are as follows:

	Revenue	% Relationship
Revenue	10,000	100
Less		
Variable cost	6,000	60
Equals		
Contribution	4,000	40
Less		
Fixed cost	2,500	
Equals		
Profit	1,500	

It is still possible to ascertain the breakeven revenue point from this statement. However, we cannot work out the unit contribution because we do not know how many bottles of water the organisation projects itself to sell. What can we do with the information we have to work out the B/E revenue point?

If we use the contribution/sales ratio we can work things out – think about this carefully and work through the next few steps slowly so that you don't miss any of the detail (it is where most of my students tend to go a little bit astray). The C/S ratio is 40 per cent. From this we know that for every £1 of revenue the company generates, 40 pence will be contributed to cover fixed costs. It follows therefore that:

- Contribution from every £1 of revenue = 40p.
- Therefore, the company will breakeven when there are enough 40ps to pay for the fixed costs (i.e. £2,500).
- £2,500/0.40 = 6,250 (i.e. the number of 40ps needed to B/E).
- As 40p of contribution can only come from £1 of sales, and as we need 6,250 lots of 40p to B/E, £6,250 of revenue is required to B/E. Therefore, the B/E revenue point is reached when sales revenue equals £6,250.

See how useful the C/S ratio is!

	Revenue	% Relationship
Revenue	6,250	100
Less		
Variable cost	3,750	60
Equals		
Contribution	2,500	40
Less		
Fixed cost	2,500	
Equals		
Profit	0	

In summary then, when your information is limited, as it was in this example, you must:

- find the contribution per £1 of revenue (use the C/S ratio);
- remember that Breakeven revenue = Fixed costs.

ILLUSTRATING BREAKEVEN ANALYSIS

It is quite easy to calculate breakeven points on a spreadsheet but often it is nice to be able to illustrate such data on a graph. Indeed, if you are ever asked to present your findings of marginal costing, and in particular breakeven, it is much better to paint a picture rather than rely on your own articulation of the key points. Constructing a breakeven graph is quite simple if you follow these steps:

1. Draw a horizontal axis to measure activity in units.
2. Draw a vertical axis to measure costs and revenue (£).
3. Plot a fixed costs line that will run parallel to the horizontal axis.
4. Plot the total costs line (VC+FC).
5. Plot the revenue line.
6. Identify the breakeven point where the revenue and the total cost lines intersect.

We can use the original breakeven example to illustrate this. Kitlocker.com sells pairs of running shoes for £25. The marginal cost per unit (i.e. per pair of shoes) is £15; we suggest that the target revenue is £18,000, making target quantity 720 units. Variable costs will now be £10,800, contribution £7,200 and profit £3,600. The marginal costing statement will now look like this:

	Quantity	Unit price	Revenue	% Relationship
Revenue	720	25	18,000	100
Less				
Variable cost		15	10,800	60
Equals				
Contribution		10	7,200	40
Less				
Fixed cost			3,600	
Equals				
Profit			3,600	

Remember that in the example the BE point in units was 360 and in revenue it was £9,000. Consequently, the graph will look like this:

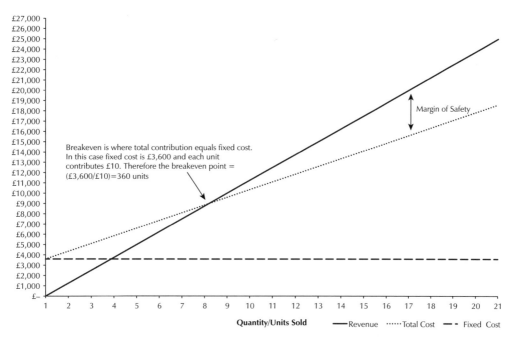

Figure 11.1 Graphical representation of breakeven

COST STRUCTURES

Balancing the levels of fixed and variable costs within total costs can often have a profound effect on the profitability of a business when trading conditions change in times of both growth and recession. Those organisations which manage their cost structure the best will be able to react more effectively in times of change. We have seen that variable costs will automatically decrease as output falls, since they are output-volume sensitive. Fixed costs, on the other hand, are not output-volume sensitive and they do not fall in line with output. Fixed costs can usually be changed by management action. For example, if Kitlocker.com use 50 per cent of their available work space, their fixed costs will remain the same (i.e. they will not reduce by 50 per cent). However, if they decide to sublet the remaining half of their unit their fixed costs will reduce, as someone else will be contributing towards them.

The problem faced by organisations is that fixed costs usually represent the productive capacity of a business (i.e. its capacity to make or sell). After any wasteful expenditure has been cut, a further reduction in fixed costs usually means downsizing the business and therefore limiting its competitiveness. Downsizing can also be a lengthy, painful and difficult process where you will have a serious impact upon the lives of others. However, given that most managers are incapable of identifying a firm's wasteful expenditure, you will find that there is usually scope to reduce fixed costs without cutting output.

To see how different cost structures work in practice we will look at an example. If a business has a large proportion of fixed costs within its total cost portfolio and experiences a sharp downfall in sales revenue, there will be no automatic reduction in fixed costs. Profits will therefore be affected. For example:

	Normal revenue	25% less revenue
Revenue	10,000	7,500
Less		
Variable cost	2,000	1,500
Equals		
Contribution	8,000	6,000
Less		
Fixed cost	7,000	7,000
Equals		
Profit	1,000	(1,000)

Remember that when revenue falls, variable costs will also fall; however, fixed costs do not alter. Therefore, in this situation the organisation moves from a position of profit to one of loss. As a manager you have the responsibility to take action and to reduce fixed costs. Generally, when we talk about cost structures the following rules apply:

- Firms with mainly fixed costs are vulnerable to a downturn in trade.
- Firms with mainly variable costs are far less vulnerable to downturns in trade.

Equally, however:

- Firms with mainly fixed costs and a proportion of spare capacity will benefit from an increase in trade.
- Firms with mainly variable costs will not benefit as much from an increase in trade.

Similar firms with different cost structures will be very differently affected by changes in the demand for their products and services. A firm's cost structure will govern how its profits will react to changes in demand.

MARGIN OF SAFETY

The impact of cost structure can be quantified by another marginal costing technique: margin of safety. This term basically means the 'distance between the breakeven revenue and sales revenue'. For you as managers, this term will be one of the key elements in your decision-making process for short-term developments. A good margin of safety means that you have room to manoeuvre and should help ensure that the odd bad decision can be alleviated. As with breakeven it is possible to calculate the margin of safety quickly and in terms of units or sales. Again it can be calculated as part of the marginal costing framework (which we will look at in a moment) or by formula:

$$\text{Target revenue (or units)} - \text{Breakeven revenue (or units)} = \text{Margin of safety (or units)}$$

To make things clear, the reason for calculating a margin of safety is to quantify how vulnerable a company (or product) is to a downturn in sales volume. A large margin of safety will often mean that, in the short term at least, a reduction in sales will not be a huge problem. However, if you have a small margin of safety, the slightest reduction in sales revenue can cause you immediate and profound problems.

To emphasise this concept and its importance as a technique for you to apply, we will look at another example. Imagine that Kitlocker.com has diversified its business into the market of gum shield production. It has two new product plans and needs to ascertain which is the best plan to use.

	Product A (£)	% Relationship	Product B (£)	% Relationship
Revenue	7,500	100	7,500	100
Less				
Variable costs	2,500	33	4,500	60
Equals				
Contribution	5,000	67	3,000	40
Less				
Fixed costs	4,000		2,000	
Equals				
Profit	1,000		1,000	

It is clear from the above that there are two different cost structures. By definition we now know that there will be different breakeven points.

ACTIVITY

What is the breakeven point in revenue for this example? (I would use the C/S ratio here to make things quicker.)

Breakeven revenue for Product A

(FC/contrib. per unit)

4,000/0.67 = 5,970

Breakeven revenue for Product B

2,000/0.40 = 5,000

We will now examine the distance between the target sales and breakeven revenue (the margin of safety) for each product.

	Product A	Product B
Target revenue	7,500	7,500
Breakeven revenue	5,970	5,000
Margin of safety	1,530	2,500

Product B is arguably the best option given that it has a wider margin of safety. Remember that in most (if not all) instances the product or business with lower fixed costs will always have a higher margin of safety. Moreover, given that it is usually impossible to predict sales, especially for a new product, the margin of safety calculation can be an important consideration.

ACTIVITY

Imagine that you have been appointed as a manager for the gum shield business operating in the previous example. The managing director has decided, with his management accountant, that both products will be sold for £1.50. Calculate, in *units*, their:

- breakeven points
- target sales
- margin of safety

Answers

	Product A	Product B
Target sales (units)	5,000	5,000
Breakeven (units)	4,000	3,333
Margin of safety (units)	1,000	1,667

APPLICATION OF MARGINAL COSTING

While, as a manager, the key functions of marginal costing are to help you establish contribution, breakeven and margin of safety there are a number of other ways we can use it to help us make short-term decisions. You may well find that you are asked to determine which marketing strategy would be more effective, whether to negotiate on price with a major customer or whether to manufacture additional items or buy them in. This chapter is intended to introduce you to the key functions of marginal costing but we will examine these other options briefly as a series of worked examples.

COMPARING ALTERNATIVE MARKETING STRATEGIES

Consider that Kitlocker.com is now involved in the production of high-performance women's swimsuits. The organisation has planned sales and revenues for the next six months:

Output	10,000
Sales price	£60.00
Total costs	£270,000

Kitlocker.com have enough spare capacity to make 12,000 more swimsuits if necessary. Although the total costs for six months, at an output of 10,000 swimsuits, is £270,000, we know that we can break down and classify some of these costs into fixed and variable groups. Below is a breakdown of the planned costs, analysed into the two marginal costing categories identified earlier. *The assumption in this illustration is that there is a 10 per cent bonus element of wages which makes them partly variable.*

	Total (£)	Fixed (£)	Variable (£)
Direct labour	50,000	45,000	5,000
Direct materials	90,000	0	90,000
Indirect materials	20,000	18,000	2,000
Machinery costs	16,000	16,000	
Building establishment	30,000	30,000	
Sales and distribution	32,000	32,000	
Administration	18,000	18,000	
Finance	12,000	12,000	
Sundries	2,000	2,000	
	270,000	173,000	97,000

First, we should establish the unit variable cost which is found by dividing the total variable cost by output. Therefore:

Unit variable cost = 97,000/10,000 = £9.70

Unit variable cost is £9.70.

Having calculated the variable cost figure, we can now transform the current sales and output plan into the marginal costing framework.

	Quantity	× Unit price	= Revenue	% Relationship
Revenue	10,000	60	600,000	100
Less				
Variable costs		9.70	97,000	16
Equals				
Contribution		50.30	503,000	84

181

short-term decision-making

Less	
Fixed costs	173,000
Equals	
Profit	330,000

The basic marketing strategy, namely to manufacture 10,000 high-performance swimsuits in six months and to sell them for £60 each, gives the company a profit of £330,000 (if all goes to plan). However, as we all know, things in business do not always go to plan. The company does, however, have the capacity to produce another 12,000 swimsuits if necessary. As managers, you may wish to consider alternative pricing policies, to make more profit or to put the pressure on competitors to develop your market position or even to gain market share. If we look at another example, what would happen if you were to reduce the price of the swimsuits by £6 to £54, and aimed to sell all 12,000 swimsuits?

We know the marginal cost of the swimsuit (£9.70), so the marginal costing layout makes it very quick and easy to see if this alternative pricing policy is viable from a profit point of view.

	Quantity	× Unit price	= Revenue	% Relationship
Revenue	12,000	54	648,000	100
Less				
Variable costs		9.70	116,400	18
Equals				
Contribution		44.30	531,600	82
Less				
Fixed costs			173,000	
Equals				
Profit (or loss)			358,600	

This is fine, since it shows that the alternative pricing policy would generate an additional £28,000 in profit (£358,000 – £330,000). However, there is a simpler method. If we consider the marginal costing theory which states 'extra contribution equals extra profit', multiplying the new unit price by the new quantity gives us the information required to compare the alternatives.

	Original	Alternative 1
Unit contribution	50.30	44.30
× Quantity	10,000	12,000
Total contribution	503,000	531,600

Assuming that you have your head screwed on it is sensible to state that the option with the highest contribution is the most profitable since the fixed costs do not change. However, let us suppose that another manager wants to beat you to the employee of the month trophy and suggests that the product price could be increased to £70, and 8,000 swimsuits could still be sold.

	Alternative 2
Unit price	£70
Less	
Unit variable cost	£9.70
Equals	
Unit contribution	£60.30
× Quantity	8,000
Equals	
Total contribution	£482,400

Is he going to beat you to the trophy? No! This alternative is a poor suggestion, as the contribution is lower than that of both the original and the first alternative.

EXTRA ORDER PROFITABILITY CALCULATIONS

In business, organisations will often be approached by their most loyal and important customers for special pricing deals. Moreover, it is not uncommon for their suggested prices to be significantly below the average cost of the items. If we look to our example above, the total cost of our 10,000 swimsuits was £270,000, which gives us an average cost of £27 per swimsuit (£270,000/10,000). Questions will arise when a new customer comes to you and says something like 'we like your product, we want 1,600 but we will only pay £44 per swimsuit'. The question here is: what should you do?

At first this would seem to be a bad idea; after all, £44 is £16 less than the sale price of £60. However, you need to remember that you have the capacity to make 12,000 swimsuits; the cost of the extra units will only be the marginal cost so the order may be worth taking providing that it increases contribution.

We need to work out what the contribution will be.

Unit price	£44
Less	
Unit variable cost	£9.70
Equals	
Unit contribution	£34.30
× Quantity	1,600
Equals	
Total contribution	£54,880

This would suggest that the deal is worth accepting, as the contribution, and therefore profit, will rise by £54,880. The full marginal costing layout would be as follows.

	Quantity	× Unit price	= Revenue	% Relationship
Revenue	10,000	60	600,000	100
Extra revenue	1,600	44	70,400	100
Less				
Variable costs		9.70	97,000	16
Extra variable costs		9.70	15,520	22
Equals				
Contribution		50.30	503,000	84
Extra contribution		34.30	54,880	78
Less				
Fixed costs			173,000	
Extra FC			0	
Equals				
Profit (or loss)			330,000	
Extra profit (loss)			54,880	

MAKE OR BUY DECISIONS

In times of growth it is usual for organisations to have a desire to expand output. Consequently, it must choose whether to expand its own production facilities (i.e. buy more machinery, employ more people) or to contract other firms to do the work for them. This can be a tricky decision, especially when you think back to the things we discussed in the cost structure section, since the organisation will not want to leave itself vulnerable to a downturn in trade. In marginal costing terms this may mean that a company can increase output without incurring additional fixed or even variable costs. The decision will be important because it will affect the strategic ability of a business to withstand times of difficulty.

When a company is expanding, one of the things it will/must bear in mind when deciding whether to expand by making or buying more items is the effect the process will have on its cost structure. This apart, the cost per unit of manufacturing (compared to that of buying) will be the major influence on the managers'/management decision. There are two possible situations managers will face when considering whether to manufacture extra items:

1. when a firm has existing, idle facilities that could be used to generate extra output;
2. when a 'green field' site would be needed to make extra output (i.e. a new facility/workforce and machines).

Output increases with idle facilities available

Under these circumstances we need only consider the extra (marginal) cost incurred. For example, imagine that the power bar business that we used earlier has two workshops, one of which is not being used. The existing fixed costs (FCs) are allocated as follows.

	Workshop 1 (in use)	Workshop 2 (idle)	Total
One month's FCs	£3,700	£1,500	£5,200

There is a new management team in place at the company and they are considering using the second workshop to produce 2,000 extra power bars. The costs and sale price are: sale price £2, three extra employees £900 per month, direct materials 75p per bar. Extra costs are therefore:

Direct labour	£900
Direct materials	£1,500
Marginal cost of extra items	£2,400

The alternative would be to subcontract the work out to another company at a cost of £1.15 per power bar. As a manager, you would need to establish whether it would be better from a cost point of view to buy in the extra output or manufacture it.

	Quantity	Unit price (£)	Make
Revenue	2,000	2	4,000
Less			
Variable cost		0.62	1,240
Equals			
Contribution		1.38	2,760
Less			
Fixed costs			1,500
Equals			
Profit			1,260

	Quantity	Unit price (£)	Buy
Revenue	2,000	2	4,000
Less			
Variable cost		1.15	2,300
Equals			
Contribution		0.85	1,700

Less

Fixed costs   1,500

Equals

Profit   200

	Quantity	Unit price (£)	Do nothing
Revenue	0	0	0
Less			
Variable cost		0	0
Equals			
Contribution		0	0
Less			
Fixed costs			1,500
Equals			
Profit (loss)			(1,500)

Obviously the company would be worst off by doing nothing, as it has to pay for the fixed costs (£1,500) per month. The second best option would be to subcontract the work, as that would cover fixed costs and achieve a profit of £200. The best option would be to produce the extra units themselves, as this yields a profit of £1,260.

Output increase needing new production facilities

The total cost of the extra output produced by the new factory must be compared with buying-in costs. Marginal and variable costs will differ here because the additional fixed costs will have to be included.

Our organisation producing running shoes may wish to consider the following alternatives:

- to build or rent a new factory and machinery, and train staff in order to make a new range of running shoes;
- to subcontract the work.

If we imagine that there is a demand to produce 12,000 pairs of shoes per year, each pair has a sale price of £25. Variable costs are £14 per unit and extra fixed costs would be £48,000 per year. If the work was subcontracted the shoes could be bought for £19. We can evaluate the two options and see that it is a much better proposition to manufacture the shoes:

	Quantity	Unit price (£)	Make
Revenue	12,000	25	300,000
Less			

Variable cost		14	168,000
Equals			
Contribution		11	132,000
Less			
Fixed costs			48,000
Equals			
Profit (loss)			84,000

	Quantity	Unit price (£)	Buy
Revenue	12,000	25	300,000
Less			
Variable cost		19	228,000
Equals			
Contribution		6	72,000
Less			
Fixed costs			0
Equals			
Profit (loss)			72,000

SUMMARY

Marginal costing is a cost accounting technique that only takes account of the variable costs of production when calculating the cost per unit. Throughout this chapter you have seen how to use a marginal costing statement to calculate important functions such as contribution, breakeven and margin of safety. The guiding principles of marginal costing and cost behaviour state that variable costs are only incurred when production (or sales) take place while fixed costs will be incurred whether trading takes place or not. You must remember, however, that we have been dealing with short-term decisions here and that costs often will, and do, change in the medium to long term.

You can use marginal costing to determine the costs of products or services, the calculation of how many units or sales you need to achieve to cover costs (breakeven), and the potential outputs and benefits of alternative projects. Moreover, you have seen that marginal costing techniques go beyond basic cost accounting and can influence marketing strategies, production methods and whether to offer incentives to customers.

Contribution is a key component of any pricing strategy and should be considered both in its absolute terms (by unit and in total) and by its relationship to sales revenue. Any change in contribution will have a direct influence on profit and therefore decisions should be implemented where an increase in contribution can be established.

QUESTIONS FOR REVIEW

1. What is the definition of a marginal cost?
2. What is the definition of contribution?
3. What is a breakeven point and how can it be measured?
4. How can cost structures have an effect on an organisation?
5. Suppose a company producing and selling mountain bikes has the following projected costs for the next three months:

	Revenue	% Relationship
Revenue	444,000	100
Less		
Variable cost	236,000	53
Equals		
Contribution	208,000	47
Less		
Fixed cost	151,000	
Equals		
Profit	57,000	

What is the breakeven point in revenue?

REFERENCES AND FURTHER READING

Collins, J. and Hussey, R. (2007) *Business Accounting: An Introduction to Financial and Management Accounting.* Palgrave Macmillan, Basingstoke.

Knott, G. (2004) *Financial Management*, 4th edn. Palgrave Macmillan, Basingstoke.

Russell, D., Patel, A. and Wilkinson-Riddle, G. (2002) *Cost Accounting: An Essential Guide.* Financial Times Press, Harlow.

CHAPTER 12

BUDGETING AND BUDGETARY CONTROL

On completion of this chapter you will be able to:

- describe the main purposes of marginal costing;
- describe the meaning of budgeting in operational, tactical and strategic contexts;
- express budget compilation in terms of a logically progressive sequence of stages;
- differentiate between continuation and zero-based budgeting and their relative appropriateness in given situations;
- apply recognised budgeting techniques to the construction of budget statements;
- analyse budgeted against actual performance using recognised evaluation techniques.

INTRODUCTION

This chapter examines the importance and the process of budgeting as a management discipline in sport. From an 'importance' perspective, budgeting is an integral part of an organisation's operational, tactical and strategic planning. Consequently it is vital that those of you looking to build a career in the sport industry should have an appropriate level of knowledge and skill in budgeting. This important skill will help you to contribute meaningfully to your organisation's business objectives. While it would be unreasonable to expect a single chapter of a book to be a one-stop shop for all you need to know about budgeting, it is possible for it to provide a sound overview of the subject.

Practical examples drawn from a variety of sports management scenarios are used to illustrate the theoretical points being made throughout the chapter. We start by using some case study material drawn from events in 2009/2010 to illustrate what can happen if budgeting is ineffective.

CASE STUDY

FIRST PRINCIPLES AND PORTSMOUTH FOOTBALL CLUB'S FINANCIAL CRISIS

Regardless of the sector of sport in which a business operates, whether it is a small voluntary sector club, a local authority swimming pool or a stock market-listed company, it is vital that an organisation's management underpin their activities by using the techniques of budgeting. There are two key questions to which all businesses should be able to respond positively.

First, 'is the selling price higher than the cost?' That is, is the organisation making a profit? For non-profit-making organisations such as members' sports clubs and local authority facilities we can modify the first question to: 'is the organisation operating within the resources allocated to it?' We understand in the context of our own lives that if we live beyond our means, that is, if we do not operate within our resources, then varying degrees of problems will follow. Initially we may experience a cash flow problem, next we might become burdened with interest payments we are unable to meet; and finally we end up being declared 'bankrupt'. The same analysis is applicable to businesses that do not operate within their resources. If we cast our minds back to the events of 2008/2009 a significant number of Football League clubs were experiencing acute financial difficulties following the collapse of the Setanta Sports contract for television rights to Premier League and Football League matches. From Setanta's perspective liquidation occurred because significantly fewer people subscribed to the service than the company had originally forecast. Less revenue than expected resulted in an inability to pay the clubs what they had been promised and led to Setanta being 'liquidated' (i.e. its assets were sold in order to release cash to pay its creditors). From the perspective of the football clubs, the Setanta deal offered a higher level of guaranteed income for a number of years. Many clubs entered into expensive financial commitments based on this guaranteed income such as players' wages and stadium improvements. When the 'guaranteed' income failed to materialise as Setanta went into administration, a number of clubs were unable to meet their own commitments and themselves became candidates for financial failure. Setanta's demise was triggered by its failure to meet a £3 million payment to the Scottish Premier League and a £10 million payment to the Premier League in England. Conditions in the contracts between the Premier League and Setanta led to an auction whereby the rights that Setanta held were sold off to the highest bidder. Sir Robin Miller, chairman of Setanta, was quoted as saying:

> This is a sad day for all concerned. Since its inspired inception a number of years ago, Setanta and its financial backers have invested hundreds of millions of pounds buying up UK and international sports rights. With the hard work and dedication of its staff, a pay-TV broadcaster was created which entertained people in three million homes with top-class sport. Unfortunately, in a difficult and highly competitive market, and despite strenuous efforts by the board and management, it has not been possible to find sufficient additional funds in the time available to ensure its survival.

Rarely has there been such a high-profile example to illustrate the point that the selling price must be higher than the cost. In the case of Setanta, the revenue generated from their three million household subscriptions was not sufficient to pay their 200 employees and the property rights holders such as the SPL and EPL. When costs exceed revenue such that a business is no longer viable, an inevitable spiral of decline follows.

The second question all businesses must answer is, 'is the business well set to continue trading?' In practical terms the second question is a reference to a firm's ability to pay its creditors as they fall due and having the autonomy to pursue policies of its own unfettered by external influences. Many business failures are not because there is limited demand for the product. One of the principal causes of business failure is that despite high demand for a product, the organisation runs out of cash and is unable to meet its obligations. In some cases, despite being profitable, a business may be 'highly geared'; that is, it has a high level of borrowing. A situation can arise whereby the providers of loans have more control over a business than the shareholders. A classic example is the way in which football clubs borrow against the value of their stadium or playing squad in order to help meet day-to-day operational costs. When the providers of loans become nervous about their debtors' ability to pay, they may call in a loan or force the business to make a decision that is not in its best long-term interests. Portsmouth Football Club incurred debts of over £60 million building up a squad of players thought good enough to compete in the Premier League in England. After winning the FA Cup in 2008, the club then went on to mount a promising campaign in the UEFA Cup, narrowly missing out on qualification for the last thirty-two following a 2-2 draw with AC Milan. Everything seemed to be going to plan for the unfashionable south coast team and yet fifteen months after playing AC Milan, the club was placed into administration, incurring a nine-point penalty which almost certainly ensured relegation. The financial warning signs had been on the wall for some time and are a classic example of what happens when businesses get into difficulty. Players and other club staff were not paid their wages on time, some of the best and highest-earning players were sold off during transfer windows; and money that should have come to the club from the Premier League was paid to clubs owed money by Portsmouth. In the meantime the club changed hands four times during the 2009/2010 season and the manager Paul Hart was sacked after a run of poor performances that left the club bottom of the Premier League. The final indignity came in February 2010 when Her Majesty's Revenue and Customs, to whom millions of pounds was owed in tax payments, filed a winding-up petition against the club in the courts, which in turn led to the club being placed into administration. In short, Portsmouth Football Club could not be described as being well placed to carry on trading, and this situation has been caused directly by the club living beyond its financial means.

Successful organisations need to operate within their resources, pay their bills as they fall due, and have effective control over their business activities. This case study illustrates what can happen when these conditions are not met. The remainder of this chapter illustrates how the use of budgeting and budgetary control techniques can help businesses to answer these two questions positively.

THE MEANING OF BUDGETING

Budgeting is a subject area that takes its roots from the field of management accounting as it helps management plan, make decisions and exercise control. Budgeting may be shown to be part of the overall planning process for a business by defining it as 'the overall plan of a business expressed in financial terms'. These plans may involve trying to achieve a pre-determined level of financial performance such as a profit of £x over the year, or having sufficient cash resources to be able to replace the equipment in a gym. Organisational business planning may be summarised as an analysis of four key questions:

1. Where are we now?
2. How did we get here?
3. Where are we going?
4. How are we going to get there?

To illustrate the link between general business planning and budgeting, the question 'where are we now?' can be modified to 'where are we now in financial terms?' Similarly the question 'where are we going?' can be modified to 'where are we going in financial terms?' To diagnose where a business *is* in financial terms requires the ability to be able to 'read' an income statement (profit and loss account), a balance sheet and a cash flow statement. To predict where a business is going is difficult (as is any attempt to predict the future), but techniques such as compiling an expected income statement (profit and loss account), balance sheet and cash flow can help to focus attention on the business essentials. Furthermore, the very process of planning ahead using budgets can help to test whether what you wish to achieve and the accompanying financial consequences are compatible or 'internally consistent'. The concept of internal consistency will be covered in the following section, but let us complete this section by being clear that the meaning of budgeting is 'the overall plan of a business expressed in financial terms'.

Budgeting as a logically sequenced planning process

A key point about budgeting is that it is an ongoing process rather than a time-limited one-off event. The actual mechanics of drawing up the numbers involved in a budget are but a small part of the overall budgeting process. By bearing in mind that budgeting is designed to help an organisation with planning, decision-making and control, it is possible to appreciate that budgeting is a continuous part of business life. This point is reinforced by viewing budgeting as steps in a logically sequenced planning process, as shown in Figure 12.1.

Figure 12.1 can be reinforced by a commentary on each of the nine stages of budgeting.

Define your business objectives

The first question to ask when involved with any financial business planning is 'in monetary terms, what are we trying to achieve?' This question should provide a clue: most sane business people would not answer by saying 'making a loss'. Losses are made in business but it is inconceivable to imagine that managers set out deliberately to make losses. Losses normally occur when there is a mismatch between what was planned and what happened in reality. Organisational objectives will vary according to the nature of the business. A community sports club which exists for the benefit of its members may desire nothing more

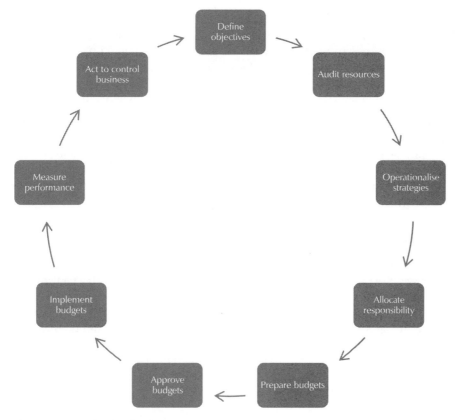

Figure 12.1 The budgeting process

than to breakeven or to make a small surplus to maintain its existing facilities. A more complex organisation such as a professional football team needs to balance the requirements of producing a successful team on the pitch (utility maximisation) with the requirements of being a commercial franchise (profit maximisation). Whatever the objectives of an organisation, they need to have certain qualities that enable them to be measured. These qualities are contained within the mnemonic 'MASTER':

Measurable   e.g. a profit of £3 million in the financial year, or simply breakeven;
Achievable   the organisation must have the capability to attain its objectives; capability means staff, other resources, and competitive advantage;
Specific   objectives must be specific (e.g. £3 million profit), not just 'to do well this year';
Time limited   objectives must have a stated date for being achieved;
Ends related   objectives must relate to achieving outputs (ends) rather than describing means (how);
Ranked   ideally objectives should be ranked in priority order.

An example of an objective meeting the MASTER mnemonic might be: 'Our first priority is to achieve a net profit of £3 million in the financial year 1 April 2009 to 31 March 2010. This target is considered to be attainable as the organisation has increased its capacity and the market is expanding.'

Audit resources

The audit of resources is a 'reality check' on the objectives. Its purpose is to ensure that the objectives and the resources required to achieve them are internally consistent. As an example, Sheffield United need around 15,000 spectators per home match to breakeven. With a stadium capacity of nearly 31,000, it is clear that 15,000 people may be accommodated at a home match so long as they are attracted to the match in the first place.

Where there is a discrepancy between the objectives and the resources available to achieve them, two courses of action are possible. First, the objectives can be changed so that they are compatible with the resources. Second, the gap between the resources available and the resources required can form the basis for prioritising capital investment such as increasing the capacity of a stadium, or identifying training and development needs to ensure that staff have the skills to deliver what is required of them.

Operationalise strategies

Having defined what you want to achieve and confirmed that you have the resources to deliver the objectives, the budgeting process evolves to consider the day-to-day tactics to be used to meet the objectives. In private health and fitness clubs these might include marketing plans, pricing policies, customer care protocols and opening hours. If organisational objectives can be regarded as 'what' we wish to achieve, then operational strategies can be regarded as 'how' we plan to achieve the objectives. Thus a football club aiming for an average match day turnover of £300,000 might set out to achieve it via operational strategies for spectators, corporate hospitality customers, programme sales, half-time draw tickets, catering and beverage sales, merchandising sales and car parking.

Allocate responsibility

The successful achievement of objectives does not occur by chance, or as a result of a mechanical exercise. Sport is primarily a service industry and the most important people in determining the extent to which objectives are met are an organisation's staff. In order for people to see where their contributions fit into an organisation's overall plan, they need to have agreed responsibility for particular areas of work. Agreed responsibility is particularly important in situations where staff can be rewarded, or indeed punished, on the basis of their performance. For example, basic performance for a sales adviser in a health club might be twenty new peak-time members per month, with incentives available if the basic target is exceeded. By contrast, a private sector company managing a leisure facility on behalf of a local authority might be punished by deductions from its management fee for not meeting the terms of its agreement, for example cleanliness standards. If it is known and clearly stated 'who is going to do what and by when', then there is the basis for a meaningful comparison of actual performance with planned or expected performance.

Preparation of budgets

It is worth noting that the actual preparation of budgets does not occur until the mid-point of the budgeting process. This is important because it makes the point that budgeting is not an isolated process and is integral to overall business planning. When preparing a budget there are two important considerations, namely 'how much' income or expenditure, and 'when' the income or expenditure will occur. To illustrate the point, if an average swimming pool is expecting 52,000 admissions per year at an average price of £4, then the answer to 'how much income will be generated?' is £208,000. However, it is unlikely that a pool will average 1,000 admissions per week for fifty-two weeks. There will be peak times such as during school holidays and half-terms, and off-peak times such as during the winter when it is cold and there are shortened hours of daylight. Thus in order to make sure that the appropriate level of resources (e.g. staff) are in the right place at the right time, it will be necessary to plan the predicted level of activity on a week-by-week or month-by-month basis. Conducting such an exercise will enable managers to plan ahead for situations where expenditure is greater than income and there is insufficient cash to meet the shortfall. Having identified situations requiring management attention, strategies can be put in place to deal with them such as negotiating an overdraft facility at the bank, rescheduling expenditure on capital items, or simply not paying creditors on time. The important point to note is that the process of budgeting identifies potential problems in advance of their occurring so that pre-emptive action may be taken.

It is unlikely that at the first time of asking the figures produced in the preparation of budgets will deliver the outcomes required. Therefore managers may be asked to revise their budgets in such a way that the desired outcome is achieved. In practice there are five ways in which a budget may be revised.

1. Increase revenue and keep costs constant. This could be achieved by increasing prices, increasing throughput, or a combination of the two methods. The key assumption here is that any increase in price will not be offset by a reduction in demand.
2. Decrease expenditure and keep income constant. This could be achieved by making savings on non-essential expenditure or reducing the quality of the service on offer (e.g. fewer staff on duty).
3. Increase income *and* decrease costs, as 1 and 2 above are not necessarily mutually exclusive.
4. Alter the financial outcome required. It may be that it is not possible to bring the required outcomes and the budget into line by using 1, 2 and 3 above. Therefore rather than alter income and expenditure, management may decide to alter the financial outcome required. This approach can work both positively and negatively. If staff provide managers with a budget that exceeds the required bottom line and the assumptions underpinning the budget are correct, then it would make sense to increase the overall budget target accordingly. A much more likely scenario is that the targeted outcome cannot be met by revisions to income and expenditure and management agree to settle for a reduced financial outcome, for example an annual profit of £2.9 million rather than £3.0 million.
5. Change the overall business objectives. It may well be the case that it is impossible to arrive at an acceptable solution to a budget using steps 1 to 4 above. Under these conditions it may be that the required outcomes and the organisation's capabilities are not compatible. The only remaining alternative is to change the organisation's objectives. As an example, it is often the case that private contractors managing local authority sport facilities are required to meet social as well as financial objectives. On occasion, pursuit of these differing aims may be mutually incompatible in the sense that programming activities for priority groups at certain times prevents revenue maximisation. Every use of resources has an opportunity cost; that is, the price of the best alternative forgone. Thus

in order to make the budget balance, it may be that some priorities which are no doubt desirable and equitable have to be sacrificed to the cause of wider business interests. For this reason, it is important that where possible objectives are ranked (see 'R' in the MASTER mnemonic above).

The significance of preparing a budget, comparing it with business objectives and taking corrective action where appropriate indicates the importance of achieving internal consistency. Using the budgeting model described thus far ensures that what an organisation wishes to achieve in overall terms and the financial consequences of doing so are consistent. If potential problems can be identified at the planning (input) stage pre-emptive action may be taken by drawing up plans to deal with adverse circumstances. Clearly this approach has a greater chance of success and is more desirable than trying to deal with situations reactively as they materialise without prior warning. The process of modelling the financial consequences of various scenarios until an acceptable outcome is achieved is known as an 'iterative' approach, or in less scientific terms, 'trial and error'.

Approval of budgets

Once an acceptable match has been achieved between an organisation's business objectives and the financial consequences of those objectives, a line needs to be drawn under the preparation of budgets stage. The point at which this line is drawn is at the approval of budgets stage, which effectively puts an end to the various iterations of the budget and leads to the formal adoption of the budget which the organisation wishes to pursue. It is recognised good practice for the approval of a budget to be formalised in the minutes of a board or committee meeting. Furthermore, budgets should be approved in advance of the financial period to which they relate. The wider significance of a budget being approved formally is that those who have compiled it and those whose performance will in part be judged by it know exactly what their responsibilities are. This in turn has two benefits. First, if you know what is expected of you, evaluation of performance can be objective rather than subjective. Second, expectation generates accountability which in turn gives managers the focus to concentrate on those things which are important in terms of meeting the organisation's objectives.

Implementation of budgets

As a logical consequence of a budget being approved, it can be implemented with effect from the date to which it applies. For example, if an organisation's financial year operates from 1 April to 31 March, it would be a reasonable expectation for the budget to be approved by the committee or board at least a month before the new financial year started. A less than ideal situation would be an organisation entering a financial period without an approved budget, which would be the managerial equivalent of trying to operate a boat without a rudder.

Measurement of performance

To reinforce the notion of budgeting being integral to overall business planning, it is vital to realise that the budgeting process does not end once the preparation and implementation phases are over. Once the budget is operational, it is essential that, periodically (say, at least monthly), a check is made of how the organisation is actually performing compared with how it planned to perform. One of the greatest motivators in life is feedback and the same is true in budgeting. Management accountants use the mnemonic CARROT as a way of categorising the features of good-quality information for feedback purposes. Each component of CARROT is explained below.

Concise   Information fed back to managers needs to be to the point.
Accurate   Feedback is used for planning, decision-making and control purposes; therefore it follows that feedback should be error free.
Reliable   Similar to 'accurate', the same results of an actual versus budget comparison should be obtained if different people carried out the analysis, i.e. the source information is robust.
Relevant   Different levels of management require different levels of information; therefore feedback should be presented in terms that are relevant to the intended recipient.
Objective   Feedback should be concerned with verifiable factual evidence and not with individual interpretation of findings.
Timely   There is a trade-off between timeliness and accuracy; none the less, feedback should be received in sufficient time for it to be of value in terms of planning, decision-making and control purposes.

Measurement of performance is not an end in itself and is only valuable as an exercise if it is used to add value to the process of management in an organisation.

Taking action to control the business

If we accept that rational decisions require information that meets the requirements of the CARROT mnemonic, the final stage of the budgeting process is to use the information to inform the direction of the organisation. It is highly unlikely that there will be a perfect match between budget and actual comparisons, so the first decision to make is whether or not overall variance is within a tolerable range. If variances are tolerable, then significant changes in policy will be unlikely. By contrast, if variances are considered to be so significant that the organisation is 'out of control' (in financial terms), then pro-active management action may be needed. On a positive note, if performance is considerably ahead of target, it may be prudent to revise targets upwards. If, however, actual versus budget comparisons reveal a significant shortfall in performance, corrective action may be needed. Such action might include extra marketing to increase sales, reducing price to stimulate sales, improving the quality of sales to boost repeat business, or more predictably, cutting costs to try and maintain profit margins.

In concluding this section it is worth making two points relating to the assertion that budgeting is a logically sequenced planning process.

1   Budgeting is a process designed to help managers make sensible decisions about running their organisations. It helps to inform decisions but clearly budgeting is not in itself a decision-making process.
2   Compiling a budget is an iterative process. It is unlikely that the first draft of a budget will produce an acceptable result. Various scenarios will be modelled and differing assumptions tested until an acceptable solution is found. Figure 12.1 is a simple model of an ideal process; in practice the numerous iterations will result in a more complicated

picture. However, the basic point is that each step of the model is a reality check on the previous step, which is designed to ensure that an organisation's overall plans and the financial consequences of those plans are internally consistent.

Although Figure 12.1 implies a step-by-step approach to compiling a budget, in reality some steps are seamless. For example, defining your objectives (step 1), conducting an audit of resources (2) and devising operational strategies (step 3) are likely to be interrelated and to occur simultaneously.

Common methods of budgeting

In this section, 'methods of budgeting' refers to types of budgeting processes and behavioural aspects of budgeting. In terms of budgeting processes there are two common ways in which budgets tend to be compiled. The most frequently used budgeting process is 'continuation' budgeting (or business as usual) and the other, somewhat rarer, process is 'zero-based budgeting' (ZBB). Continuation budgeting refers to situations whereby the business objectives of an organisation do not change significantly from one financial period to the next. Under these circumstances, it makes perfect sense to continue with essentially the same business objectives and hence the same approach to budgeting. An example of a continuation budget might be a voluntary sector sports club whose main aim is to breakeven and to provide a service to the membership. If the club's basic operations lead to a situation whereby the selling price is higher than the cost, then apart from increasing membership subscriptions and bar prices to keep up with inflation, there is no point wasting time and resources on a more complicated approach to the club's finances. Continuation budgeting is also referred to as 'incremental' or 'decremental' budgeting. Incremental budgeting refers to a situation whereby an organisation increases its income and expenditure, usually by the rate of inflation, in order to pursue its existing policies. Decremental budgeting refers to a situation whereby an organisation agrees to either a standstill level of funding (a cut in real terms) or an absolute decrease in funding. When faced with a decremental budget, managers have the problem of deciding whether to pursue existing policies with fewer resources; to reduce funding to all policies by the same relative amount ('the equal misery' approach); or to cut funding to some activities in order to preserve the more highly ranked priorities (see R in the MASTER mnemonic above). An example of a simple continuation budget for a professional rugby club is shown in Figure 12.2.

The basic assumptions in Figure 12.2 are that the club will pursue the same policies from one year to the next and will increase income and expenditure by the rate of inflation (in this case 3 per cent). Thus all that has happened to the numbers in the budget is that they have increased by 3 per cent. There are some advantages and disadvantages of using continuation budgeting and these are highlighted below.

Advantages of continuation budgeting

- Continuation budgeting is intuitively simple and easy to understand.
- It is an effective use of resources if business objectives, infrastructure and strategies have remained unchanged.
- It is quick and easy to update figures and budget templates that are readily to hand.
- It requires fewer staff resources and therefore costs less than zero-based budgeting.

Figure 12.2 Rugby club continuation budget

INCOME	This year	Inflation	Next year
Season ticket sales	1,080,000	3%	1,112,400
Other ticket sales	250,000	3%	257,500
Television revenue	900,000	3%	927,000
Sponsorship	160,000	3%	164,800
Catering	220,000	3%	226,600
Merchandising	130,000	3%	133,900
Total income	2,740,000	3%	2,822,200
EXPENDITURE			
Players' wages	1,700,000	3%	1,751,000
Ground expenditure	218,000	3%	224,540
Marketing activities	136,000	3%	140,080
Administration	342,000	3%	352,260
Other expenses	302,000	3%	311,060
Total expenditure	2,698,000	3%	2,778,940
PROFIT/(LOSS)	42,000	3%	43,260

Disadvantages of continuation budgeting

- The overall rate of inflation within a country does not necessarily equal the rate of inflation within a particular industry and therefore the use of the headline inflation figure to increase budgets is somewhat crude.
- Continuation budgeting does not encourage growth in real terms. In Figure 12.2 the net position is that the business stands still. Businesses need to grow in real terms to remain competitive and to have the resources to maintain their operating infrastructure.
- Changes may be occurring within the marketplace which require change such as the application of internet technology and e-marketing. By not taking advantage of business opportunities as they present themselves, standing still may actually be going backwards relative to your competitors.
- There is the danger that if income and expenditure budgets are not challenged occasionally then targets are 'soft' rather than a fair test of an organisation's capabilities. Managers can build 'slack' (unnecessary expenditure) into budgets which can be 'rewarded' when budgets for the following year are confirmed without detailed scrutiny.

Despite the fact that continuation budgeting is by far the most commonly used budgeting technique, if an organisation is facing a fundamental change to its operating circumstances, a more analytical approach may be needed. Rather than starting with the previous year's budget and updating it, the zero-based budget starts with a blank piece of paper and challenges every item of income and expenditure. An example of zero-based budgeting questions might be:

KEY TERMS

BUDGET

The business or overall plan of an organisation expressed in financial terms.

CASH BUDGET

An analysis of how the cash available to an organisation is expected to change over a given period of time.

CONTINUATION BUDGET

Budgets compiled on the basis of no change in policies or priorities (i.e. business as usual).

VARIANCE

The difference between actual performance and planned performance.

ZERO-BASED BUDGETING

A method of budgeting which starts with the priorities of an organisation and allocates resources to those priorities according to their rank order of importance.

1. What is the purpose of this expenditure?
2. On what exactly will this expenditure be made?
3. What are the quantifiable benefits of this expenditure?
4. What are the alternatives to this proposed expenditure?
5. What would be the outcome of cutting this expenditure completely?

In order for funds to be allocated to a given item of expenditure, a robust defence would have to be made for the expenditure through the five questions listed above. If some expenditure was not defendable, then it might be cut and re-allocated to more deserving areas of an organisation's activities. As an example, consider the case of a large professional football club that runs its own laundry to wash and iron players' kit. The laundry will make use of staff, space, equipment, energy and consumables – all of which cost money. Furthermore, in the long run equipment will need to be replaced and service contracts will have to be in place in case machinery breaks down. If commercial laundry facilities were available locally, which could match the quality of service provided in-house at a cheaper price, then not only would

the club save money, it could also use the staff, space and other resources released on more important business objectives. Clearly using the zero-based approach would be a more rigorous way of questioning existing business practices than simply accepting that the club has always provided an in-house laundry and will continue to do so.

The purpose of zero-based budgeting is the allocation of resources in a systematic manner which is consistent with an organisation's wider business objectives. It makes an implicit assumption that people within an organisation act rationally and prioritise business objectives rather than personal agendas – sometimes this can be a very ambitious assumption. Compared with continuation budgeting, zero-based budgeting is resource intensive and therefore can be wasteful if there has been no significant change in business objectives and operating procedures. It is therefore unsafe to make sweeping generalisations about one budgeting process being better than another. As in many instances of using applied management techniques, the best methods are the ones most appropriate to the circumstances faced by an organisation. Therefore, if a business is stable with no major changes on the horizon, continuation budgeting might be the best method to use. By contrast, if a business requires a major strategic overhaul, then zero-based budgeting might be the best method to use. As with many things in life, compromise can help to keep most of the people happy for most of the time. So, too, a business could use continuation budgeting most of the time, but once every three or five years a zero-based approach could be used to challenge the status quo and re-allocate resources to where they are most needed.

In addition to being familiar with methods of budgeting such as continuation or zero-based approaches, it is also important to realise the human dimension of budgeting. Sport is a people business and ultimately the extent to which business objectives are realised depends on the extent of staff motivation towards meeting targets. One of the great de-motivators in life is having targets imposed upon you from above (top-down) without consultation. Equally, for management there is nothing more depressing than letting staff set their own budgets and finding out that the so-called 'bottom-up' budgets do not deliver the organisation's overall business objectives. The compromise approach is a participatory budgeting style whereby all staff members whose performance will in part be judged by meeting the budget have some influence in the compilation of the figures by which they will be judged. There are no hard-and-fast rules about when to use 'top-down', 'bottom-up' or 'participatory' methods. Good managers need to have a broad range of skills and techniques in their managerial toolboxes. Furthermore, these skills and techniques should be used in a context-sensitive manner, contingent upon the particular circumstances of the business and its operating environment.

APPLYING BUDGETING TO WORKED EXAMPLES

Business organisations report a summary of their financial transactions in three standard formats:

1. the income statement (previously called the profit and loss account (or income and expenditure statement in the case of non-profit organisations));
2. the balance sheet;
3. the cash flow statement.

As you know, the income statement is a measure of an organisation's financial performance; the balance sheet is a measure of financial position; and the cash flow statement illustrates how the cash available to an organisation has changed over a given period of time. In financial terms, the answers to the questions 'where are we now?' and 'where are we going?' may be seen by constructing an income statement, balance sheet and cash flow statement to show the change between the starting point and the ending point. In this section, examples of each financial statement are modelled and issues relating to them discussed. Perhaps most importantly, the linkages and non-linkages between the statements are also illustrated.

The income statement

Figure 12.3 repeats the first two columns from Figure 12.2 and shows how a small rugby club might produce a summary of its income statement. The key message emerging from Figure 12.3 is that the club is planning to make a profit of £42,000 during the financial year.

The problem with Figure 12.3 is that a year is a long time and it is unlikely that income and expenditure will occur at the same rate throughout the year; that is, the budget does not tell you when profits or losses will occur. Many businesses are seasonal and will have peaks and troughs in terms of their level of activity. This in turn has implications for other areas of management such as staff scheduling, the purchase of fixed assets and cash flow management. If the data in Figure 12.3 were to be allocated over twelve months on the basis of when such income and expenditure were predicted to occur, the monthly budget would resemble the example shown in Figure 12.4.

INCOME	This year
Season ticket sales	1,080,000
Other ticket sales	250,000
Television revenue	900,000
Sponsorship	160,000
Catering	220,000
Merchandising	130,000
Total income	2,740,000
EXPENDITURE	
Players' wages	1,700,000
Ground expenditure	218,000
Marketing activities	136,000
Administration	342,000
Other expenses	302,000
Total expenditure	2,698,000
PROFIT/(LOSS)	42,000

Figure 12.3
An income statement

	Aug	Sept	Oct	Nov	Dec	Jan	Feb	March	April	May	June	July	Total
INCOME													
Season ticket sales	540,000	540,000	0	0	0	0	0	0	0	0	0	0	1,080,000
Other ticket sales	30,000	24,000	22,000	32,000	40,000	36,000	30,000	18,000	18,000	0	0	0	250,000
Television revenue	0	0	400,000	0	0	100,000	0	0	0	0	400,000	0	900,000
Sponsorship	80,000	0	0	0	0	0	40,000	0	0	0	0	40,000	160,000
Catering	18,000	22,000	20,000	24,000	28,000	26,000	20,000	14,000	16,000	12,000	10,000	10,000	220,000
Merchandising	12,000	10,000	12,000	16,000	32,000	6,000	4,000	6,000	4,000	10,000	10,000	8,000	130,000
Total income	680,000	596,000	454,000	72,000	100,000	168,000	94,000	38,000	38,000	22,000	420,000	58,000	2,740,000
EXPENDITURE													
Players' wages	150,000	150,000	150,000	150,000	150,000	150,000	150,000	150,000	158,000	114,000	114,000	114,000	1,700,000
Ground expenditure	100,000	8,000	12,000	10,000	20,000	8,000	4,000	4,000	12,000	30,000	4,000	6,000	218,000
Marketing activities	8,000	0	0	24,000	24,000	0	0	0	0	0	40,000	40,000	136,000
Administration	34,000	28,000	28,000	28,000	28,000	28,000	28,000	28,000	28,000	28,000	28,000	28,000	342,000
Other expenses	24,000	24,000	24,000	24,000	24,000	24,000	24,000	24,000	24,000	24,000	24,000	38,000	302,000
Total expenditure	316,000	210,000	214,000	236,000	246,000	210,000	206,000	206,000	222,000	196,000	210,000	226,000	2,698,000
PROFIT/(LOSS)	364,000	386,000	240,000	−164,000	−146,000	−42,000	−112,000	−168,000	−184,000	−174,000	210,000	−168,000	42,000
Cumulative	364,000	750,000	990,000	826,000	680,000	638,000	526,000	358,000	174,000	0	210,000	42,000	

Figure 12.4 Rugby club annual budget sub-analysed by month

Two important points emerge from Figure 12.4. First, simply by looking at the profit or loss per month it is clear that seasonality is a factor in the club's financial fortunes. Large amounts of income are received during the first three months of the financial year in the form of season ticket sales and television revenues, and as the year progresses, expenditure exceeds income from November until May. Second, a simple table of figures is not particularly helpful to somebody reading the budget. It would be much more helpful if the numbers were explained by a series of notes such as the examples given below.

Income

Season ticket sales will occur in August and September and we expect 4,320 fans to purchase a season ticket at an average price of £250 (£1,080,000) (last year 4,000 sales @ £240 = £960,000).

Expenditure

Players' wages are based on core costs of £114,000 per month, plus an average of £36,000 per month in bonus payments during the playing season. There is an additional one-off payment of £8,000 budgeted for April in the event of the playing squad avoiding relegation.

In practice, it would be expected that all items of income and expenditure would be qualified by a written explanation. By providing a brief written commentary to the key figures and assumptions that underpin the budget, it is possible for those people who look at it to have a much clearer idea of the organisation's plans. If the club planned to make a profit of £42,000 (financial performance), then it follows that the club's overall financial position would increase by £42,000. This may be verified by examining the club's opening and closing balance sheets as shown in Figure 12.5.

The income statement in Figure 12.4 shows the club making a profit of £42,000 and the balance sheet in Figure 12.5 shows the club's net worth increasing by £42,000. This is not a coincidence. The income statement (financial performance) 'explains' the change in an organisation's financial position (balance sheet). Although an analysis of the income statement should be carried out monthly, it would be unusual to analyse the balance sheet with the same frequency.

Having established that the income statement and the balance sheet are linked, it is worth demonstrating that profit and cash are not linked. Simply because an organisation has made a profit of £42,000 does not mean that the organisation has an extra £42,000 in cash to spend. This may be demonstrated easily using the data in Figures 12.4 and 12.5. The profit made during the year was £42,000, yet cash has changed by +£184,000 (opening cash £90,000, closing cash £274,000). Why is this the case? There are three reasons why cash (liquidity) and profitability are not directly linked.

Expenditure is recognised on an income statement when it is incurred rather than when it is paid. Thus, immediately an invoice is received, it is logged as being an expense, even though it may not actually be paid until thirty or even ninety days later. The same is true for income: a business will recognise a sale as income on receipt of an order, not when the client actually pays for the goods or services supplied. This is known as the accruals or matching principle. Thus in Figure 12.4, the budget figures refer to when income and expenditure are incurred and not actual movements in cash.

FIXED ASSETS	31.07. This year	Change	31.07. Next year
Intangible assets	150,000	−50,000	100,000
Tangible assets	900,000	−100,000	800,000
	1,050,000	−150,000	900,000
CURRENT ASSETS			
Stock	12,000	2,000	14,000
Debtors	60,000	12,000	72,000
Cash	90,000	184,000	274,000
	162,000	198,000	360,000
CREDITORS < 1 YEAR	112,000	2,000	114,000
Net current assets	50,000	196,000	246,000
CREDITORS > 1 YEAR	110,000	4,000	114,000
NET ASSETS	990,000	42,000	1,032,000
CAPITAL & RESERVES			
Share capital	200,000	0	200,000
Income statement	790,000	42,000	832,000
TOTAL CAPITAL	990,000	42,000	1,032,000

Figure 12.5 Opening balance sheet, change, and closing balance sheet

Income statements do not include the purchase or sale of fixed assets (capital expenditure). Thus a football club might make a profit of £42,000 and actually reduce the cash available to it as a result of investing in new players or stadium improvements. By the same logic it would be possible to make a loss and to increase cash, for example by selling a member of the playing squad.

Income statements contain non-cash transactions such as depreciation, which is a way of spreading the cost of an asset over its useful life. If a top professional footballer is purchased on a four-year contract for £10 million, this is equivalent to an annual cost of £2.5 million. The way of recording this transaction would be to reduce cash by £10 million and to increase fixed assets by £10 million. This makes no difference to the net worth of the business as one asset, cash, has been exchanged for another asset, a player. At the end of each year of the player's registration, fixed assets would be reduced by £2.5 million until the cost of the player was written off. However, the 'writing off' of the value of a player is a paper transaction in the sense that no cash is involved. The actual movement of cash was recorded when the player was bought for £10 million.

As a result of profitability and liquidity not being identical, and of the importance of cash to businesses, it is common practice to produce a cash budget that documents the actual movements of cash during a financial year. The cash budget provides a link between the opening cash balance, the income statement, the balance sheet and the closing cash balance.

In the interests of simplicity, if we assume that the income statement in Figure 12.4 has been compiled on a cash basis and there is no need to account for depreciation, a basic cash budget for the club might look like the example shown in Figure 12.6.

The important point of note in Figure 12.6 is that it documents how opening cash of £90,000 increased during the year by £184,000 to result in a closing cash balance of £274,000. These important figures are highlighted in Figure 12.6. The main reason why cash increased considerably in excess of profit (£42,000) was because of the sale of fixed assets (£220,000). The final column in Figure 12.6 shows where the data for the cash budget were obtained and confirms that the cash budget is a link between the opening balance sheet, the income statement for the financial period under review, and the closing balance sheet. The sale of fixed assets (usually playing staff) is a classic method used by football clubs to balance their books and to ease cash flow problems. From a management perspective, the information in Figure 12.6 indicates that at no point will the club run out of cash and furthermore there will be a regular cash surplus. This cash surplus could be invested in an interest-earning current account in order to generate further income for the club – a good example of success (sensible cash management) breeding success (extra income derived from interest on cash investments).

For most sport managers, budgeting tends to start and end with a budgeted income statement, sub-analysed on a monthly basis (Figure 12.4). This is a perfectly acceptable level of skill for most managers. However, for those with ambitions to assume full responsibility for all aspects of an organisation's financial performance, skills are also needed to be able to produce and act upon budgeted balance sheets and cash flow statements.

In the final section of this chapter, the review of budgeting is concluded with an example of measuring actual performance against budget.

COMPARING ACTUAL AND BUDGETED PERFORMANCE

The ultimate purpose of budgeting is to assist managers in the planning, decision-making and control of a business. To achieve this aim, periodic comparison of actual performance compared with planned or budgeted performance is required. Figure 12.7 is an example of how such a comparison might be presented to the managers of an organisation.

The layout of Figure 12.7 has a deliberate structure to it and each component is explained in turn below:

- 'Actual' income and expenditure refers to entries made to an organisation's accounting system which are supportable by documentary evidence such as invoices, receipts, staff time sheets, etc. 'Actual' figures are drawn from the financial accounting systems and can be supported by an audit trail of evidence.
- 'Incurred' (or 'committed') expenditure refers to expenditure which relates to the financial period in question that we know has been made, but as yet has not been billed for. These sorts of data can be picked up from documentation such as purchase order forms. In order to produce timely budget reports, it is sometimes not possible to wait until all of the paperwork relating to expenditure in a period has been received. Thus in order to reflect a more realistic picture of events, the 'Incurred' column is used to log known expenditure that is not formally in the books of account. The 'Incurred' column tends to be used for expenditure only – it would be unusual to have incurred income.

	Aug	Sept	Oct	Nov	Dec	Jan	Feb	March	April	May	June	July	Total	Data Source
Opening cash for month	90,000	458,000	802,000	1,147,000	976,000	839,000	753,000	732,000	564,000	425,000	240,000	442,000	274,000	Balance sheet
Profit/loss for month	364,000	386,000	240,000	-164,000	-146,000	-42,000	-112,000	-168,000	-184,000	-174,000	210,000	-168000	42,000	Income statement
Change in stock	0	2,000	-1,000	-1,000	2,000	-6,000	1,000	1,000	2,000	-2,000	2,000	-6000	-2,000	Balance sheet
Change in debtors	4,000	-6,000	10,000	-8,000	1,000	-2,000	6,000	1,000	4,000	-6,000	-6,000	-1000	-12,000	Balance sheet
Change in creditors < 1 year	0	2,000	-4,000	2,000	4,000	-6,000	2,000	-2,000	4,000	-8,000	-6,000	12,000	2,000	Balance sheet
Purchase of fixed assets	0	-40,000	0	0	0	-30,000	0	0	0	0	0	0	-70,000	Balance sheet
Sale of fixed assets	0	0	100,000	0	0	0	80,000	0	40,000	0	0	0	220,000	Balance sheet
Change in creditors > 1 year	0	0	0	0	0	0	0	0	0	0	0	4,000	4,000	Balance sheet
Change in cash	368,000	344,000	345,000	-171,000	-137,000	-86,000	-21,000	-168,000	-134,000	-190,000	202,000	-168000	184,000	Cash budget
Closing balance for month	458,000	802,000	1,147,000	976,000	839,000	753,000	732,000	564,000	430,000	235,000	442,000	274,000		Balance sheet

Figure 12.6 Abbreviated cash budget

Figure 12.7 Actual versus budget comparison

INCOME	Actual	Incurred	Total	Budget	Variance	Direction	Note
Season ticket sales	544,000		544,000	540,000	4,000	F	1
Other ticket sales	28,000		28,000	30,000	–2,000	U	1
Television revenue	0		0	0	0		
Sponsorship	86,000		86,000	80,000	6,000	F	2
Catering	19,000		19,000	18,000	1,000	F	
Merchandising	14,000		14,000	12,000	2,000	F	
Total income	691,000	0	691,000	680,000	11,000	F	3
EXPENDITURE							
Players' wages	154,000		154,000	150,000	4,000	U	4
Ground expenditure	97,000	1500	98,500	100,000	–1,500	F	
Marketing activities	10,000		10,000	8,000	2,000	U	5
Administration	32,000	2500	34,500	34,000	500	U	5
Other expenses	26,000		26,000	24,000	2,000	U	5
Total expenditure	319,000	4,000	323,000	316,000	7,000	U	
PROFIT/(LOSS)	372,000	–4,000	368,000	364,000	4,000	F	6

- The 'Total' column is simply the sum of the 'Actual' and the 'Incurred' columns.
- 'Budget' refers to the approved budget for a given financial period, in this case for the first month (August) of the budget shown in Figure 12.4.
- 'Variance' is the difference between the 'Total' column and the 'Budget' column.
- 'Direction' is a reference to whether the variance on any given line of the budget is favourable (F) or unfavourable (U). One characteristic of good information is that it is relevant to the intended recipient. For non-finance specialists, spelling out whether a variance is favourable or unfavourable is a helpful aid to understanding the underlying meaning of the figures.
- 'Note' is a cross-reference to a written qualitative explanation of a variance. Numbers in isolation do not explain a variance and therefore it is sometimes useful for a written explanation to accompany some of the more significant variances.

To illustrate how qualitative explanations can help to explain the meaning of variances, presented below are the notes that might have accompanied the actual versus budget comparison in Figure 12.7. Note how it is written in the form of a report and may easily be cross-referenced to Figure 12.7.

REPORT

To: Club Directors
From: Management Accountant
Date: 10 September 20XY
Re: Actual vs. budget notes for month of August

Note 1: Season ticket sales/other ticket sales

Season ticket sales (2,176 at £250) are sixteen ahead of target (2,160 at £250) and it seems that the overall target of 4,320 will be exceeded. More season ticket sales have been achieved by persuading people who previously attended the club on an ad hoc basis. Therefore there has been a direct trade-off between season ticket sales and other ticket sales. We expect overall ticket sales for the season to be £16,000 ahead of budget.

Note 2: Sponsorship

Following the club's promising start to the season, a new sponsor has been found for the club's kit which will be worth £6,000 per year. Overall sponsorship revenues are expected to exceed budget by this £6,000.

Note 3: Total income

Total income is £11,000 ahead of target in the period. As explained in Notes 1 and 2, these are considered to be genuine performance over budget. However, it is not all net gain (see Note 6 below).

Note 4: Players' wages

The successful start to the season has led to bonus payments of £4,000 over and above the expected level. So long as the club continues to be successful, extra ticket sales and match day activity should more than compensate for bonus payments to players.

Note 5: Marketing activities/administration/other expenses

The increase in the club's activity at the start of the season has led to overspends on marketing, administration and other expenses. However, extra expenditure has been made in order to obtain extra revenue.

Note 6: The bottom line

The club is £4,000 ahead of budget for the period as a result of increased profitable activity. This is primarily as a result of generating extra revenue (£11,000). Should this promising start to the year continue, then it is likely that the club will exceed its overall profitability target of £42,000.

Signed

Management Accountant

Any director reading the above report would be able to grasp the basic point that the club was performing ahead of budget and had made a promising start to the year. At this stage the actual versus budget comparison would be noted and no action would need to be taken, other than to congratulate and encourage those responsible for delivering the better-than-planned performance.

SUMMARY

The purpose of this chapter has been to provide an overview of budgeting as a management discipline and to examine the role of budgeting in the context of overall business planning. The first principles of business are that organisations need to operate within the resources allocated to them and to be in a position whereby the business is well set to continue trading. Budgeting can help in this process by expressing in financial terms where a business hopes to be at some time in the future.

Budgeting is a management accounting discipline and helps to provide information for planning, decision-making and control purposes. Budgeting is a logically sequenced planning process starting with the definition of 'MASTER' objectives and finishing with a feedback or control loop. Furthermore, there are two commonly used methods of budgeting, namely continuation budgeting and zero-based budgeting. They have different objectives and their use is dependent upon the circumstances faced by a business.

Businesses report a summary of their financial transactions in the standard formats of income statement, balance sheet and cash flow statement. It is good practice to produce budgets (or plans) for all of these financial statements so that managers can gain a comprehensive overview of a business's financial affairs. To reinforce the point that budgeting is a continuous process, regular (monthly) checks should be made of how an organisation actually performed compared with how it planned to perform. Where significant variances are found, these should be highlighted and explained so that non-finance specialists can grasp their underlying meaning.

QUESTIONS FOR REVIEW

1. What are the two most common methods of budgeting?
2. What are the two types of continuation budget?
3. What is the purpose of a decremental approach to the budgeting process?
4. A budget is an organisation's plan expressed in financial terms. True or false?
5. How many steps should there be in an effective budgeting process?

REFERENCES AND FURTHER READING

Bill, K. (ed.) (2009) *Sport Management*. Learning Matters, Exeter.
Schwarz, E., Hall, S. and Shibli, S. (2010) *Sport Facility Operations Management*. Butterworth-Heinemann, Oxford.
Stewart, B. (2007) *Sport Funding and Finance*. Butterworth-Heinemann, Oxford.
Trenberth, L. (ed.) (2003) *Managing the Business of Sport*. Dunmore Press, Palmerston North.

CHAPTER 13

INVESTMENT APPRAISAL AND LONG-TERM DECISION-MAKING

On completion of this chapter you will be able to:

- explain the importance and purpose of investment appraisal;
- communicate the differences between short-term and long-term decision-making;
- calculate the key measures of investment appraisal: payback, accounting rate of return, net present value and the internal rate of return;
- understand and communicate the time value of money and its impact upon decision-making.

INTRODUCTION

When we considered short-term decision-making in Chapter 10 the majority of the decisions we dealt with were to do with revenue expenditure. By contrast, this chapter will examine long-term decisions based on capital expenditure that should help determine profits which reach into the future. Capital expenditure is different from revenue expenditure (labour and material costs) as it is generally concerned with the purchase of large capital items such as machinery, plant and equipment, land and buildings or even another organisation. The benefits of such expenditure should last for a number of years; hence they need to be quantified.

The purpose of this chapter is to introduce you to long-term decision-making and to examine the four main tools which will enable you to make decisions based on the financial outputs that the expenditure should derive. There are of course parallels to short-term decision-making, as you will often find that you can make a choice between alternatives and compare costs and revenues. However, due to the fact that you are analysing the impact of expenditure (and revenue) in the longer term we need to factor in external forces such as inflation so that we can establish the real cost or profit.

THE PURPOSE OF INVESTMENT APPRAISAL

Investment appraisal is a technique that can be used to ascertain the profitability of long-term projects to establish whether they are worth undertaking in the first place. In essence this will enable you to determine that projects are truly financially viable and, if there are alternatives, which project is best in the long term. This is an important consideration as some projects may return a profit in the short term but fall short of other projects' potential earnings in the longer term.

Capital expenditure involves the outlay of considerable amounts of money on a project; for example, Kitlocker.com purchasing a new embroidery machine, a local swimming pool acquiring a new computer booking system or a private health club installing a new fitness suite. Such projects therefore involve the purchase of new fixed assets that will have a long-term impact upon the organisation.

> **KEY TERM**
>
> ### (CAPITAL) INVESTMENT APPRAISAL
>
> The evaluation of proposed investment projects which will have a lasting effect on an organisation. It helps to determine which project is likely to give the highest financial return.

While short-term decisions may gain a few brownie points, or even a promotion or two, they are not likely to earn the benefits that have the potential to generate significant increases in revenue and profit. Indeed, investment decisions are critical for business growth, for owners and managers, and in many cases for the growth of our economy. Such decisions are likely to have the following characteristics:

- a life span of more than two years;
- to be strategic in nature;
- to involve medium to high levels of expenditure;
- to consider external factors such as inflation and interest rates.

Unlike short-term decision-making techniques where there are two principal tools – contribution and breakeven analysis – long-term decision-making often involves a minimum of four techniques. These in turn will be covered in the remainder of this chapter and, unlike short-term decision-making where you can choose the measure that best suits you, it is worth applying all four techniques to each project in order to achieve a more rounded view. The techniques are:

1. the payback method;
2. the accounting rate of return;
3. net present value;
4. the internal rate of return.

Each of these techniques varies in the degree of difficulty which is required to calculate the answers. However, they are all solvable when you use a simple spreadsheet or scientific calculator. Both the payback and accounting rate of return methods are what a management accountant would term 'conventional capital investment appraisal techniques' whereas the net present value and internal rate of return techniques are termed 'discounted cash flow techniques' which involve the time value of money.

Before we move on, it is worth summarising the key points here. Investment appraisal involves the comparison of the cost of a project now (i.e. the investment today) with the expected net benefits (i.e. financial returns) in the future. The principal functions of investment appraisal therefore are:

- to test the viability of one or more projects;
- to compare different or competing projects that require funding to achieve the same goals;
- to rank projects competing for limited amounts of finance (such as a lottery funding bid), which may set out to achieve different goals.

Given that the following techniques all look into the future it is important to note that you need sound, predicted data on which to base your calculations. In making any investment decision, there will always be a risk that the predicted data may be inaccurate and unreliable. These techniques will not provide you with a crystal ball for predicting the future – you would need Mystic Meg or another fortune teller for that!

PROJECT DATA

The starting point for any investment decision is project data. Project data will involve the following key items of information that will enable any investment appraisal technique to take place:

- the investment required (£);
- the estimated project life (years);
- expected cash inflows from trading (revenues);
- expected cash outflows from trading (costs);
- the net cash flows, i.e. inflows minus outflows;
- any residual value.

It is usual for project data to be displayed on a spreadsheet as this makes it easier to apply the techniques. A typical layout for project data would be as follows:

Kitlocker.com embroidery machine	Cash inflows (£)	Cash outflows (£)	Net cash flows (£)
Investment		10,000	−10,000
Year 1	5,000	1,000	4,000
Year 2	5,000	1,000	4,000
Year 3	5,000	1,200	3,800
Year 4	4,000	1,400	2,600
Year 5	4,000	1,900	2,100
Residual value	1,000		1,000
Project lifetime surplus			7,500

The example above details a potential investment for Kitlocker.com and the purchase of a new embroidery machine. This machine has an investment cost of £10,000. The cash inflows would relate to the revenue generated by the machine from customers purchasing garments that had been embroidered, while the cash outflows would involve the cost of running the machine. The project lifetime surplus provides us with a quantifiable figure that determines the project's profit or loss over its lifetime (in this case five years).

Throughout this chapter we will use this basic layout and add to it for each measurement technique. This will involve adding new columns (and even removing some when you are comfortable with how things work). However, we need to remember two final points before applying anything new. All the investment decisions in this chapter are based on the assumptions that all investments would occur on day 1 of a project (which means we don't have to split costs over different time periods), all trading inflows and outflows occur on the last trading day of the year (for the same reason), and taxation and inflation have to be ignored due to the fact that they vary from project to project and industry to industry. Before moving on, why not attempt the following project data activity to ensure that you are comfortable with how the figures are calculated?

ACTIVITY

Calculate the missing information for the following project:

New booking system	Inflows (£)	Outflows (£)	Net cash flows (£)
Investment		10,000	
Year 1	20,000	7,500	
Year 2	40,000		36,000
Year 3		10,000	25,000
Year 4	23,000		−5,000
Year 5	50,000	40,000	
Residual value	2,500		
Project lifetime surplus			

Hopefully your answer should look something like this:

New booking system	Inflows (£)	Outflows (£)	Net cash flows (£)
Investment		10,000	−10,000
Year 1	20,000	7,500	12,500
Year 2	40,000	4,000	36,000
Year 3	35,000	10,000	25,000

Year 4	23,000	28,000	−5,000
Year 5	50,000	40,000	10,000
Residual value	2,500		2,500
Project lifetime surplus			71,000

PAYBACK PERIOD

The payback period is our first, most widely used and straightforward investment appraisal technique. It is a measure that all sport managers should be aware of and one that should not be difficult to apply or interpret (as you will see below). Each project will be considered solely from the cash flows that it receives and pays, and therefore the total amount of time that it takes to pay back its initial investment. You can probably appreciate here why it is the most widely used technique that we will cover, since all owners and managers of an organisation will want to know how quickly a project will return its investment. This will allow you to establish when the project will effectively breakeven and determine how long it will be before the investment begins to make a profit and therefore a financial return on investment. As a measure, it is useful in appraising when different projects will pay back, as it will allow you to see when you are able to invest in other projects.

KEY TERMS

PROJECT DATA

Predicted information that will determine the investment required in the project, the life span of the project, cash inflows, cash outflows, net cash flows and any residual value.

PAYBACK PERIOD

The time required for the predicted net cash flows to equal the capital invested in a project.

Often managers will prefer to choose projects that pay back the fastest, though other considerations such as overall profit and the time value of money are ignored. At this point it is worth looking at an example so that we can see how this works in practice. We will use the first example from Kitlocker.com.

Kitlocker.com embroidery machine	Cash inflows (£)	Cash outflows (£)	Net cash flows (£)
Investment		10,000	−10,000
Year 1	5,000	1,000	4,000
Year 2	5,000	1,000	4,000
Year 3	5,000	1,200	3,800
Year 4	4,000	1,400	2,600
Year 5	4,000	1,900	2,100
Residual value	1,000		1,000
Project lifetime surplus			7,500

As you should be able to see, the embroidery machine will pay back its £10,000 initial investment midway through the third year. In this case we would conclude that the project will pay back at the end of Year 3 (remember that we consider inflows and outflows on the last day of trading).

The main advantages of using the payback method of investment appraisal are that it is simple and easy to calculate, it can compare risky projects quickly, and it helps determine which project to choose if short-term gains are desired over long-term ones. However, given that it is often difficult to estimate and time future cash flows, it ignores net cash flows after the payback period, it ignores the size of the investment and it ignores the time value of money, it is an investment appraisal technique that should not be used in isolation.

ACTIVITY

When does the new booking system project pay back its initial investment?

New booking system	Inflows (£)	Outflows (£)	Net cash flows (£)
Investment		10,000	−10,000
Year 1	20,000	7,500	12,500
Year 2	40,000	4,000	36,000
Year 3	35,000	10,000	25,000
Year 4	23,000	28,000	−5,000
Year 5	50,000	40,000	10,000
Residual value	2,500		2,500
Project lifetime surplus			71,000

Your answer should have been: at the end of Year 1. Using the payback method in isolation would suggest that this project is worth undertaking given its rapid return of investment which will free up cash for other projects within twelve months.

THE ACCOUNTING RATE OF RETURN

Given that the payback period is concerned with cash flow, the next investment appraisal technique in this chapter focuses on profits. The accounting rate of return considers the overall profitability of a project – its lifetime surplus – and relates the average yearly surplus to the average investment. Consequently the accounting rate of return is a more sensible and conventional measure of success as it will express in percentage terms the relationship between profit and investment. In all cases the project with the highest accounting rate of return will be preferred. This method of investment appraisal is again easy to calculate and while there are one or two different ways of attempting the calculation the most logical method is by way of four formulas contributing to five steps (again these are easy to use on a spreadsheet). The formulas should be calculated in sequence and one at a time. They are as follows:

1. Calculate the average yearly surplus of the project:
   Project lifetime surplus / number of years of the project

2. Calculate the net investment:
   Initial investment – residual value

3. Calculate the average investment
   (Net investment + residual value)/2

4. Calculate the accounting rate of return
   Average yearly surplus (the answer to 1)/average investment (answer to 3)

5. Express the answer as a percentage.

It is important to calculate step 3 as we need to identify the average amount of capital invested over the course of the project, since the initial capital outlay will not be tied up for the duration of the project.

> **KEY TERM**
>
> **ACCOUNTING RATE OF RETURN**
>
> Relates the average yearly surplus of a project to the average investment to measure the overall profitability of a project (its lifetime surplus).

Let us return to our embroidery machine and see what the accounting rate of return is.

Kitlocker.com embroidery machine	Cash inflows (£)	Cash outflows (£)	Net cash flows (£)
Investment		10,000	−10,000
Year 1	5,000	1,000	4,000
Year 2	5,000	1,000	4,000
Year 3	5,000	1,200	3,800
Year 4	4,000	1,400	2,600
Year 5	4,000	1,900	2,100
Residual value	1,000		1,000
Project lifetime surplus			7,500

The accounting rate of return calculations will be:

1. Calculate the average yearly surplus of the project:
   Project lifetime surplus / number of years of the project
   £7,500 / 5 = £1,500

2. Calculate the net investment:
   Initial investment − residual value
   £10,000 − £1,000 = £9,000

3. Calculate the average investment:
   (Net investment + residual value)/2
   (£9,000 + £1,000) / 2 = £5,000

4. Calculate the accounting rate of return:
   Average yearly surplus (the answer to 1)/average investment (answer to 3)
   £1,500 / £5,000 = 0.3

5. Express the answer as a percentage:
   30%

In this example the accounting rate of return may be calculated as being 30 per cent – a very good return. However, while this method of investment appraisal again uses simple calculations and considers the entire life of the project, as with the payback period the accounting rate of return ignores the time value of money, there is no single definition of how to calculate the figures, averages are often misleading, no account is given of when profits manifest themselves and there is no guidance on whether an acceptable level of return is good. This results in the technique being left as part of a bigger picture for investment appraisal.

Go back to the 'new booking system' example and using the formulas calculate the accounting rate of return.

New booking system	Inflows (£)	Outflows (£)	Net cash flows (£)
Investment		10,000	–10,000
Year 1	20,000	7,500	12,500
Year 2	40,000	4,000	36,000
Year 3	35,000	10,000	25,000
Year 4	23,000	28,000	–5,000
Year 5	50,000	40,000	10,000
Residual value	2,500		2,500
Project lifetime surplus			71,000

You should have calculated the following accounting rate of return:

1. Calculate the average yearly surplus of the project:
   Project lifetime surplus/number of years of the project
   £71,000 / 5 = £14,200

2. Calculate the net investment:
   Initial investment – residual value
   £10,000 – £2,500 = £7,500

3. Calculate the average investment
   (Net investment + residual value)/2
   (£7,500 + £2,500)/2 = £5,000

4. Calculate the accounting rate of return:
   Average yearly surplus (the answer to 1)/average investment (answer to 3)
   £14,200 / £5,000 = 2.84

5. Express the answer as a percentage:
   284%

NET PRESENT VALUE: A DISCOUNTING METHOD

Having considered the two most basic investment appraisal techniques, we have found that there are some limitations to each. Due to the long-term nature of investment decisions, understanding lifetime surpluses and payback periods is one thing. However, neither technique appreciates the time value of money. If you consider this point for a moment you should begin to understand it. Think about the following example: which would you choose, £50 now or

£50 in one year's time? Even when you ignore risk and inflation you should have said that you would take £50 now as it has more value to you given that it can be used productively. You could, for example, invest it to earn interest or use it to buy stock that you will sell for a profit. The basic principle here is that the £50 is used productively and not spent in the local pub. It is based on the concept that cash received at an earlier date is worth more than a similar amount received in the future. In the same way, because cash that will be paid out at a later date is not available for investment today it is worth less than a similar amount received today.

KEY TERMS

TIME VALUE OF MONEY

The concept that cash received today is worth more than the same amount received at a later date owing to the opportunity cost of capital.

OPPORTUNITY COST OF CAPITAL

The interest forgone because the cash was not available for investment purposes today.

The longer anyone has to wait for money the less it is worth. By way of an example, let us go to another scenario. Imagine that a close friend of yours wanted to borrow money from you now and promised to pay you £50 in one year's time; how much would you be willing to lend if the interest rate was 10 per cent? Part of your decision-making process would obviously be whether you expected to get the money back; if you consider that the debt may turn bad you may wish to charge a higher rate of interest. By contrast, if you think that your friend will make good his promise you may be willing to lend £45.46. In one year's time this would give you interest of £4.54 to make the sum of £50 that your friend has promised to pay. In order to understand this more clearly and to emphasise the importance of the time value of money, we need to look more closely at the concepts of compound interest and discounting.

COMPOUND INTEREST

Compounding is the calculation of the future value of a sum of money invested today at a given rate of interest. Interest is then added periodically to the capital sum invested so that interest in future periods is earned on the compounded sum (i.e. the interest earned also earns interest in subsequent periods). In compounding and discounting calculations the percentage interest rate should be expressed as a decimal; for example, 5 per cent should be expressed as 0.05 – this makes it much easier to apply the calculations and will save you the odd headache later on. As with all investment appraisal techniques, you can do the calculations on a spreadsheet. Let us look at an example.

Imagine that you get some money from the bank of Mum and Dad and decide to invest £1,000 at an annual rate of 5 per cent (0.05) for four years. We can calculate the future value of your £1,000 using the following steps:

	£
Capital invested at start of Year 1	1,000
Add interest for Year 1 (1,000 × 0.05)	50
Value of investment at end of Year 1	1,050
Add interest for Year 2 (1,050 × 0.05)	53
Value of investment at end of Year 2	1,103
Add interest for Year 3 (1,103 × 0.05)	55
Value of investment at end of Year 3	1,158
Add interest for Year 4 (1,158 × 0.05)	58
Value of investment at end of Year 4	**1,216**

Because your £1,000 is locked into the savings account for four years the amount of interest will grow on an annual basis. Therefore the future value, in four years' time of your £1,000 investment, at a compound interest rate of 5 per cent per annum, will be £1,216, returning £216 profit to you (before any tax has been taken by HMRC of course).

Now, going through these steps just to work out a future value could be a little boring – just imagine if you were working out the future value of a mortgage that adds compound interest over twenty-five or thirty years! Consequently you will find that tables of compounding 'factors' are available to save time. If, however, you don't have the tables (given that we don't tend to carry them around in our back pockets) we can use a multiplier which may be calculated by a (relatively) easy formula. This formula is as follows:

$$\text{Compounding factor} = (1 + \text{Interest rate})^{\text{number of years}}$$

Note here that ' ^ ' is the mathematical symbol that means 'to the power of'.

We can use the formula to ascertain the future value of your £1,000 from the previous example. Remember that the investment was for four years and at an annual interest rate of 5 per cent.

$$\text{Compounding factor} = (1 + 0.05)^4$$
$$\text{In reality this means} = 1.05 \times 1.05 \times 1.05 \times 1.05$$
$$= 1.216$$

Therefore your £1,000 investment multiplied by the compounding factor equals:

$$£1,000 \times 1.216 = £1,216$$

DISCOUNTING

Compounding is useful if we want to project calculations into the future. However, when making investment decisions, cash flows for different years need to be converted into a common value (i.e. converted into their respective values at the same point in time). The point in time chosen is the 'present' or 'today' – the time at which the decision is taken. This means that all cash flows are converted to their 'present values' or 'values today'. In order to achieve these values we need to discount future values to present values. Discounting is therefore a technique that allows a fair comparison of competing projects which have different life spans.

Discounting is based on the same mathematical principle as compounding, but while compounding increases present value to future value (i.e. calculates the future value of £1 invested today), discounting decreases future values to present values (i.e. calculates the present value of £1 received in the future). It therefore follows that discounting is the opposite of compounding (Figure 13.1).

Using the example of your investment of £1,000 at a rate of 5 per cent (0.05) per annum, the present values of future sums can be calculated as follows:

Future value		Present value
£1,050	Received in one year's time	= £1,000
£1,103	2	= £1,000
£1,158	3	= £1,000
£1,216	4	= £1,000

The present value of £1,216 to be received in four years' time is £1,000 when the interest rate is 5 per cent per annum. The principle here is that you can forecast future income and adjust it to today's value, a present value, so that you can compare it with the initial investment to determine whether it is financially viable. There are two techniques for investment appraisal that use this concept:

1 net present value: this provides an absolute measure for project performance;
2 the internal rate of return: this provides a relative measure for project performance.

Both of these techniques require cash flows (from our project data) to be discounted (or adjusted) to a present value and then compared with the initial capital outlay. As with compounding, we can use 'discount factors' to help calculate the appropriate sum.

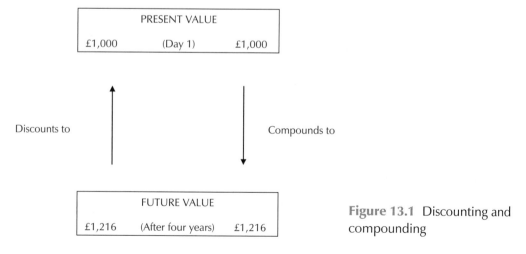

Figure 13.1 Discounting and compounding

DISCOUNT FACTORS

Discount factors (i.e. the 'multipliers' which can be used to calculate the present value of any future cash flows at a given rate of interest) are often calculated using a longhand method (in the same way as compounding). In our example we can calculate the discount factors for your £1,000 investment at an interest rate of 5 per cent per annum for a fixed period of four years as follows:

$$£1,000/£1,050 = 0.9524 \text{ for Year 1}$$

The factor of 0.9524 is the multiplier used to calculate the present value of any future cash flows to be received at the end of one year when the interest rate is 5 per cent per annum.

$$£1,000/£1,103 = 0.9070 \text{ for Year 2}$$

This factor of 0.9070 is the multiplier to be used to calculate the present value of any future cash flows to be received at the end of two years when the interest rate is 5 per cent per annum.

$$£1,000/£1,158 = 0.8638 \text{ for Year 3}$$

This factor of 0.8638 is the multiplier to be used to calculate the present value of any future cash flows to be received at the end of three years when the interest rate is 5 per cent per annum.

$$£1,000/£1,216 = 0.8227 \text{ for Year 4}$$

This factor of 0.8227 is the multiplier to be used to calculate the present value of any future cash flows to be received at the end of four years when the interest rate is 5 per cent per annum.

DISCOUNTING TABLES AND FORMULA

Again, as with compounding, discounting tables may be used to calculate the present value of future cash flows. These tables provide the discounting factors at various rates of interest and for various time periods. They will show, for example, that the discounting factor to be used to calculate the present value of £1 received or paid in four years' time where the interest rate is 5 per cent per annum is 0.8227. It should be noted that discounting always decreases the value of cash flows. The discounting factors, therefore, will always be less than 1.

However, to make our life a little easier given that we won't normally have sight of long tables, we can use a formula to calculate the discount factors. The formula is a slight variation on the compounding one, as this time we are discounting:

$$1/(1+\text{Interest rate})^{\wedge}\text{number of years}$$

NET PRESENT VALUE

The net present value technique, or investment appraisal, uses discounting to convert the expected future cash flows of a project into present-day values. The discount factor that is chosen will always be based on the required interest rate. As a result, the net present value method identifies how much better the return on an investment project will be than an alternative project. Because the discount rates calculated by the formula in the previous section are for £1 we need to multiply the cash flow for a particular year to determine the present value. Once a present value is established for each year for the cash inflows it is compared with the initial capital outlay and an absolute value (net present value) is determined. Providing that the net present value (NPV) is positive, the project may be deemed to yield a higher return than the initial investment after considering the time value of money. Consequently the project would be worth undertaking. As with most measures in investment appraisal, the higher the value, the better the project.

We will illustrate NPV and the associated discount factors using our project data layout (with an extra column or two) for Kitlocker.com and the purchase of the embroidery machine. In this example it is assumed that the interest rate is 10 per cent per annum. You will notice that we have an additional column for the discount factors (these are calculated using the formula) and another for the present values (these are calculated by multiplying the net cash flows by the discount factor for the appropriate year. The discount factor for the investment year is always 1.000 (due to the fact that it is invested today and does not need to be discounted) and the discount factor for any residual value will always be the same as the final year of the project (it is assumed that once the project is finished the asset will not be used).

Kitlocker.com embroidery machine	Cash inflows (£)	Cash outflows (£)	Net cash flows (£)	10% Discount factor	Present value (£)
Investment		10,000	−10,000	1.0000	−10,000
Year 1	5,000	1,000	4,000	0.9091	3,636
Year 2	5,000	1,000	4,000	0.8264	3,306
Year 3	5,000	1,200	3,800	0.7513	2,855
Year 4	4,000	1,400	2,600	0.6830	1,776
Year 5	4,000	1,900	2,100	0.6209	1,304
Residual value	1,000		1,000	0.6209	621
Project lifetime surplus			7,500	NPV	3,498

The NPV for the embroidery machine is calculated to be £3,498, by some margin less than the project lifetime surplus. However, having taken into account the time value of money this investment would still yield a positive return and should therefore be considered seriously.

Due to the fact that the net present value method uses cash flows rather than accounting profits, takes into account the time value of money, considers the timing of cash flows and uses relatively simple rules, it is often seen as a more effective way of appraising projects. However, as with all long-term investment decisions the predicted revenues may change, it fails to recognise any business risk and is a little longer winded to work out than the previous two techniques.

> **KEY TERM**
>
> ## NET PRESENT VALUE
>
> The difference between the sum of discounted values of the predicted net cash flows and the capital invested in a proposed long-term investment project.

USING NPV TO EVALUATE TWO OR MORE PROJECTS

Using NPV to compare the viability of two or more projects should by now be common place in the sport industry. Indeed, when you consider the amounts of money that have been earmarked for the development of the London 2012 Olympic site it seems obvious that the planners must have applied some investment appraisal to make a decision on which design to use. On a smaller scale we can use this technique to compare the viability of several projects that are competing for limited capital resources. Imagine that the embroidery machine from our Kitlocker.com example is only one of two projects they are considering investing in, the other being a new heat press. We can use NPV to compare the two projects so that we can make the best decision for the use of the limited funds available.

Kitlocker.com heat press	Cash inflows (£)	Cash outflows (£)	Net cash flows (£)	10 % discount factor	Present value (£)
Investment		10,000	–10,000	1.0000	–10,000
Year 1	5,000	1,000	4,000	0.9091	3,636
Year 2	6,000	1,000	5,000	0.8264	4,132
Year 3	6,000	1,000	5,000	0.7513	3,757
Year 4	5,500	1,000	4,500	0.6830	3,074
Year 5	1,000	2,000	–1,000	0.6209	–621
Residual value	0		0	0.6209	0
Project lifetime surplus			7,500	NPV	3,978

While both projects yield the same project lifetime surplus we can see that the heat press has a higher net present value. Given that both projects have similar payback periods, it may be sensible for the company to invest in the heat press instead of the embroidery machine.

ACTIVITY

Calculate and compare the net present values, at an annual interest rate of 5 per cent, for the new booking system that we examined earlier and a café refit.

New booking system	Cash inflows (£)	Cash outflows (£)	Net cash flows (£)	5% discount factor	Present value (£)
Investment		10,000	−10,000		
Year 1	20,000	7,500	12,500		
Year 2	40,000	4,000	36,000		
Year 3	35,000	10,000	25,000		
Year 4	23,000	28,000	−5,000		
Year 5	50,000	40,000	10,000		
Residual value	2,500		2,500		
Project lifetime surplus			71,000	NPV	

Café refit	Cash inflows (£)	Cash outflows (£)	Net cash flows (£)	5% discount factor	Present value (£)
Investment		10,000	−10,000		
Year 1	20,000	15,000	5,000		
Year 2	48,000	20,000	28,000		
Year 3	55,000	25,000	30,000		
Year 4	33,000	28,000	5,000		
Year 5	23,000	15,500	7,500		
Residual value	5,500		5,500		
Project lifetime surplus			71,000	NPV	

Hopefully your answers will resemble those given below and you should have said that the new booking system appears to be a better investment.

New booking system	Cash inflows (£)	Cash outflows (£)	Net cash flows (£)	5% discount factor	Present value (£)
Investment		10,000	−10,000	1.0000	−10,000
Year 1	20,000	7,500	12,500	0.9524	11,905
Year 2	40,000	4,000	36,000	0.9070	32,653
Year 3	35,000	10,000	25,000	0.8638	21,596
Year 4	23,000	28,000	−5,000	0.8227	−4,114
Year 5	50,000	40,000	10,000	0.7835	7,835
Residual value	2,500		2,500	0.7835	1,959
Project lifetime surplus			71,000	NPV	61,834

Café refit	Cash inflows (£)	Cash outflows (£)	Net cash flows (£)	5% discount factor	Present value (£)
Investment		10,000	−10,000	1.0000	−10,000
Year 1	20,000	15,000	5,000	0.9524	4,762
Year 2	48,000	20,000	28,000	0.9070	25,397
Year 3	55,000	25,000	30,000	0.8638	25,915
Year 4	33,000	28,000	5,000	0.8227	4,114
Year 5	23,000	15,500	7,500	0.7835	5,876
Residual value	5,500		5,500	0.7835	4,309
Project lifetime surplus			71,000	NPV	60,373

INTERNAL RATE OF RETURN

The internal rate of return method of investment appraisal is based on the same principles as net present value. It differs, however, in that it attempts to establish the interest rate at which the investment will return a net present value of zero. As the cost of capital rises the NPV will fall, as we have seen in the examples above. The internal rate of return (IRR) requires the calculation of net present value using substituted costs of capital to determine those costs of capital resulting in a net present value of 0. For a project to be viable, therefore, the IRR percentage determined must be greater than the cost of capital for the project. In simple terms, I like to think of IRR in the same way as breakeven and margin of safety. The interest rate that results in an NPV of 0 is the point of breakeven and the margin of safety is the distance away from that figure. When evaluating different projects that are competing for limited funds this method helps factor risk into the decision-making process. Moreover, when comparing projects the project with the highest IRR is preferred.

> **KEY TERM**
>
> **INTERNAL RATE OF RETURN**
>
> The interest rate at which the sum of the discounted values of the predicted net cash flows is equal to the capital invested in the proposed project.

As with previous methods, the best way to make sense of IRR is to apply it to an example. Given the success we have had so far, we can go back to Kitlocker.com and the embroidery machine. First, we can see the NPV at the specified interest rate per annum, 10 per cent. This yields an NPV of £3,498.

Kitlocker.com embroidery machine	Cash inflows (£)	Cash outflows (£)	Net cash flows (£)	10% discount factor	Present value (£)
Investment		10,000	−10,000	1.0000	−10,000
Year 1	5,000	1,000	4,000	0.9091	3,636
Year 2	5,000	1,000	4,000	0.8264	3,306
Year 3	5,000	1,200	3,800	0.7513	2,855
Year 4	4,000	1,400	2,600	0.6830	1,776
Year 5	4,000	1,900	2,100	0.6209	1,304
Residual value	1,000		1,000	0.6209	621
Project lifetime surplus			7,500	NPV	3,498

What we need to do here is work out at what interest rate the NPV will be almost 0. Consequently we need to increase the interest rate – this will have a decreasing effect on NPV. So let us try an annual interest rate of 20 per cent.

Kitlocker.com embroidery machine	Cash inflows (£)	Cash outflows (£)	Net cash flows (£)	20% discount factor	Present value (£)
Investment		10,000	−10,000	1.0000	−10,000
Year 1	5,000	1,000	4,000	0.8333	3,333
Year 2	5,000	1,000	4,000	0.6944	2,778
Year 3	5,000	1,200	3,800	0.5787	2,199

Year 4	4,000	1,400	2,600	0.4823	1,254
Year 5	4,000	1,900	2,100	0.4019	844
Residual value	1,000		1,000	0.4019	402
Project lifetime surplus			7,500	NPV	810

It is clear that we are getting there, as we have managed to reduce the NPV to just £810. We should now try a slightly higher interest rate again, perhaps 25 per cent.

Kitlocker.com embroidery machine	Cash inflows (£)	Cash outflows (£)	Net cash flows (£)	25% discount factor	Present value (£)
Investment		10,000	−10,000	1.0000	−10,000
Year 1	5,000	1,000	4,000	0.8000	3,200
Year 2	5,000	1,000	4,000	0.6400	2,560
Year 3	5,000	1,200	3,800	0.5120	1,946
Year 4	4,000	1,400	2,600	0.4096	1,065
Year 5	4,000	1,900	2,100	0.3277	688
Residual value	1,000		1,000	0.3277	328
Project lifetime surplus			7,500	NPV	−214

This time we are a little too high, as the adjustment has led to a loss, i.e. an NPV of −£214. We now know that the interest rate at which this project will yield a 0 NPV lies somewhere between 20 and 25 per cent. Using a bit of common sense it seems that the rate will be closer to 25 per cent than 20 per cent, so we will try an interest rate of 24 per cent.

Kitlocker.com embroidery machine	Cash inflows (£)	Cash outflows (£)	Net cash flows (£)	24% discount factor	Present value (£)
Investment		10,000	−10,000	1.0000	−10,000
Year 1	5,000	1,000	4,000	0.8065	3,226
Year 2	5,000	1,000	4,000	0.6504	2,601
Year 3	5,000	1,200	3,800	0.5245	1,993
Year 4	4,000	1,400	2,600	0.4230	1,100
Year 5	4,000	1,900	2,100	0.3411	716
Residual value	1,000		1,000	0.3411	341
Project lifetime surplus			7,500	NPV	−23

At an interest rate of 24 per cent the project yields as near to 0 as we need it to; in this case an NPV of –£23. Granted we could use a spreadsheet and continue to crunch the numbers to get to an absolute 0 but for the purposes of what you will need, this is close enough. For those of you who really want to know, this project has an NPV of 0 at an interest rate of 23.885 per cent! This method of calculating IRR is called the 'trial-and-error method' for what I imagine is an obvious reason.

ACTIVITY

Calculate the internal rate of return for the new booking system example.

New booking system	Cash inflows (£)	Cash outflows (£)	Net cash flows (£)	5% discount factor	Present value (£)
Investment		10,000	–10,000	1.0000	–10,000
Year 1	20,000	7,500	12,500	0.9524	11,905
Year 2	40,000	4,000	36,000	0.9070	32,653
Year 3	35,000	10,000	25,000	0.8638	21,596
Year 4	23,000	28,000	–5,000	0.8227	–4,114
Year 5	50,000	40,000	10,000	0.7835	7,835
Residual value	2,500		2,500	0.7835	1,959
Project lifetime surplus			71,000	NPV	61,834

New booking system	Cash inflows (£)	Cash outflows (£)	Net cash flows (£)	5% discount factor	Present value (£)
Investment		10,000	–10,000		
Year 1	20,000	7,500	12,500		
Year 2	40,000	4,000	36,000		
Year 3	35,000	10,000	25,000		
Year 4	23,000	28,000	–5,000		
Year 5	50,000	40,000	10,000		
Residual value	2,500		2,500		
Project lifetime surplus			71,000	NPV	

Using the trial-and-error method of IRR, you should have reached the following conclusion – a huge interest rate of 183 per cent which represents a significant margin of safety.

New booking system	Cash inflows (£)	Cash outflows (£)	Net cash flows (£)	183% discount factor	Present value (£)
Investment		10,000	–10,000	1.0000	–10,000
Year 1	20,000	7,500	12,500	0.3534	4,417
Year 2	40,000	4,000	36,000	0.1249	4,495
Year 3	35,000	10,000	25,000	0.0441	1,103
Year 4	23,000	28,000	–5,000	0.0156	–78
Year 5	50,000	40,000	10,000	0.0055	55
Residual value	2,500		2,500	0.0055	14
Project lifetime surplus			71,000	NPV	6

Discount methods of investment appraisal are a much fairer way of making long-term decisions as they take into consideration the overall profitability of projects and the timing of cash flows. However, applying the correct interest rate is crucial and can have a huge influence on your calculations.

SUMMARY

Investment appraisal is the study of long-term decision-making and will usually involve the purchase of large capital items. The benefits of such purchases are likely to have a financial impact upon the organisation for a number of years, so the decision-making process needs to be precise. Investment appraisal has four main techniques that may be used to determine the financial viability of projects and choose between alternative projects when there is competition for limited finance. The four methods of investment appraisal are as follows:

1. payback period;
2. the accounting rate of return;
3. net present value;
4. the internal rate of return.

The payback period focuses on early cash flows and gives you an idea about how soon the initial investment is likely to be recovered by calculating the number of years it is expected for the project to breakeven. The accounting rate of return on the other hand examines the overall profitability of the project during its lifetime and identifies the average profit as a percentage to the average investment. Both methods, however, ignore the important consideration of the time value of money.

The time value of money can be included in investment appraisal techniques through the use of net present value and the internal rate of return. Both methods use discounting as a means of establishing the true profit of a project. Net present value provides an absolute measure of return while the internal rate of return provides a relative measure of return. Both methods use discount factors that can be easily calculated on a spreadsheet using a discount factor formula.

QUESTIONS FOR REVIEW

1. Why is investment appraisal useful for long-term decision-making?
2. What are the four main methods of investment appraisal?
3. What is the formula for calculating discount factors?
4. What are the main limitations of the payback period and the accounting rate of return?
5. What is the limitation of project data?

REFERENCES AND FURTHER READING

Collins, J. and Hussey, R. (2007) *Business Accounting: An Introduction to Financial and Management Accounting*. Palgrave Macmillan, Basingstoke.

Russell, D., Patel, A. and Wilkinson-Riddle, G. (2002) *Cost Accounting: An Essential Guide*. Financial Times Press, Harlow.

Trenberth, L. (ed.) (2003) *Managing the Business of Sport*. Dunmore Press, Palmerston North.

CHAPTER 14

SPORT FUNDING AND FINANCE

> **On completion of this chapter you will be able to:**
> - explain the importance of funding in sport;
> - appreciate the need for being strategic in your pursuit of funding;
> - understand and explain the main sources of funding;
> - communicate the process by which funding can be secured in the public sector;
> - understand and apply key performance indicators to plans in order to secure funding.

INTRODUCTION

Funding in sport is often taken for granted by managers, academics and students. However, securing and managing funds is often one of the main challenges for any organisation. Indeed, in the public and voluntary sectors it is the management of external funds that enables the organisation to survive. While the funding of major sport organisations such as professional sport teams is beyond the scope of this chapter we do need to recognise that many of you will, at some point in your careers, be asked to bring in money to your organisation. Some of you will work in organisations that sell goods, so the reinvestment of profits can be used to fund new ideas; however, many of you may work on sport development projects, community projects or in small and medium-sized enterprises, which means that you will need to write funding bids and business plans.

Consequently, this chapter will focus on the most common ways of securing funding – from funding bodies and through sponsorship. We will examine in some detail the process by which funding is gained and the key issues that affect the funding bodies and those in the market for such funds. Financial support is often finite, so you may find that you need to attract a variety of different sources. Your income structure, similar to your cost structure (which we considered in Chapter 11), will need to be well balanced in case one type of fund is reduced or withdrawn altogether.

FUNDING OPTIONS

All organisations require funding of some description, whether that funding is generated by the organisation itself, by way of reinvestment, or whether that funding comes from an external partner such as a funding body, sponsor or fundraising event. As trading organisations grow they will, at some point, be faced with the problem that expansion cannot be financed entirely from funds generated from internal operations, while voluntary sport teams may reach a point where membership subscriptions are insufficient to help the club take the next step in their development plan. Consequently a decision will need to be made on how to meet the funding gap and on the most effective type of finance to meet the organisation's requirements. To this end there are two main categories of funding: commercial finance and non-commercial finance. Typically, commercial finance will involve organisations applying for finance that charges interest, while non-commercial finance is based on grants. The respective funding options within these two categories will now be explored.

NON-COMMERCIAL FINANCE OPTIONS

Non-commercial funding in many cases can be the difference between whether a project proceeds or not. The most common form of funding in this category is a grant that may be applied for directly to a particular funding body such as the government, local authority, governing body, public sector agencies or (in the case of the UK) the National Lottery Fund. Grants of this nature may often be used to negate the need for commercial borrowing and will therefore mean that you do not have to pay interest on the funding. Moreover, it is typical for local clubs, for example, to apply for funding from multiple bodies and agencies. In the UK it is estimated that there are well over 500 different types of grant schemes covering a wide range of sport and leisure-related areas and while it would be impossible to write about all of the different funding options in this category here, we can look briefly at some of the larger, more popular funds, including:

- central and local government funding;
- sport council funding;
- national governing body funding;
- the National Lottery;
- Awards for All;
- Innovation Fund.

Central and local government funding

Central exchequer funding comes about following direct subsidies from public budgets, special taxes, loans with low interest rates, payment for renovation of existing facilities and structures and land sales or donations. For a government-funded project the criteria for funding may mean that you have to prove that you are addressing some sort of social problem, participation agenda or other key target. This may mean that you will need to divert some of the funds into addressing particular issues other than your principal goal. It may, however, be exactly what you need, as you will be able to apply for funds that directly relate to your mission statement.

Local authorities acting independently or in partnership with sports councils or governing bodies can make capital grants to local clubs that help them achieve their own objectives (see above). Many local authorities have an active programme to encourage and develop sporting activities, both recreational and competitive. There will, however, usually be a specific focus on developing sporting activities as part of a wider community initiative. In addition to these funds, it may also be the case that local councillors have 'ward' money that may be given to a club or society. In the UK the majority of funding for sport is channelled through local government, national sporting governing bodies and the National Lottery Fund. Similar arrangements exist in most other parts of the world too.

Sport council funding

Most sporting governing bodies have a responsibility to increase participation levels in particular social groups, high-performance sport and sporting events. If your organisation can 'tap in' to such priorities you will stand a greater chance of receiving the funding you require. It is common for applications for government funds to be highly competitive, and therefore usual that only the most competitive and agenda–addressing bids receive funding. Indeed, even when funding applications are accepted by such funds, the application is expected to achieve a 100 per cent return on the investment (i.e. £2 is achieved for every £1 of investment). As a rule of thumb you may therefore have to demonstrate that you can generate at least 65 per cent of the cost of your project elsewhere.

The strength of the government-funded model is that it will not be compromised by a commercial imperative for high profits. Instead it will be driven to provide more community access and equity. However, such funds are weakened by the fact that there are often insufficient incentives to maximise efficiency and to provide maximum accountability.

National governing body funding

While the main sport councils have a number of core funding themes, central government funds are also allocated to national governing bodies in all sports. As a result, many governing bodies will have their own grant schemes. This is, however, dependent on the size of the governing body, so before making an application you should first check that they offer grant aid or that they know of other funding sources for your sport.

In England, Sport England is investing £130 million in thirty key sports. This investment is distributed in conjunction with the advice and strategic direction of national governing bodies and a range of additional partners. The thirty sports include football, athletics, rowing, swimming, netball, squash, cricket, rugby union, badminton and triathlon.

As with sports council funding, a key strength lies in the fact that the fund will not be compromised by a commercial imperative for high profits. Instead, these funds are driven by the desire to provide more community access and equity, and are weakened by the fact that there are insufficient incentives to maximise efficiency and to provide maximum accountability.

The National Lottery

In the United Kingdom many sports clubs have been successful in their bids to various National Lottery funding organisations for projects such as new facilities, equipment, coaching, youth projects and so on. Lottery-funded programmes attract huge interest and are now increasingly competitive, so you will need to ensure that any application is very strong (see 'The funding process' on p. 244 to help with this). The projects that are awarded capital funding range from local to international, and priority is given to those projects that influence whole communities. Revenue projects, by contrast, are available to support elite sportsmen and women, to assist with training, coaching and travel. There are, however, hundreds of different Lottery sources and programmes, and these will need to be followed up by you for your particular needs.

Awards for All

Awards for All is a much smaller grants scheme for projects requiring between £500 and £10,000 of lottery funding. Its principal goal is to improve local communities and the scheme provides mainly revenue grants to help support coaching programmes or training courses, publicity materials, equipment, start-up costs and volunteers' expenses. Applications for these grants may be made at any time of the year by not-for-profit organisations and the grant must be used within one year.

Innovation Fund

The Innovation Fund provides medium to large awards to organisations that demonstrate they are or can address specific barriers to growing and sustaining participation in sport. The fund is targeted at projects that offer higher returns for higher risk (as you might expect from an innovative approach). Successful projects would be identified as market leading, and the aim is to turn the project from a special item into business as usual so that there can be a sustained impact. There are normally two rounds of applications per year, and financial contribution from a partner is often encouraged.

CASE STUDY

NON-COMMERCIAL FINANCE AND FOUNDATION X

Project overview

Foundation X wished to provide accessible and appropriate multi-sport sessions for young people aged 11 to 16. The sessions would provide local people and participants with the opportunity to volunteer and gain sporting qualifications. The project would deliver two coaching sessions per week in six different areas. A personal development programme would run alongside the sessions to encourage the use of sport to develop a stronger sense of volunteering and an employable, coaching, workforce.

Project impact

The project would:

- increase participation in sport and increase sustained levels of physical activity;
- widen access to sporting opportunities by targeting priority groups;
- provide volunteering, training and pathways to employment through sport;
- increase educational and vocational attainment;
- enhance the quality of coaching provision;
- encourage economic regeneration via sport in the target areas.

Project cost

The project has a lifetime of eighteen months and would cost £170,000. This cost would include salary costs, coaching costs, vehicle costs, training and education, management fees, administration, and insurance and facility hire. Partnership funding would be secured worth £65,000.

Grant requested

Foundation X requested 50 per cent of the total project cost: £85,000.

Funding body comments

It was appreciated that this project would indeed increase the number of participants in the six areas identified in the funding application. Moreover, the project would target gaps in sporting provision and provide a sustainable link to other partners. Alongside these objectives the project would also fit into the funding bodies' strategic goals.

Funding body recommendation

The recommendation was to fund 40 per cent of the total project cost based on the conditions that Foundation X could demonstrate its impact and identify additional partnership funding to cover the outstanding funds.

CONCLUSION

This case study illustrates the process and outcome of a non-commercial funding application. It is common for funding bodies to (1) fund less than the requested amount, (2) expect additional funding to come from a partner organisation, and (3) request that an impact assessment be conducted to ensure that the project delivered what it stated it would. It is also clear that, by providing a strategic application which considered the funding bodies' objectives as well as its own, Foundation X was successful in its bid for funding.

COMMERCIAL FINANCE OPTIONS

As we have already discovered, the fundamental difference between non-commercial and commercial finance options is the return that is required for the funding. By their very nature, non-commercial funding requires you to influence agendas and community-oriented goals. By contrast, commercial finance options will normally expect a monetary return as well. Such a requirement means that commercial funding is often withdrawn at speed, is reviewed regularly and makes you much more accountable. While commercial finance can be generated by increasing equity stakes (i.e. the owner of the organisation injecting more money into the business with a view to future profit), most commercial finance centres on borrowing (hence you should know how to use the gearing ratio covered in Chapter 9). Interest will usually be paid to the lenders and will be offset against business profits. Lenders will have no voting rights or direct influence (or control) over management. However, they will require security over the organisation's assets and in some instances personal guarantees. Due to its business focus a commercially driven fund option will be concerned about the containment of cost, efficiency and innovation, and will expect you to embrace and implement such practice. For the purposes of this chapter we will explore four key funding options:

1 bank loans;
2 debt finance;
3 leasing;
4 share issues.

Bank loans

Probably the best-known source of finance to you, given the number of credit cards you have in your wallet or purse, and the most widely used source of short-, medium- and long-term commercial finance, is a traditional bank loan. These can either be personal loans to help you or business loans to help both start-up and existing organisations. It is a flexible form of finance with interest being charged at regular intervals throughout the trading period. At their most basic level organisations will be given an overdraft facility on their standard account to manage short-term cash flow problems. In such cases interest rates are fixed much higher than the prevailing bank base rate.

More formal business loans may be offered to finance particular activities and should be negotiated based on sound and robust business plans. Interest rates will tend to be much lower than those on overdrafts, and you are expected to manage payments through revenues and profits that you or the organisation generates. Defaulting on repayments can be costly and may affect future applications.

Debt finance

Debt financing is an increasingly common source of finance in the sport industry, especially in professional team sports such as professional football. Debt financing basically involves the sale of an organisation's debts (or lending) to a third party. This type of finance provides, at its basic level, working capital and improves cash flow – similar to a traditional loan. However, debt financing is much more flexible than a standard overdraft or loan, as it can be renegotiated and paid back at will. They are often arranged on the basis of future revenues, hence the attraction of professional football, and are easy to secure. The main problem with finance of this style is that it often comes with a hefty interest rate and therefore places huge pressure on the financed organisation to generate profits to service the debt. Surprisingly, many see this as a positive method of growth, as it focuses objectives and forces organisations to eradicate waste and maintain efficient, highly profitable businesses. If we go back to our Manchester United Football Club case study we can see how debt finance has been used.

CASE STUDY

DEBT FINANCE AND MANCHESTER UNITED FOOTBALL CLUB

When Malcolm Glazer launched his takeover of Manchester United Football Club he did so using a significant amount of debt finance, and while this finance has been renegotiated in recent years, events of 2010 have illustrated what is really going on inside the boardroom of Old Trafford.

To finance the takeover, the Glazer family originally borrowed money from three hedge funds. It was one of three types of money worth about £275 million to complete the buyout. These loans came with very expensive strings attached, including the fact that rather than having to pay off the loan and the interest each year, the interest simply rolls up and is added to the final bill.

Even allowing for the £175 million that the club paid off at the time of their first refinancing exercise in 2006, and the recent exercise which converted a number of loans into a £500 million bond, key figures estimate that by the time all of the loans mature they will be worth about £600 million due to an interest rate jump to 16.25 per cent.

Despite this, the football club have no intention of paying off their most expensive debts in the short term. The £500 million bond has liberated their wallet and they have predicted cash reserves of £150 million. This money, however, will remain in the commercial operation so that they can exploit, still further, their expanding fan base across the globe. The refinancing has removed the immediate pressures of the original debt and the club has begun to focus on new strategic options such as the sale of sponsorship rights globally and the sale of mobile marketing rights to different territories.

Such a bold move not to repay the loans may seem strange. Granted, some of the reluctance to use cash reserves to repay borrowing might not go down too well with the fans of the club, but it should also be seen as a commercial masterstroke which should enable the club to continue to grow and ultimately repay its debts without too much problem when they mature.

Leasing

Leasing is, ostensibly, a contract between two parties for a specified time period of an asset, for example a car. Leasing is a good way of securing assets that you would not be able to afford outright but that you require to grow your business. It is normal that the lease will pay for the repair and maintenance costs but this is not always the case. The decision to lease or buy is normally determined by an organisation's cash flow; by leasing an asset that organisation can use funds that would otherwise be tied up. Leases can be arranged for a range of assets including premises, machinery, vehicles and fixtures and fittings – you just need to find the right organisation that will lease the assets at a price you can afford.

Share issues

The final type of commercial finance option that we consider is share issues. This is something that will rarely provide an opportunity to you, as it requires the organisation to be listed on the stock exchange. Providing that the organisation is listed it can offer more shares to the public in order to raise funds. There are four main ways of achieving this: a rights issue, a public issue, an offer for sale and placing. We will deal with each of these in turn.

A rights issue gives existing shareholders the right to purchase new shares in proportion to their existing holding. Usually these shares will be issued at a discount on the market price given that they will dilute share capital anyway (as there are more shares available). By contrast, a public issue occurs when an organisation offers its shares to the general public. The shares are offered at a fixed price and the public apply to purchase the shares they require.

An offer of sale involves new shares being offered to the public, usually by advertisement by a financial institution which has previously bought the shares from the organisation. Consequently the shares will become available at a higher price. Finally, placing shares means that shares are sold privately by financial institutions to selected people.

ALTERNATIVE FINANCE OPTIONS

While most finance is driven by the commercial and non-commercial arrangements outlined above, there are three further options available to you that influence the sport industry in particular. These options are:

1 sponsorship;
2 public–private partnerships (PPPs);
3 fundraising.

Sponsorship

In addition to traditional commercial finance, sport is regularly supported by sponsorship arrangements. Such arrangements will involve sponsors funding, providing goods/services and/or supporting you in your aims and objectives. Sponsorship is a critical communications tool for both the sponsor and the sponsee, and may be used as a public relations tool and for marketing and promotions, thus improving your competitive edge. All such benefits need to be considered when approaching potential sponsors, as you need to ensure that they provide you with the correct function. However, sponsors, particularly in the sport industry, now expect a return on their investment which is measurable. As a result you will need to provide a detailed analysis of how the partnership can support the sponsor, link with its objectives and help develop its market position. Sponsorship is now a mutually beneficial exercise rather than one-way traffic.

By way of an example, organisations that sponsor major sporting events will do so due to the global audience to which their brands gain exposure. The World Cup has a global audience of 40 billion viewers, so Coca-Cola, as a worldwide, leading brand, wants to associate itself with such excellence. However, in order to personalise and localise its image and activity, Coca-Cola also supports grass-roots sport to reinforce its global message.

Sponsors are looking for sports properties that can make a valuable and quantifiable contribution to existing or planned brand communications. To do so, the sponsorship must have a good fit with the event and its target audience. Any prospective sponsor must be approached professionally, as commercial sponsorship can be extremely difficult to find and requires a lot of work to service it. Consequently you need to carefully target prospective sponsors and then design an approach specifically tailored to each sponsor's needs.

Public–private partnerships (PPPs)

One way of overcoming the weaknesses of both government and private funds while maintaining their respective strengths is to create a funding structure that embraces them both. Such an arrangement is called a public–private partnership where the government and private sector drive the project as a joint venture. This mixed management system will still require you to be strategic in your application but will offer you a more rounded level of support. It does, however, require a fine balancing act, given the various personal ambitions. Public and private entities must understand, respect and acknowledge their potential differences. The public sector partner will want to meet the needs and wants of their target population, including social benefits and outcomes. On the other hand, the private sector partner will look to maximise financial return and will therefore want to target their efforts into providing the greatest opportunity to earn revenues and make profits. Hardly a match made in heaven, I am sure you will agree. Moreover, the public sector will want to ensure that you adhere to their guidelines whereas a private sector partner will be more flexible and potentially more innovative with their solutions. The final challenge is that both parties will want to look after themselves and may end up competing against each other throughout the partnership.

CASE STUDY

PUBLIC–PRIVATE PARTNERSHIPS IN THE LONDON BOROUGH OF GREENWICH

The London Borough of Greenwich has been involved in a PPP for more than twelve years with a leisure trust called Greenwich Leisure Limited (GLL). A ten-year programme of investment is in place to address the capital requirements of the service. Increases in income are reinvested and this has resulted in improved facilities for customers, and has also increased participation. The subsidy paid by the council to run its leisure facilities reduced from £2.5 million in the early 1990s to £900,000 in 2005. Membership increased from 7,000 to 70,000 during the same period. The partnership encourages staff, customers and community groups to be involved in the planning and development of programmes and new services. There are three main projects.

The Healthwise Project

This partnership between GLL, Greenwich Primary Care Trust, Woolwich Development Agency and the Healthy Greenwich Network was brought together as part of a wider physical activity for health programme for the area, which is designed to develop an integrated and innovative approach to improving health outcomes by increasing levels of activity.

GLL and Charlton FC

GLL and Charlton FC work in partnership with Greenwich Community College and have accessed European funding to develop sporting, recreational and employment opportunities for the local community. The funding enabled the redevelopment of the ground, including the rebuilding of the West Stand incorporating a fitness centre and gym boasting 1,300 members, and a new North Stand which houses the London Leisure College.

The London Fitness Network

The London Fitness Network is a strategic alliance of the London leisure trusts engaged in delivering not-for-profit leisure services to their communities. The partnership includes eight independent trust organisations with over sixty leisure centres across London providing a joint membership service.

Fundraising

Our final funding option is the option of fundraising. Fundraising is mainly about people, whether they are giving you money, organising events, using your service or managing your committees. A really good fundraiser therefore will be known, liked and trusted by the right kinds of people. Fundraising is therefore hard work, time-consuming and sometimes a thankless task. However, it is possible, as you will know by the hundreds and thousands of fundraising events that take place regularly, for example fun runs, school fetes or quiz nights.

It is far easier to raise money for something specific than to appeal for administrative costs or general funds. Donors prefer to feel that their money is going to something tangible and in which they are generally interested. While a guide to how fundraising works is beyond the scope of this chapter it is worth outlining a few key points:

- Identify a tangible item for the fundraising.
- Outline the long-term bonus and impact of the fundraising.
- Be realistic and achievable in your goals, giving the funder confidence that you will meet your intended outcomes.
- Provide good value so that your project stands out as being well-thought out.
- Be topical: try to link your project to current issues and concerns.
- Make your project relevant to the funder so that it meets their interests and priorities.
- Don't be afraid of hard work: fundraising is tough, often demoralising and an organisational nightmare.

THE FUNDING PROCESS

Whatever funding strategy you go with, it is possible to apply a basic funding process checklist which will enhance your chances of securing funding. Certainly in most government funding schemes a three-stage process (see Figure 14.1) will be used to assess the suitability of the application. It follows therefore that we should apply this model to the other funding options (with the exception of fundraising, given the practicalities involved). Stage one will usually be the 'enquiry' stage where applications will be vetted for their initial suitability; this might involve an expression of interest, a telephone conversation, or a short letter or e-mail outlining your requirements. Providing that your request meets the approval of the funding body, you will follow it up with a formal application for funding before your bid is passed on to stages two and three.

In order to pass stages one and two you should be able to answer the following questions:

- Can you explain why your project is needed?
- Can your project clearly deliver against the funding body's priorities?
- Have you considered any alternatives to fund the project? If not, why not?
- Can you communicate the project's aims and objectives, and more importantly its planned output?
- How will you measure the project against self-imposed key performance indicators? (We will examine these later in the chapter.)
- Can you provide an accurate, and prudent, cost breakdown for your project (like a budget that we covered in Chapter 12)?
- Have you carried out an assessment of risk associated with the project and what mechanisms have you put in place to deal with them?
- Do you have an implementation plan so that the funding body can see how the funds will be used and when they will be used?
- What is the sustainability of your project?

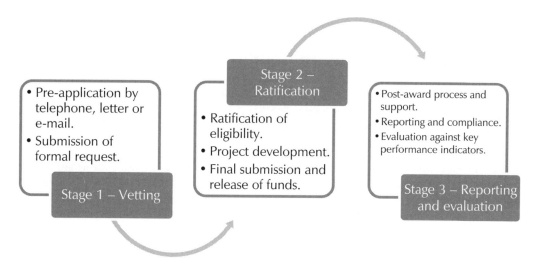

Figure 14.1 The funding process

Providing that your application passes the initial vetting process, which it should given that you will have been strategic in both your selection of funding body and in the nature of your request so that you demonstrate an awareness of the wider goals of the funder, you will move on to stage two: ratification. This stage involves some further development of your project plan, often in conjunction with the potential funding body. This should ensure that any shared goals are met and that the funding is allocated correctly. It will also give the funding body time to appraise the application fully, and establish when and how they can provide funding. It would not be uncommon for a funding body to offer support services at this point which would develop the partnership and ensure that the project maintains its momentum.

Once the project has been developed fully the funds should be allocated. Many sport organisations consider this to be the time to celebrate, but it is often just the starting point. From here on the project will move into stage three which is where it needs to be managed properly, be accountable for the use of resources and begin to show a return on investment. The most effective way to manage and review any project is through the use of monitoring and evaluation, or, to use more common terminology, apply and report the outcome of key performance indicators.

MONITORING AND EVALUATION: KEY PERFORMANCE INDICATORS

Performance on any project, let alone a funded one, should be assessed and managed at regular intervals. Indeed, it is an effective method of keeping a project on track, ensuring that predicted revenues and costs are controlled and making future decisions on the most up-to-date information. Essentially, monitoring and evaluation are about the need to enhance performance so that both you and the funding body can see that the project is meeting its aims and objectives. Monitoring and evaluation also enable you to manage expectations (in much the same way as budgeting appraisal does – see Chapter 12) through clearly defined targets and the measurement of performance against these targets (in the same way that ratio analysis does). Finally, it will allow your managers to assess how well you are doing in managing the project!

The number and type of key performance indicators (KPIs) will vary depending on the size and scale of the project and the requirements and expectations of the funding body and you. They are also a useful tool once funding has been secured and can help with improving sustainability. Evaluating KPIs is the most effective way of making decisions in the short term as you can react quickly if something goes wrong or exploit areas that are going particularly well.

The main issue with using KPIs is that they really only provide quantitative information as a measurement of performance, and as a result fail to identify the reason why things are happening. This means that you may find you need to follow up results quickly with some sort of qualitative exercise. Nevertheless, if you can ensure that your KPIs follow these principles you shouldn't go far wrong:

- Only focus on relevant information. Does the information help you explain or manage performance?
- Set up hierarchical KPIs. Prioritise key aims and objectives so that you achieve the most important things.
- Use them. If you are not meeting targets then the funding body may decide to pull out of the project, leaving you with a funding gap.
- Use KPIs in association with targets. Such targets should be challenging but not insurmountable.
- Appreciate their value and ensure that the project team does too.

SUMMARY

As I have mentioned, there will be many more fundraising options and examples for you to consider when approaching funding and finance in your career. This chapter was only intended to give you a flavour of what to expect and some of the key messages and questions to consider. However, regardless of what you now know about funding and finance in sport, you need to appreciate that they will be required by nearly every sport organisation at some point in their development. They can fund major and minor projects, can be driven by non-commercial, commercial and other means, and has a definitive process. Moreover, the challenge for any manager is to be able to evaluate his or her funded project using key performance indicators. These will keep the project on track and enable you to react quickly to environmental changes.

QUESTIONS FOR REVIEW

Given the discursive and signposting nature of this chapter and the fact that it is the final chapter in the book, there are no questions for review.

REFERENCES AND FURTHER READING

Bill, K. (ed.) (2009) *Sport Management*. Learning Matters, Exeter.
Botting, N. and Norton, M. (2003) *The Complete Fundraising Handbook*. Directory of Social Change, London.
Masterman, G. (2007) *Sponsorship for a Return on Investment*. Butterworth-Heinemann, Oxford.
Masterman, G. (2009) *Strategic Sports Event Management*, Olympic edn. Butterworth-Heinemann, Oxford.
Schwarz, E., Hall, S. and Shibli, S. (2010) *Sport Facility Operations Management*. Butterworth-Heinemann, Oxford.
Stewart, B. (2007) *Sport Funding and Finance*. Butterworth-Heinemann, Oxford.
Trenberth, L. (ed.) (2003) *Managing the Business of Sport*. Dunmore Press, Palmerston North.

APPENDIX A: ADDITIONAL CASE STUDY

Once you have completed Chapter 1, consider the following.

Earlier you examined some information about Tottenham Hotspur Football Club. While this book focuses on sport it will also be useful to have a look at a leisure organisation.

Arena Leisure plc stage 25 per cent of all horse-racing in the United Kingdom. They own, run and manage a portfolio of racecourses to provide a solid base for the future development of the group. They maintain a continued focus on improving their fixture list which includes seventy-five race meetings at Southwell, twenty-three race meetings at Folkestone, ninety race meetings at Lingfield Park, twenty-seven race meetings at Royal Windsor, twenty-one race meetings at Worcester and ninety-seven race meetings at Wolverhampton. In addition, they aim to increase overall attendances at their courses, currently around 750,000 people a year, and to expand their non-racing facilities such as gambling, sport and leisure clubs and television.

To answer the following questions you will need to go online and download their annual report. It may be found at www.arenaleisureplc.com.

QUESTIONS

- Is the organisation meeting its corporate statement?
- How has the business performed over the past year?
- What are its future prospects?

Once you have completed Chapter 7 consider:

Go back to the Arena Leisure case study that we looked at in Chapter 1 and conduct the same analysis as we have done for Spurs. If you have not already done so, go online and download their annual report. It may be found at www.arenaleisureplc.com.

Once you have completed Chapter 9 consider:

Go back to the Arena Leisure case study that we asked you to look at in Chapters 1 and 7, and conduct the same analysis as we have done for JJB. If you have not already done so, go online and download their annual report. It may be found at www.arenaleisureplc.com.

additional case study

APPENDIX B: ANSWERS TO REVIEW QUESTIONS

CHAPTER 1

1. Managers use financial information to make decisions and to evaluate the success of such decisions.
2. You could have suggested any three from the following list:
    - owners of a company;
    - trade contacts;
    - providers of finance;
    - Her Majesty's Revenue and Customs;
    - employees;
    - customers.
3. Types of businesses are: sole traders, partnerships, private company and public company. They may also be 'for-profit' and 'not-for-profit' organisations.
4. Financial accounting examines 'historical information'.
5. False. The balance sheet shows what assets the company owns and what liabilities it has. The profit and loss account (income statement) reports the profit (or loss) made by the company.

CHAPTER 2

1. Hopefully you remembered some of the following accounting concepts:
    - reliability;
    - comparability;
    - going concern;
    - accruals;
    - materiality;
    - business entity;
    - money measurement;
    - dual aspect;
    - historical cost.

2   The blanks should have been filled in as follows:

    a   dual aspect
    b   going concern
    c   materiality
    d   business entity
    e   accruals
    f   money measurement.

3   Financial Reporting Council, International Accounting Standards Committee and the stock exchange.

4   True or false answers below:

    a   True
    b   False: liabilities are amounts owed by the business to other people
    c   True
    d   True
    e. False: creditors are liabilities and are therefore amounts owed by the business.

CHAPTER 3

1   For the following questions complete the 'T' accounts:

    a   The owner of the firm introduces capital of £15,000 in cash.

    Cash A/C

DEBIT	CREDIT
15,000	

    Capital A/C

DEBIT	CREDIT
	15,000

    b   Goods for resale are purchased, by cash, for £6,000.

    Purchases (stock)

DEBIT	CREDIT
6,000	

    Cash A/C

DEBIT	CREDIT
	6,000

c The rent bill arrives for the gym amounting to £3,500. Note the bill has not yet been paid.

Rent

DEBIT	CREDIT
3,500	

Trade creditors

DEBIT	CREDIT
	3,500

d New machinery costing £10,000 is purchased for cash.

Machinery

DEBIT	CREDIT
10,000	

Cash A/C

DEBIT	CREDIT
	10,000

e Cash sales amount to £21,000. Note we will deal with the reduction in stock later.

Sales

DEBIT	CREDIT
	21,000

Cash A/C

DEBIT	CREDIT
12,000	

f The business buys £5,000 of goods for resale on credit.

Purchases (stock)

DEBIT	CREDIT
5,000	

Trade creditors

DEBIT	CREDIT
	5,000

g New vehicles are brought for £30,000. A deposit of £13,000 is paid and the rest is put on credit. Note: we have to record the full double entry here, so we need to split the asset up into two parts.

Motors

DEBIT	CREDIT
13,000	
17,000	

Cash A/C

DEBIT	CREDIT
	13,000

Traded creditors

DEBIT	CREDIT
	17,000

2 The following table illustrates where everything should go.

Assets	Liabilities
Stock	Bank overdraft
Cash	Amounts owing to creditors
Trade debtor	Mortgage
Motor vehicle	Amounts due on stocks purchased

3 Complete the gaps in the following table:

	Assets £	Liabilities £	Capital £
(a)	16,200	8,500	**7,700**
(b)	21,000	**9,925**	11,075
(c)	**23,350**	4,560	18,790
(d)	12,350	4,350	8,000
(e)	65,800	**10,800**	55,000

252
answers to review questions

CHAPTER 4

1. It is the residue of the cost of the asset minus the depreciation to date. Note: we have called it a residue because we cannot find a good word to describe it, since it is not a 'real' item: it is cash (the purchase price of the asset) less an accounting estimate (a figure used to match a share of the value of the asset to the periods it was used in). The net book value is not what you can sell the asset for.
2. There is no change: depreciation is not cash.
3. Interest receivable is the amount of interest that an organisation would receive. Monies received are income and not expenses. Interest payable is an expense.
4. Interest payments are payments for the interest on a loan: the interest accrues on the amount of the loan outstanding (the capital). Capital payments are payments that reduce the amount of capital outstanding.
5. Yes: discounts are allowed as an expense.

CHAPTER 5

1. Errors of omission and commission, compensating errors. Errors of principal and errors of original entry.
2. An arithmetic check to ensure that the double-entry rule has been applied correctly. Debits should equal credits.
3. The answers are:
   - Trade debtors: balance sheet (current asset).
   - Cash and bank: balance sheet (current asset).
   - Bank loans: balance sheet (non-current liability).
   - Rent: income statement (expense).
   - Wages: income statement (expenses). If they are owed they would also be in the balance sheet (current liability).
   - Loan interest paid: income statement (expense).
   - Trade creditors: balance sheet (current liability).
4. No. It will be shown in the balance sheet as a fixed asset.
5. Profit increases capital.
6. No. The van is an asset. The loan is a liability (it is money that is owed).
7. The values would be:
   - Van (asset): £10,000. This is the cost of the van and would go on the balance sheet.
   - Depreciation (expense): £2,000. This is the depreciation charge for the second year and would be taken to the income statement.
   - Provision for depreciation: £4,000. This would go to the balance sheet and would allow the calculation of the net book value of the van (£6,000).
8. No. It lists a summary of the transactions (i.e. the balances on each account).

'T' accounts for the trial balance activity

To help make this logical (if you got the activity wrong) you will notice that there is a reference column included in the accounts. This represents the question number so that you can follow exactly what we have done.

Cash A/C

Ref.	DEBIT	Ref.	CREDIT
1	7,000	2	3,500
4	1,000	5	2,000
6	10,000	8	4,250
9	1,500	10	100
		11	100
		12	1,500
		C/d	8,050
	19,500		19,500
B/d	8,050		

Capital A/C

Ref.	DEBIT	Ref.	CREDIT
		1	7,000
C/d	7,000		
	7,000		7,000
		B/d	7,000

Rent A/C

Ref.	DEBIT	Ref.	CREDIT
2	3,500		
		C/d	3,500
	3,500		3,500
B/d	3,500		

Purchases (stock)

Ref.	DEBIT	Ref.	CREDIT
3	5,000		
		C/d	5,000
	5,000		5,000
B/d	5,000		

Trade creditors' A/C

Ref.	DEBIT	Ref.	CREDIT
8	4,250	3	5,000
C/d	750		
	5,000		5,000
		B/d	750

Loan A/C

Ref.	DEBIT	Ref.	CREDIT
		4	1,000
C/d	1,000		
	1,000		1,000
		B/d	1,000

Fixtures and fittings A/C

Ref.	DEBIT	Ref.	CREDIT
5	2,000		
		C/d	2,000
	2,000		2,000
B/d	2,000		

Sales A/C

Ref.	DEBIT	Ref.	CREDIT
		6	10,000
C/d	12,500	7	2,500
	12,500		12,500
		B/d	12,500

Trade debtors' A/C

Ref.	DEBIT	Ref.	CREDIT
7	2,500	9	1,500
		C/d	1,000
	2,500		2,500
B/d	1,000		

Interest payable (loan interest)

Ref.	DEBIT	Ref.	CREDIT
10	100		
		C/d	100
	100		100
B/d	100		

Wages (admin) A/C

Ref.	DEBIT	Ref.	CREDIT
11	100		
		C/d	100
	100		100
B/d	100		

Drawings A/C

Ref.	DEBIT	Ref.	CREDIT
12	1,500		
		C/d	1,500
	1,500		1,500
B/d	1,500		

CHAPTER 6

1. (i) An accrued expense is an amount that is owed but has not yet been paid. For example, a company's telephone charges will be billed quarterly in arrears. If the company's year end is part-way through a quarter they will estimate the phone charges that they think will have accrued and include these in the accounts. (ii) A prepaid expense is the opposite of the above (i.e. it has been paid in advance (for example, car insurance)).
2. They would be adjustments to the respective accounts (and would be shown on the balance sheet as prepayments and current liabilities).
3. Only the period August to March is in this accounting period. Thus only eight-twelfths of the payment is for this year; so of the £12,000 paid, only £8,000 is for this year. The other £4,000 is a prepayment and will be charged as an expense in next year's accounts.

4   Gross profit is profit before deducting operating expenses; interest and tax have been deducted. It is calculated as: Gross profit = Sales revenue minus cost of sales.
5   Net profit is Sales revenue minus all expenses. It is calculated as: Gross profit minus all other expenses.

CHAPTER 7

1   The income statement reports the operating results of the organisation for the year. It shows, in financial terms, the activities of the organisation.
2   The balance sheet is a statement of the organisation's assets and liabilities. However, it is only a 'snapshot': it shows the situation at the time it was compiled. As soon as there is a transaction it will change.
3   No, no and no. No way! *No!* The answer is *No!* Cash is cash: it is real, you can see it, you can spend it and you can touch it. Profit is not real: it is the 'residue' that remains after all expenses for a period have been deducted from incomes for a period. Note the answer says 'for a period' and not 'in a period'. This is because of the accruals concept.

CHAPTER 8

1   Income statement (profit and loss account), balance sheet and cash flow statement.
2   Introductory material, directors' reports, financial statements and notes to the accounts.
3   Notes to the accounts provide additional, more specific information relating to key items contained within the main financial statements.

CHAPTER 9

1   Ratio analysis is used to measure and compare the performance and financial health of an organisation from year to year or against similar companies.
2   The five key areas are: growth, profitability, ROCE, liquidity and investment ratios.
3   ROCE is the return on capital employed and therefore shows the 'reward' that has been gained by using the capital in the organisation.
4   Liquidity is a measure of how quickly an organisation could cover its immediate liabilities if it demanded payment. It can be measured by the current ratio and the quick (acid test) ratio.
5   Hopefully you covered three of the points we discussed earlier in the chapter. These included the following:

- There are no universally agreed definitions for the formulas and terminology used.
- Some data may not be available, so you may have to use less precise material.
- Comparisons with other companies in the industry may be difficult if their data is not published – how do you really know how you are doing?
- The sport and leisure industry is always in a period of rapid change, and therefore some analysis is out of date before it is completed owing to the changes in the operating environment.
- Non-financial factors are not considered in ratio analysis.

CHAPTER 10

1. The purpose of cost accounting is to assist managers to make decisions which will have an impact upon the future financial success of an organisation.
2. Financial accounting is required and is governed by law, and provides information on past performance. By contrast cost accounting examines forward-looking information which provides information for managers to plan, make decisions and exercise control.
3. A variable cost tends to vary according to the level of activity. Examples of variable cost would include direct product materials and casual labour (i.e. paid by the hour).
4. A direct cost can be traced in full to a product or service. An indirect cost cannot, but is incurred in the course of making or providing a product.
5. A cost centre is a designated location, function, activity or item for which costs are collected (e.g. a marketing department and a cost unit is a unit of production for which costs are collected, such as the hire of a squash racket).

CHAPTER 11

1. A marginal cost is the cost incurred in making one more unit.
2. Contribution is the amount of money left over from sales revenue once variable costs have been paid. This money is what is left to pay fixed costs.
3. The breakeven point is the point at which an organisation will not make a profit or a loss and may be explained as the breakeven point in revenue or the breakeven point in units.
4. Cost structures can have a profound effect on a business in times of growth and during a downturn in trade. Organisations where the majority of cost is fixed will find it difficult during periods of economic recession but will be able to react more quickly in times of growth.
5. You need to use the C/S ratio:

$$C/S \text{ ratio} = 47\%$$

Therefore, contribution per £1 of revenue = 47 pence.

Breakeven revenue = Fixed costs/Contribution per £1 of sales

151,000 / 0.47

= £321,277

Thus:

	Revenue	% Relationship
Revenue	321,277	100
Less		
Variable cost	170,277	53
Equals		
Contribution	151,000	47

	Revenue	% Relationship
Less		
Fixed cost	151,000	
Equals		
Profit	0	

CHAPTER 12

1. Continuation budgeting and zero-based budgeting.
2. Incremental and decremental.
3. No change in business strategy or priorities.
4. True.
5. Eight: define business objectives, audit resources, operationalise strategies, allocate responsibilities, prepare budgets, implement budgets, measure performance and take action to control the business.

CHAPTER 13

1. Investment appraisal helps us to evaluate the long-term benefits and financial viability of proposed investment projects with a view to determining which is likely to give the highest financial return.
2. Payback period, accounting rate of return, net present value and internal rate of return.
3. 1/(1 + interest rate) ^ number of years.
4. They do not take into consideration the time value of money.
5. It is predicted data and may change in the long term.

GLOSSARY OF TERMS

Below you will find all of the key terms that are covered in this book in one place. This will help you understand the terminology throughout instead of having to keep flicking back through previous chapters. You will also find some additional terminology, just in case I have assumed incorrectly that you know what I'm are talking about.

Account: a record that is kept as part of an accounting system. It will be a record of the transactions and will be recorded in monetary values.

Accounting: identifying, collecting, measuring, recording, summarising and communicating financial information.

Accounting equation: Assets – Liabilities = Capital.

Accounting rate of return: relates the average yearly surplus of a project to the average investment to measure the overall profitability of a project (its lifetime surplus).

Accruals: the accruals basis of accounting requires the non-cash effects of transactions and other events to be reflected in the financial statements for the accounting period in which they occur and not during the period when the cash is paid or received.

Annual report: the financial statements, directors' report, auditor's report and other information published by an organisation on an annual basis.

Asset: item or resource that has a value to the business and things that are used by the business and for the business. Normally we will classify assets as either fixed or current. The basic difference is that a fixed asset is something that the business intends to keep and use for some time, whereas a current asset is held for the business to convert into cash during trading. Some good examples are business premises, motor vehicles that are fixed assets, and stock and cash, which are current assets.

Asset disposal: the term used to describe the sale of fixed assets when they reach the end of their useful life.

Bad debts: a debt that the company has decided is unlikely to be paid.

Balance sheet: a list of all of the assets owned by a business and all of the liabilities owed by a business at a specific point in time. It is often referred to as a 'snapshot' of the financial position of the business at a specific moment in time (normally the end of the financial year).

Borrowings: amounts of finance the company has borrowed from lenders in the form of overdraft facilities and loans, etc.

Breakeven point: the level of activity at which there is neither a profit nor a loss. It can be measured in terms of units of production or sales revenue.

Budget: the business or overall plan of an organisation expressed in financial terms.

Business entity concept: dictates that a line is drawn between the business and its owner(s): the business and its owner(s) are two separate entities.

Capital: generally considered to be the owners' stake in the business and may also be called equity. To take this a step further, it is also the excess of assets over liabilities.

Cash budget: an analysis of how the cash available to an organisation is expected to change over a given period of time.

Cash flow statement: a financial summary of all of the cash receipts and payments over an accounting period.

Closing stock (inventory): the value of stock (inventory) that is held at the end of a period.

Consistency concept: similar items within a single set of accounts should be given similar accounting treatment, and the same treatment should be applied from one accounting period to the next for similar items so that one year's results are comparable to the next.

Continuation budgeting: budgets compiled on the basis of no change in policies or priorities, i.e. business as usual.

Contribution: the sales value less the variable costs and based on the assumption that the sales value and the variable costs will remain constant.

Contribution/sales ratio: the relationship between contribution and sales revenue. It also means the percentage of sales revenue that is left over as contribution.

Corporate statement: a statement of an organisation's goal for the financial period that allows us to see how the organisation has performed over the financial period.

Cost accounting: the process of collecting, processing and presenting financial data to ascertain the cost of the cost centres and cost units.

Cost behaviour: all of the costs outlined above will, and do, behave in different ways. Cost behaviour is the study of the way in which costs fluctuate and the rationale for such variation. If we strip this back to basics, then the basic principle of cost behaviour is that as activity rises, costs will normally rise too.

Cost centre: a designated location, function, activity or item for which costs are collected (e.g. the marketing department).

Cost of sales: the cost of goods sold during the period. For a retailer this will be calculated as Opening stock + Purchases – Closing stock. For a manufacturing company it will include all of the production costs.

Creditor: an entity or person to whom money is owed.

Debtor: an entity or person who owes money to the business.

Depreciation: a notional charge made in the accounts to represent the use of an asset. It also serves to reduce the value of an asset in the balance sheet.

Direct costs: a fundamental method in cost classification is to establish which costs are direct and which costs are indirect. Direct costs can be easily identified (or traced) in full to a product, service or department.

Dividends: amounts of money paid to shareholders from profits earned by a company. It is usual for the total payment to be paid in two instalments: an interim payment part-way through the year and the final payments at the year end. Dividend payments are discretionary: they do not have to be paid.

Double-entry rule/bookkeeping: the principle that every financial transaction involves two items.

Dual aspect concept: each transaction conducted by a business will affect two items within the business.

Expenses: the reverse of income. All money spent in relation to the company's activities.

Financial accounting: the preparation of information for external use, mainly concerned with reporting on past events.

Financial statements: the complete set of accounts. This will include the balance sheet (this shows the organisation's assets and liabilities), income statement (the profit and loss account) and the cash flow statement. Also included will be notes on the accounting policies used and significant activities.

Fixed cost: an item of revenue expenditure that will be unaffected by changes in the level of production or sales activity in the short term.

Going concern: the information presented in the financial statements is prepared on the basis that the organisation will continue to operate for the foreseeable future.

Gross profit: Sales income minus the direct cost of the goods or services sold to customers, i.e. sales minus cost of sales.

Historical cost concept: dictates that the value of items that a business owns must be based on their original cost and must not be adjusted for any subsequent changes in price or value.

Income: all money that is received or receivable.

Income statement (P&L account): a statement showing the profits (or losses) recognised during a period. The profit is calculated by deducting expenditure (including charges for capital maintenance) from income.

Indirect costs: by contrast, an indirect cost that is incurred in the course of making a product or delivering a service cannot be traced in full to that product or service. Indirect costs are often termed overheads.

Intangible fixed asset: a fixed asset that has no physical existence. Examples are goodwill, patents and trademarks.

Internal rate of return: the interest rate at which the sum of the discounted values of the predicted net cash flows is equal to the capital invested in the proposed project.

Inventory: *see* **Stock**.

(Capital) Investment appraisal: the evaluation of proposed investment projects which will have a lasting effect on an organisation. It helps to determine which project is likely to give the highest financial return.

Liabilities: amounts owed by the business to people other than the owner. Normally we will see liabilities classified as either payable within one year (current liabilities) (e.g. bank overdrafts, supplier accounts) or payable after one-year (non-current liabilities) (e.g. longer-term bank loans).

Limited company: a company registered with the Registrar of Companies whose shareholders enjoy limited liability.

Limited liability: legal protection given to the shareholders of a limited company. When a company cannot pay its debts the shareholders will not be liable to contribute more than their initial investment towards the overall debt.

Liquidation: quite simply the process by which a limited company ceases to exist. It is a legal status rather than a financial position.

Liquidity: the term used to describe the ability of an organisation to generate sufficient cash to meet its liabilities as they fall due.

Loans: money borrowed or lent. In an organisation's accounts it normally means amounts borrowed, as amounts lent are usually called investments. Loans are normally arranged by banks and will be noted as long-term (non-current) liabilities.

Management accounting: providing information that is focused primarily on the needs of management and will therefore additionally look to the future, and will cover planning and control aspects. Management accounting is not a statutory requirement.

Marginal cost: the extra cost of making one more unit in a given period of time (often referred to as the variable cost per unit of production).

Materiality concept: only items of significance are included in the financial statements. An item is significant if its omission or misrepresentation could influence the economic decisions of those using the financial statements.

Money measurement concept: only items of monetary value can be recorded in the financial statements.

Net present value: the difference between the sum of discounted values of the predicted net cash flows and the capital invested in a proposed long-term investment project.

Nominal ledger ('T' account): an accounting record which summarises the financial affairs of a business containing details of assets, liabilities, incomes and expenditures.

Opening stock (inventory): the value of stock that is held at the beginning of a financial period.

Operating profit: the profit of a business which is generated from its ordinary activities.

Opportunity cost of capital: the interest forgone because the cash was not available for investment purposes today.

Overdraft: the amount owing to a bank on a current account.

Partnerships: two or more people enter into business together. The liability will be shared between the owners and at least one of them will have unlimited liability for the debts they may incur.

Patent: the exclusive right to use an invention. The value of a patent may be carried in the accounts as an intangible asset.

Payback period: the time required for the predicted net cash flows to equal the capital invested in a project.

Profit: a positive residue between sales income and total expenses for a financial period.

Profit centre: a designated location, function, activity or item for which costs and revenues are collected (e.g. trading activities (sales)).

Profit and loss account (income statement): a statement showing the profits (or losses) recognised during a period. The profit is calculated by deducting expenditure (including charges for capital maintenance) from income.

Project data: predicted information which will determine the investment required in the project, the lifespan of the project, cash inflows, cash outflows, net cash flows and any residual value.

Prudence concept: states that revenue and profits are not anticipated but are recognised only when they are realised.

Public company: a plc has shares, which can be purchased by anyone on the stock exchange. Ownership is therefore open to anyone who wants to buy shares. Plcs have legal requirements in that they have to produce annual reports and accounts and file them with Companies House. They must have two directors.

Residual value: the value of a fixed asset after it has been fully depreciated. It may often be the same as an item's scrap value.

Return on capital employed (ROCE): the ratio of profit before interest and tax to capital used to earn the profits. It shows the 'reward' that has been gained by using the capital in the organisation.

Sales: the amount shown on the income statement indicating the value of goods and services supplied to customers.
Semi-variable costs: in reality few costs are ever completely fixed or variable. Many will have fixed elements to them or fixed charges that need to be paid before you can access better deals. Semi-variable costs therefore have a fixed and variable element to them. Such costs are affected by output and we can use the example of mobile telephone contracts to see how this works in practice. Contracts will have a standing charge, say £25 per month, and if you go over your inclusive allowance or use your phone abroad you will incur additional (variable) charges based on usage.
Shareholder: someone who owns shares in an organisation. Collectively all of the shareholders own the organisation concerned.
Sole trader: one person owns the business. There is no legal separation of identity between the business and the owner.
Stepped costs: these are fixed over a certain range of output but will increase as capacity is reached. For example, your salary may stay constant irrespective of what you have to do in your job until an additional shift is added or more staff are recruited.
Stock: items held by a company for sale, conversion to a product for sale or consumption in production. Now also referred to as 'Inventory'.
Tangible fixed asset: a fixed asset that has a physical existence. Examples are vehicles, furniture, buildings and equipment.
Time value of money: the concept that cash received today is worth more than the same amount received at a later date because of the opportunity cost of capital.
Total cost: fixed costs + variable costs.
Trademark: a word or symbol that identifies specific goods or services. The value of a trademark may be carried in the accounts as an intangible asset.
Trial balance: a list of nominal ledger ('T') account balances. It is used primarily as a measure to see if credit balances equal debit balances. Ultimately it will offer some reassurance that the double-entry rule has been applied correctly.
Turnover: another term for the sales figure on an organisation's income statement.
Unlimited liability: the opposite of limited liability. At least one of the shareholders (be it a sole trader or partnership) will be liable for the total debt their company incurs.
Variable cost: an item of revenue expenditure that will vary with the level of production or sales activity.
Variance: the difference between actual performance and planned performance.
Zero-based budgeting: a method of budgeting which starts with the priorities of an organisation and allocates resources to the priorities according to their rank order of importance.
Zyzzyva: a tropical American weevil. You will now be able to impress your family and friends by your knowledge of accounting and the last word in the dictionary!

INDEX

account 4
accounting 4, 5, 17
accounting equation 45
accounting policies 115
accounting rate of return 29
Accounting Standards Board 34
Accounting Standards Committee 25
accruals 30, 91
acid test 141
annual reports 112, 122
asset disposal 74, 75
assets 8, 18; current 33, 45, 99; non-current 45, 99; *see also* fixed assets
Awards for All 237

bad debts 70, 71
balance sheet 7, 8, 18; growth analysis 133; interpreting 101
borrowing 9, 10, 28, 143
breakeven 164, 171; analysis 176; point 172
British Triathlon Federation 108
BSkyB 10, 27
budget 160, 189
business entity concept 31

capital 34, 43, 45, 84
capital employed, return on 134, 136
cash 10, 18
cash budget 200, 205
cash flow statements 104, 140
closing stock 52, 84, 88
Combined Code 36
Companies Act 95
Companies House 16
company law 22
comparability 29
compounding 221
consistency concept 30
continuation budget 198

contribution 168
contribution/sales ratio 169
corporate governance 36
corporate statement 5
cost accounting 154, 155
cost behaviour 160, 165
cost centre 160
cost of sales 69, 84
credit facilities 71, 129
creditors 74, 84, 101
current assets 33, 45, 99
current liabilities 63, 118, 140
current ratio 140

debt finance 145, 239
debt ratio 413
debtors 52, 68
defensive position ratio 124, 143
deficits 108, 115
depreciation 64, 115, 157
direct cost 157, 162
directors report 113
discount factor 223, 224
discounting 223
discounts 68, 69
dividends 103, 114
double-entry bookkeeping 42, 82
dual aspect concept 31, 41, 44

earnings per share 147
electricity bills 91
employees 14, 104, 114, 185
expenses 30, 49, 52

final accounts 63, 69, 78
financial accounting 17, 155
financial information 5, 8, 10, 13
Financial Reporting Standards 24; FRS 1 104; FRS 01 34; FRS 18 29

financial statements 3, 4, 18, 107, 113, 122
fixed assets 8, 33
fixed cost 157, 162
F-TRIADS 37
funding options 235
fundraising 235, 243

gearing ratio 145
going concern 30
gross profit 88, 89
gross profit ratio 134
growth 131, 148, 213
Glazer, Malcolm 13, 27, 240

Her Majesty's Revenue and Customs 14, 222
historical cost concept 31

income 31, 49, 52
indirect cost 157
innovation fund 237
interest payments 14, 143
International Accounting Standard (IAS) 17, 95
internal rate of return 214, 228
investing activities 101, 106
investment appraisal 213
investment ratios 130, 147
income statements 4, 18, 19, 202
intangible fixed assets 8, 33

key reports 113

leasing 241
ledger accounts 49
legal identity 15
legal requirements 16, 18
liabilities 19, 33; current 99, 118; non-current 99, 118, 136
limited companies 16, 19
limited liability 15, 16
liquidation 16, 190
liquidity 104, 105, 123
liquidity ratios 140
loan interest 61
loans 13, 27
long-term solvency 143

management accounting 18, 153, 155
marginal cost 164, 165
materiality concept 31
mispostings 88, 90
money measurement concept 31
monitoring and evaluation 245

national governing body 236
National Lottery 237
net book value 65

net present value 214, 220
net profit 66, 89
non-trading organisations 108
notes to the accounts 15, 97, 99, 115
not-for-profit organisations 107, 147

opening stock 84, 90
operating activities 105, 113
operating profit ratio 135
opportunity cost of capital 221
overdraft 11, 33, 239
overhead 89, 157, 165
ownership 16, 26, 64

partnerships 42, 238
patent 34
payback period 216, 219
prepayments 92
price/earnings ratio 147
prime ratio 137, 139
private companies 15, 16
profit 25, 30, 91, 96, 98, 107
profit and loss account 5, 19, 115, 192, 201
profit centre 160
profitability ratios 134
project data 214
prudence concept 29–30, 38, 72, 90
public companies 16
public–private partnership 242

quick ratio 141

ratio analysis 124, 129; defensive position 143; growth 131; investment 147; limits of 149; liquidity 140; profitability; return on capital employed 136
reference columns 54
relevance 29
reliability 29
residual value 214, 225
return on capital employed 136; secondary analysis 139
returns 10, 73, 214
revenue 96, 105
rules of financial accounting 22

sales 49, 107; cost of sales 84, 88
semi-variable cost 158
share issue 148, 241
shareholder 15, 22, 191, 241
shares 16; buying and selling 26, 27; dividends 103, 146; earnings per share 147
sole traders 16
solvency 123, 140
sponsorship 25, 34, 123, 241

sport council 236
statutory requirements 18
stepped cost 159
stock 30, 52
stock exchange 26
stock valuations 84
straight line depreciation 65, 157
surplus 17, 84, 108, 193

'T'-accounts 49
tangible fixed assets 33
time value of money 214, 219, 225
total cost 159, 177

trading statements 83
trial balance 78
turnover/capital employed 138
takeovers 13, 27, 240

unincorporated businesses 15
unlimited liability 16
user groups 14, 124

variable cost 158, 165, 167
variance analysis 197, 200, 209

zero-based budget 198, 200, 210